THE ORTHODOX CHURCH

By the same author, from SVS Press:

THE ORTHODOX CHURCH
Its Past and Its Role in the World Today

by
JOHN MEYENDORFF

with selected revisions by
Nicholas Lossky

Fourth Revised Edition

ST VLADIMIR'S SEMINARY PRESS
CRESTWOOD, NY 10707
1996

Library of Congress Cataloging-in-Publication Data
Meyendorff, John, 1926-1992
    The Orthodox Church.
    Revised translation of L'Eglise orthodoxe.
    Bibliography: p.
    Includes index.
1. Orthodox Eastern Church—History. I. Title.
BX290.M413   1981   281.9   81-4978
ISBN 0-913836-81-8   AACR2

THE ORTHODOX CHURCH
Its Past and Its Role in the World Today

Fourth revised edition, 1996

First published in 1960 under the title
L'Eglise Orthodoxe: hier et aujourd'hui, by Éditions du Seuil

ISBN 0-913836-81-8

This revised and augmented edition is the work of Professor Nicholas Lossky, a longtime friend of John Meyendorff, who spared neither his time nor his effort in producing it. He has my deepest gratitude for this achievement. Also I add a note of thanks to Michael Plekon for translating Prof. Lossky's text from the French.

— Marie Meyendorff

PRINTED IN THE UNITED STATES OF AMERICA

CONTENTS

Foreword to the Fourth Edition

The search for unity constitutes one of the most characteristic and also most positive aspects of modern Christian history.

"As you, Father, are in me and I am in you, may they also be one in us, so that the world may believe that you have sent me" (John 17:21).

This prayer of the Head of the Church establishes a dependence of cause and effect between the unity of Christians and their witness in the world: in order for the world to believe, the faithful of Jesus Christ must make manifest their unity in God and appeal to their non-Christian brothers and sisters to share in this unity. No, the historical reality runs the risk of making the world believe the contrary, that the Father has not at all heard the prayer of His Son, that the redemptive work of Christ has brought not peace but discord, that the Gospel is no more than one doctrine among others, which, up to the present, has been unable to conquer humanity as a whole.

This is the scandal of which Christian missionaries were the first to become aware. They nourished a current of thought called "ecumenical," which raised the problem of unity for the Christian conscience. They asserted that, in practice, this problem did not concern just the specialists, but that it had to do with the Gospel itself and its efficacy in the modern world, and finally, it had to do with a response to the will of God Himself. Originally the personal initiative of certain pioneers in the beginning of the century, today ecumenism is the preoccupation of all the Churches. It is in the light of the spectacular progress of this movement that we seek to present in this book the history, doctrine and particular message of the Orthodox Church.

Further on below we will examine the historical circumstances which progressively shattered the unity of the Greco-Roman world, after this world had received the apostolic preaching in the first century, and which contributed to divide Christians of the East from those of the West. It is evident that today these circumstances are largely overthrown by the events for which our planet is the theater. The political and economic centers of our world have been displaced and even the traditional concepts of "East" and "West" belong now more to history than to our present reality. Orthodox communities are today numerous throughout the part of the world called "the West," and conversely the Roman Church as well as the confessions of the Reformation are present in the Near East, the Balkans and in Russia. It has become banal today to affirm that our planet is small, that we must give up the isolation of our cultures and our traditions. As for the the countries of Asia and Africa, these look for the Gospel in its authentic purity and the Church in her divine reality, ignoring the medieval quarrels which have torn Christianity apart. All this incontestably announces an era in which the ecumenical problem should be posed in its essential content as a debate *about the faith*. History itself challenges us to free ourselves of the secondary problems sociologically tied up in the old versions of Christianity, by putting before us the the very *same* problems, imposing the identical solutions. That all of us are not yet members of the one and only Church of Jesus Christ constitutes then, a fact which ought to—or necessarily will one day—be explained by substantial reasons. Our contemporaries or our descendants will find it more and more difficult to accept the justification of schisms for reasons other than those of *faith*. And it is here, without a doubt, that we come upon one of the positive features of our era: the flight from false problems and the search for the real ones. What a magnificent occasion for us Christians to search our consciences and finally to engage in a real debate about unity!

In this debate, the Orthodox Church occupies a peculiar position. She remains, indeed, a stranger to the most serious collision which modern Christianity knows: that which continues to divide the Roman Church from the communities issuing from the Reformation. In this regard, she remains the Church of continuity and tradition. This is the sense which she gives to the adjective which most often is used to designate her: that of *Orthodoxy*.

In the course of the dogmatic controversies which followed the Constantinian peace, the Greek words *catholicos* and *orthodoxos* concurrently served to designate those who held onto the true doctrine. The first of these adjectives, used for the first time in the first century by St. Ignatius of Antioch (*Smyrneans* 8,2) to describe the Christian Church—the Catholic Church—reflects the fullness, the universality and also the communal nature of the Christian message: in the face of all "particular" opinions, the Church proclaims a doctrine which is a totality and which is destined for all to hear and believe. The destiny of this term in Christian literature and theology was so great that it was adopted in the very symbols of the faith and finally by the composers of the Creed of Nicea-Constantinople: "one, holy, catholic and apostolic Church." In the West, the term was used most generally: one would speak of both "Catholic" Christians and of the "Catholic" faith. In the East, by contrast, the term "catholic" was used to designate the Church, while individual Christians were most often called "Orthodox," "those of true faith," in opposition to the heretics. Finally, during the Middle Ages, one spoke more and more of the "Orthodox Church," now in contrast to Roman "Catholicism."

In the ecumenical debate, the Orthodox Church then presents herself as the guardian of the true faith, that of the apostles and the Fathers of the Church. As a condition of union, she proposes

a return of all Christians to this one unique faith, the faith of the
first ecumenical councils.

But this pretension and hope might well seem to be utopian.
This return to the sources, necessary for reestablishing unity, does
it not seem to be like only an artificial return to a past now gone?
And, what is more, the historical weaknesses of Eastern Orthodoxy, which has claimed to have preserved this heritage from the
past, does not make such a return particularly attractive. What
then would be the justification for such a return?

In this book, we will try to show that it would be inexact to
pose the problem in this way. While Orthodoxy speaks of a
"return to the sources," this does not have so much to do with a
return to the past as with the permanence and fidelity of Revelation. This Revelation judges not only the past, but also the present
and the future of both East and West. One of the most basic
problems for theologians today is knowing how to discern between the holy Tradition of the Church—an expression adequate
or appropriate to Revelation—and the human traditions which
express Revelation only imperfectly and, very often, which even
oppose and obscure it. How many of these human traditions
should the Orthodox abandon before other Christians will accept
their claim of having the true and unique Tradition? The merit,
that is, the historical merit of the Christian East, is to have largely
allowed an open door to such an examination of conscience.

Fortunately, the Orthodox Christian East has always succeeded in avoiding the tragic pitfall of considering any human
institution, or even any human formulation of Christian dogma,
as being absolute and infallible as such. Indeed, even Scripture is
God's word, but spoken by human beings, so that the living Truth
which it contains must be understood not only in its literal
meaning but also through the power of the Spirit, which inspired
the authors and continues to inspire the faithful in the body of the

Church. Historical knowledge and critique are therefore necessary for the understanding of how inspiration occurs.

Our book, therefore, will have a double goal: that of presenting the Orthodox Church—its past and its present state—to Western readers who, with rare exceptions, have only a very limited knowledge of her, and that of enticing the Orthodox themselves to an examination of conscience which they very much need.

In our presentation, we will follow the historical development of the Orthodox Church from the apostolic time to our own. It is the interpretation we will give to the stages of this history which will permit the reader to understand the essential dogmatic positions of Orthodoxy. The basic dogmas about Scripture and Tradition, about the Church and about ecclesiastical authority will thus be defined in the opening chapters. At the conclusion of the book, we will return to certain other doctrinal aspects in the forms in which they are expressed today.

This is therefore not a systematic exposé of Orthodox faith which we are attempting here but a general introduction to the past and present life of the Orthodox Church.[1]

---

1 Chapter VIII ("The Orthodox Church Today") contains a description of Orthodoxy such as it was in the 1960's, when the book was published. Even though the majority of what is described remains important for our understanding of the contemporary situation, a postscript here will try to update this information. Our postscript here restates the essentials of what Fr. John Meyendorff himself prepared in 1981 for the publication of the 3rd edition of his book in English. According to his own suggestion, we take the liberty here of recommending that the reading of VIII be done in conjunction with the postscript. The latter comments on recent happenings between the Orthodox Church and Rome, complementing what is discussed in X ("Ecclesiological Positions"). [Note by Nicolas Lossky.]

Chapter 1

THE APOSTLES. HOLY SCRIPTURE. THE APOSTOLIC FATHERS. THE EARLY CHURCH.

"It was in the fifteenth year of the emperor Tiberius' reign, when Pontius Pilate was governor of Judaea, when Herod was prince in Galilee, his brother Philip in the Ituraean and Trachonitid region, and Lysanias in Abilina, in the high priesthood of Annas and Caiaphas, that the Word of God came upon John, the son of Zachariah, in the desert" (Luke 3:1-2). It is in this exact, historically accurate way that the Evangelist St. Luke begins his account of the messianic work of Jesus. Christianity, as a matter of fact, is based on a historically attested intervention of God in the concrete affairs of mankind, namely, the incarnation of his Son. We find the same concern for historical accuracy in the Creed, which tells us that Christ suffered "under Pontius Pilate." Why should this relatively obscure provincial official be mentioned in a short, solemn statement of the Christian faith, except in order to impress upon us the fact that Jesus was indeed a real historical person, a man like all of us, a Jew who suffered under the Roman yoke like all his compatriots, and to emphasize the fact that living men had heard him, had seen him with their own eyes, and had touched him with their hands (cf. 1 John 1:1)?

This historical nature of the messianic work is also attested by the way in which the Gospel was transmitted to the Greco-Roman world and later generations. When he was about to leave his disciples and ascend to heaven, the Master solemnly declared to them: "The Holy Spirit will come upon you, and you will receive strength from him. You are to be my witnesses in Jerusalem and throughout Judaea, in Samaria, yes, and to the ends of the earth" (Acts 1:8).

Like all other historical facts, the acts performed by Jesus—and especially the most extraordinary act which God ever performed in him: his resurrection on the third day—must be attested by witnesses: "There were Peter and John, James an Andrew, Philip and Thomas, Bartholomew and Matthew, James the son of Alphaeus and Simon the Zealot, and Judas the brother of James. All these, with one mind, gave themselves up to prayer, together with the women, and Mary the Mother of Jesus, and his brethren" (Acts 1:13-14). They were rather dull-witted witnesses, at best, those twelve fishermen from Galilee—who were only eleven after the betrayal of Judas—and the few close relatives of Jesus. After the tragedy of Golgotha, after the Resurrection, after all that the Master had told them regarding his kingdom, they still persisted in asking him when he intended to restore the monarchy of David (Acts 1:6). However, they had followed him from the beginning of his ministry: this was the necessary condition for being a member of the apostolic college, as is clear from the account of the election of Matthias to succeed Judas: "There are men who have walked in our company all through time when the Lord Jesus came and went among us, from the time when John used to baptize to the day when he, Jesus, was taken from us. One of these ought to be added to our number as a witness of his resurrection" (Acts 1:21-22).

Eager as they were to serve as witnesses of the risen Master, they were not fully capable as yet of grasping the overwhelming universality of the ministry with which they had been invested. It was only after a promise which Jesus had repeatedly made had been fulfilled that they were able to exchange their Galilean dialect for the universal language of the Gospel: the Holy Spirit alighted on each of them and they "began to speak in strange languages, as the Spirit gave utterance to each" (Acts 2:4). Only then did Peter feel himself authorized to announce to Israel the beginning of the true messianic reign, the fulfillment of the prophecies: "Let it be known, then, beyond all doubt, to all the house of Israel, that God has made him Master and Christ, this Jesus whom you crucified" (Acts 2:36).

In order to establish the community of the New Covenant, it was necessary both to have eyewitnesses of the risen Christ and for the Holy Spirit to descend on the infant Church in order to make this witness plausible and its fruits immediately evident to all: "And about three thousand souls were won for the Lord that day" (Acts 2:41).

To this day the Church lives only by the witness of the Apostles and thanks to the Holy Spirit, who dwells in it from the day of Pentecost: it is thus both "holy" and "apostolic." The Spirit, actually, has *added* nothing to the work performed by Christ, for "it was God's good pleasure to let all completeness dwell in him" (Col 1:19). The Spirit "bears witness, because he is the truth" (1 John 5:6): "And he will bring honor to me," said Jesus, "because it is from me that he will derive what he makes plain to you" (John 16:14). The coming of the Spirit therefore does not make the human witness of the Apostles with respect to the historical resurrection of the Lord superfluous: it places a seal upon it and authenticates it.

This last point is particularly important when we consider the significance of the *books* of the New Testament and the formation of the canon of Holy Scripture. The four Gospels, the book of Acts, the epistles of Paul, and the Apocalypse are primarily concerned with furnishing information concerning the person of Jesus Christ, the nature of his sacrifice, and the fact of the Resurrection: they constitute, in other words, a written account of the message of the Apostles. Their authority comes both from their apostolic origin and from their inspiration. Tradition insists, as a matter of fact, on the apostolic origin of the Gospels of Mark and Luke, although their authors were not members of the college of the Twelve and probably did not know Jesus; in order to establish the authenticity of these Gospels it appeals to the authority of Peter and Paul, whose preaching was taken down by Mark and Luke. This rather elastic conception of authenticity has allowed the inclusion in the canon of such works and the Epistle to the Hebrews or the apocalypse, with regard to which their have been doubts since the earliest times of the Church: hence we may say that apostolic authenticity does not necessarily mean material authenticity, but that it is a guarantee, vouched for by the Holy Spirit, of the apostolic origin of the contents of the Holy Books.

As a matter of fact, the witness of the Apostles would have been valueless without the miracle of Pentecost, unless the Spirit had come not merely to the Twelve but to the entire Church. The Church is thus founded not only *by* the apostles but *on* them, as well as in the Holy Spirit. It occurred to no one to add to the Scriptural canon a work that was not of apostolic origin, because the Spirit does not reveal anything except Christ, to whom the Apostles witnessed. But it is the Spirit who defines the canon of Scriptures in the Church and preserves the Church through the centuries in truth and in faithfulness to its Head.

These are the basic elements of the Orthodox conception of Scripture and Tradition. Scripture includes the *totality* of the apostolic witness and nothing can be added by way of completing our knowledge of the person of Jesus, his work, and the salvation which he brought us; but this written witness regarding Christ was not launched in a void—after the manner of the Koran, which, according to Islamic tradition, fell from heaven and is read by men in a form fixed once and for all—but was given to a community which had been founded by these apostles and which had received the same Spirit. This community is the Church, which has received the Scriptures and acknowledges in it the Truth, fixed in its limits for all time, and interprets this corpus of writings with the help of the Spirit. This interpretation and its acknowledgment are what is known as Tradition.

The early history of the Church is described in the books of Acts, written by St. Luke, and author of the third Gospel. The book is divided, somewhat schematically, into two rather unequal parts: the first part (chapters 1 to 9) is concerned with the primitive Church at Jerusalem, its foundation at Pentecost, its internal organization, and the activities of its leaders; the second part comprises the rest of the book and has to do no longer with the Church at Jerusalem but with the person of the Apostle of the Gentiles, whom Luke here calls Paul (Acts 8:9), whereas in the previous chapters he was known as Saul.

The community of Jerusalem is governed by the college of the Twelve, but in this college the apostle Peter clearly occupies the first place: he speaks in the name of all and acts as head. It is probable that the famous words of Jesus on the road to Caesarea reported by the Jerusalemite Gospel of Matthew relate to this predominant role of Peter at Jerusalem: "Thou art Peter, and upon this rock I will build my Church" (Mt 16:18).[1] The Church of Jerusalem, of course, was not one church among many; it was actually *the* Church, the only Church, the "remnant" of Israel, foretold by the prophets, which had received the Messiah. The Church of the Gentiles, for which Paul would be the special Apostle, could only be a "wild olive" grafted on the authentic olive tree (Rom 11:17). Governed by the twelve Apostles, the original Judaeo-Christian community was an anticipation of the heavenly Jerusalem, the holy city that will descend from heaven and concerning which the seer of the Apocalypse says: "The city wall, too, had twelve foundation stones: and these too bore names, those of the Lamb's twelve Apostles" (Apoc 21:14). History and eschatol-

---

1 See my article "Sacrement et hiérarchie dans l'Église. Contribution orthodoxe à un dialogue oecumémique sur la Primauté romaine," in *Deiu vivant*, no. 26 (1954), pp. 81-91; also V. Kesich, "The Problem of Peter's Primacy in the New Testament and the Early Christian Exegesis," in *St. Vladimir's Seminary Quarterly*, vol. 4, nos. 2-3 (1960), pp. 2-25.

ogy are so intimately bound up with each other in the first chapters of the book of Acts that it is difficult to isolate the distinguishing features of each. In Peter's speech, the day of Pentecost, the coming of the Spirit, is interpreted as the fulfillment of the eschatological prophecy of Joel, and the life of the infant community is portrayed as a constant miracle: "They used to gather together with one accord in Solomon's Porch. No one else dared join them, although the people held them in high honor" (Acts 5:12-13).

Chapter 12 brings this exceptional period in the history of the Church to a definite close. The college of the Twelve ceased to exist: Herod caused "James, the brother of John, to be beheaded" (Acts 12:2), and no one thought of replacing him by electing a successor in order to keep up the symbolical number of Twelve, as they had in the case of Judas. Peter, after his arrest and miraculous escape, "left them and went elsewhere" (Acts 12:17). He will retain his personal authority as "First Apostle," but this authority will not be regarded as absolute, since he will be directly contradicted by Paul (Gal 2). Moreover, at Jerusalem the first place will henceforth be assumed by James, the brother of the Lord (Acts 15), who was not a member of the college of the Twelve. The part played by Peter in the foundation of the Church will be perpetuated—as we shall see later on—by the episcopal office, but he will henceforth be confined to being the "Apostle of the Circumcised" (Gal 2:7-8), a ministry which, unfortunately, was not destined to have a brilliant future inasmuch as Israel would definitely reject its Messiah, the miserable "remnant" which actually did receive him being finally swallowed up by the disaster of AD 70 which swept over Palestine.

From then on the future will belong historically to the Apostle of the Gentiles, Paul, to whom chapters 13 to 28 of the book of Acts are devoted. As a result of his missionary journeys through the Mediterranean basin Christian communities will spring up everywhere. All "churches of God," like that of Jerusalem before them, will receive the Gospel and the Holy Spirit. However, the community in Palestine was always regarded by Paul an enjoying a peculiar authority and a special primacy because of its early foundation even after the college of the Twelve had left Jerusalem. He tried in particular to get its approval—after a great deal of trouble—for the basic principle underlying his mission to the Gentiles, and he never forgot the collection "for the brothers of Judaea," a symbol and expression of the unity of the Church. However, for him, every church was the "Church of God," in which "there was neither Greek nor Jew." He insisted that all Christians who lived in one place should belong to one church, a point that was a source of friction with the parallel mission to the Jews which did not share this view. He was indignant with them at Corinth where they wished to form two distinct communities: "Each of you has a cry of his own: I am for Paul, I am for Apollo, I am for Cephas, I am for Christ, What, has Christ been divided up?" (1 Cor 1:12-13). Christians, as a whole, "form" Christ; they are one indivisible body which ought to be evident in its entirely and its fullness in each church.

These frictions with Jewish Christians do not seem to have affected Paul's relations with Peter, the Apostle of the Circumcised. According to Tradition, both Apostles came to Rome and bore witness by their blood, perhaps only a few months apart, to the unversality of salvation in Jesus Christ. This communion of the two "first Apostles"[2] in death in the capital of the Empire—the first of Twelve who presided over the Church at Jerusalem, and the first Apostle of the Gentiles—contributed greatly to the prestige of the Roman Church, where the memory of their teaching and presence remained alive and where their relics would soon be venerated.

Among the earliest witnesses to the Resurrection we also find

---

2 The Byzantine liturgy regularly refers to Peter *and* Paul as *koryphaioi* (leaders).

the mysterious figure of the "beloved disciple," John, the son of Zebedee. He too, like Peter and Paul, is regarded as the author of certain books of the New Testament and is associated with a particular locality, namely Ephesus. John was one of the outstanding members of the apostolic college, personally very close to Peter, and because of this he played a very important role in the life of the primitive Church at Jerusalem. His intimacy with the Master seems to have conferred on him a kind of spiritual primacy among the Apostles, a primacy which some have opposed or compared to the more institutional primacy of Peter, and which is reflected in the pages of his Gospel.[3] Nevertheless, his name is mentioned only once in the epistles of Paul: John is referred to along with James and Peter as one of the "columns" of the Church of Jerusalem (Gal 1:9). We do no know whether he later assisted Peter with the Jewish mission of this church. According to Tradition he resided during the latter years of his life at Ephesus—a church founded by Paul (Acts 19:8-9)—but he does not appear to have been connected with any kind of opposition to Pauline doctrine. His works, the last to be included in the New Testament canon are strongly marked by the author's own personal, visionary conception of the Christian message, and the Byzantine Church has therefore accorded him the title of "the Theologian." John emphasizes particularly the sacramental side of this message, and it is not unreasonable to conclude, as some have done, that the monarchic episcopate derives from the Johannine tradition.[4]

In our time, Protestant exegesis is coming to admit more and more the importance of the sacramental element in the life of the early Church.[5] Now it is beyond dispute that baptism and the Eucharist, the essential elements in the earliest Christian preaching,

---

3 See Mgr. Cassien, "Saint Pierre et l'Église dans le Nouveau Testament," in *Istina*, no. 3 (1955), pp. 261-304.

4 See J. Colson, *L'Évêque dans les communautés primitives: tradition paulinienne et tradition johanique de l'épiscopat des origines à saint Irénée* (Paris, 1951).

5 See for example O. Cullmann, *Early Christian Worship* (London: SCM Press, 1953).

are acts of a ritual and corporate nature and presuppose a certain organization of the community which celebrates them. Our present knowledge of the primitive eucharistic prayer points to a close parallel between Jewish worship in the time of Christ, especially the prayers—preserved in the Talmud—that were recited by certain Jewish brotherhoods when common meals were celebrated, and its Christian counterpart. Christ and his disciples formed one of these brotherhoods and celebrated such a ritual meal described for us briefly by the Evangelists, in the course of which Jesus blessed bread and wine, declaring them to be his Body and his Blood, and directed his disciples to "do this" in remembrance of him.

The fact that we find liturgical elements of contemporary Judaism in the earliest Christian anaphoras is a clear indication of the apostolic origin of the Christian rite of the Eucharist: that is to say, the earliest communities celebrated the Supper in the same way that is was celebrated by Jesus in the Upper Room. But this still leaves us with the problems of determining who presided over these Christian gatherings and therefore took the place of the Jewish head of the family or president of the fraternity. This problem has a particular relevancy for us, because the Last Supper, as the prototype and origin of the Christian Eucharist, was presided over by the Master in person, and consequently the president of the Christian assembly would be the logical person to pronounce the words which He pronounced and to perform the acts which He performed.

The problems can be solved almost certainly, it would seem, for the primitive community at Jerusalem. The first twelve chapters of the Acts show clearly that the Apostle Peter was the head of the Apostolic college and the head of that church. This role of Peter at Jerusalem appears to follow naturally from the words of the Lord: "Thou art Peter, and upon this rock I will build my Church" (Mt 16:18); "When, after a while, thou has come back to me, it is for thee to be the support of thy brethren" (Lk 22:32);

"Feed my sheep" (Jn 21:15-17). Jesus was himself the Rock and
the Shepherd, but he gave to one of his disciples the power to
perform this ministry: the Apostle Simon Peter was the disciple
who performed this function in the primitive Jewish-Christian
community at Jerusalem, which came to be regarded as the
unique model for all future Christian churches.

But Peter left Jerusalem "for another place" (Acts 12:17) and
was replaced by James as the head of the Church at Jerusalem.
From then on, the Apostles—the Eleven (James, brother of John,
being dead: Acts 12:2), Paul, and certain others—were the itinerant witnesses of the risen Christ: everywhere they went they
founded Christian churches, leaving to others the responsibility of
presiding over them and performing the sacramental rites. The
Apostle Paul, for example, celebrated the rite of baptism only on
extraordinary occasions, for, he said, "Christ did not send me to
baptize; he sent me to preach the Gospel" (1 Cor 1:14-17). For
the postapostolic period, the *Didache* specifically states: "Let each
Apostle, when he comes to you, be received like the Lord; but let
him remain only one day, or two days in case of need; if he
remains three days, he is a false prophet" (9:4-5). After Peter and
the other members of the apostolic college had ceased to preside
over the Church of Jerusalem, the apostolic ministry became
itinerant, and no ancient document has survived indicating that
the Apostles personally presided over any particular church. St.
Irenaeus of Lyons in the second century, for example, describes
the role of the Apostles as being that of "founders" or "builders":
"After having founded and built the Church, the blessed Apostles
entrusted to Linus the charge of the episcopate...Anacletus succeeded him. After him, in the third place from the Apostles, it is
to Clement that the episcopate fell... "(*Against the Heresies*, iii.3).

A sharp distinction thus came to exist between the apostolate—an itinerant and universal witness—and the episcopal office, or a sacramental, administrative, and *local* function.

The book of Acts and the epistles of Paul seem to assume that there was a certain collegiality in the government of the earliest churches: we hear of *episkopoi* (overseers), *perbyteroi* (elders), *proistamenoi* (presidents), in the plural. By the end of the first century, however, all the churches were presided over by one person, the *episkopos,* or bishop. Did a revolution take place in the organization of the Church? No, for there is no evidence of any protest being made by Christians of the earliest period against the establishment of a "monarchic" episcopate. As a likely explanation we must remember that the sacramental orientation of the primitive Christian community naturally called for and presupposed the existence of a single head.

The whole life of the community, as a matter of fact, was centered around the celebration of the Eucharist. Now the Supper has to be presided over by one person, the image of the Lord. This function of president was performed by Peter at Jerusalem. Since all the local churches founded by the apostles were essentially identical in organization with the Church of Jerusalem and were reproductions, as it were, of the same communal and eschatological prototype, this primitive community, as described in the first twelve chapters of the book of Acts, served as a model for all the rest, and Peter himself, when reporting at Jerusalem on the baptism of Cornelius and other pagans, declared that "the Holy Spirit fell upon them, just as it was with us in the beginning" (Acts 11:15; cf. 10:44, 47; 11:17). St. Ignatius of Antioch, the earliest and principal witness to the monarchic episcopate (about AD 100) describes the Christian church at Magnesia or Smyrna as having a single bishop—the image of God—who was assisted by the "prebyterium," which corresponded to the college of Apostles at Jerusalem: "I conjure you, have a heart to do all things in the divine concord, under the presidency of the bishop who holds the place of God, the presbyters, who hold the place of the senate of the Apostles, and the deacons who are so dear to me, to whom has been entrusted the service of Jesus Christ" (*Magn.* vi.1); "Let us all revere the deacons like Jesus Christ, as well as the bishop who is the image of the Father, and the presbyters as the senate of God and as the assembly of the Apostles" (*Trall.* iii.1).

The essential point about the ecclesiology of St. Ignatius is that the local church is not regarded as a *part* of the body of the Church but as the whole, having at its head the Lord himself and *all* the Apostles. If St. Ignatius is aware of an apostolic succession in the Church, it is to be found in the collegial ministry of the presbyters. The bishop's function is to represent the Father, to be the source and unique center of church unity, as the Father is the source of the Divinity.

Moreover, the episcopal office, by definition the function of a single individual, was thought of in the primitive Church as a continuation in each church of the ministry which Peter performed at Jerusalem. It is in this sense that we must interpret the words which Christ addressed to Simon Peter on the road to Caesarea. The great exponent of this idea in the third century was St. Cyprian, the bishop of Carthage. For St. Cyprian the episcopate is "one" by virtue of the identity of faith—the faith of Peter—of all the churches and all the bishops sit on the one chair (*cathedra una*), namely, that of Peter, by confessing this true faith.[6] Representing the "image of the Lord" in the Christian community, the bishop thus appeared not only as the consecrator of the Eucharist but as the teacher of true doctrine.

The definite hierarchic structure of the early Christian communities is thus determined by their sacramental nature.

The Sunday eucharistic gathering, the meal in common which serves to proclaim and anticipate the joyous feast of the Kingdom to come, is the moment when the Church fully became the Church, for it was then that all communicated in the Lord, then

---

6 There is a consensus today regarding the interpretation of St. Cyprian's famous treatise *De catholicae ecclesiae unitate* in this sense; cf. in particular the translated text in *Ancient Christian Writers*, no. 25, with notes by M. Bévenot (Westminster, MD: 1957); also P. T. Camelot, "Saint Cyprien et la primauté," in *Istina*, no. 4 (1957).

also that baptism was conferred, instruction in the faith was given, and bishops and presbyters were elected; it was then too that bishops came from neighboring communities to consecrate new bishops; it was then that discussions were held regarding the common problems facing the community. Nothing, not even the persecutions, was allowed to interfere with Christian participation in the Sunday Supper of the Lord. Because these Christian gatherings were rather sizable, they were inevitably known to the Roman police, and the corporate worship of the *religio illicita* thus had the effect of making Christians vulnerable to attack by their enemies. Yet they insisted upon meeting together for worship, and refused to substitute any kind of personal or private prayer for the corporate gatherings. The reason for this was simply that they regarded these liturgical gatherings as belonging to the very essence of their faith. Like the Church at Jerusalem, "they occupied themselves continually with the Apostles' teaching, their fellowship in the breaking of the bread, and the fixed times of prayer" (Acts 2:42). They could not give up this custom without violating the commandment of the New Covenant.

The cautious historian of course must be wary about painting too bright a picture of the early Christians and portraying them as perfect in all respects. Yet, as long as the fledgling status of the new Church lasted, as long as being a member of the New Covenant entailed a certain risk or at least a conscious effort to profess the faith, it was natural that the faithful should be more aware than later generations of the true nature of the Christian community. In this sense and in this only, the Church of the first three centuries can be said to be the golden age of Christianity—and also, to a certain extent, a criterion by which to judge the rest of Christian history.

Unfortunately we cannot linger over this interesting formative period but must content ourselves with having pointed out some of its salient features, of particular importance because of their influence on later church history.

Church very extensive judicial authority, and turned over to it the control of public welfare. Magnificent churches were raised over the holy places of Christianity and the tombs of the martyrs, and their new capital, Constantinople or the New Rome, was adorned no longer with temples to Victory or Justice, as in the pagan past, but with churches dedicated to Christ-Wisdom (Hagia Sophia) or Divine Peace (Hagia Eirene).

In adopting the new religion and employing it more and more as the basis for their policies, the emperors were clearly trying to inject new life into the state, and above all, to assure the unity of the Empire. Secure at last in the enjoyment of imperial protection, the Church opened its gates wide to the masses who sought admittance, and when Justinian closed the last pagan university at Athens in 539, he could justly pride himself on being the head of a completely Christian state, for the boundaries of his political power coincided with those of the Church. The people of God, taken as a whole, were thought of as united under the scepter of a single monarch: Church and state were no longer two separate entities, concerned about defining their mutual relations, but one single society governed by two hierarchies: the ecclesiastical and the political, the latter headed by the emperor.[1] The status of Christianity in the East during the medieval period was thus practically identical with its status in the West, except for the fact that in the East no one succeeded in gathering into his hands the supreme power over both temporal and spiritual affairs as the popes did in the West.

The Byzantine emperors, it is true, made certain efforts along these lines, particularly from the time of Justinian. The politico-religious unity which they dreamed of bringing about was being constantly threatened by dogmatic controversies, for the universal Church which they regarded as a prop for the Empire was distress-

---

1 For the theocratic ideas of Justinian, see A. Schmemann, "Byzantine Theocracy and the Orthodox Church," in *St. Vladimir's Seminary Quarterly*, vol. 1, no. 2 (1953).

ingly divided, first by the Arian controversies, and then by the endless later christological disputes. In order to restore church unity the emperors had recourse to the method of holding ecumenical councils, but this proved to be time-consuming and the outcome was sometimes uncertain. From the time of Justinian they began to embark on the dangerous path of issuing dogmatic decrees on their own, but they at once came up against a stubborn fact: the Church was not disposed to recognize their claim to infallibility.

Besides, Justinian and his immediate successors had much too good a grasp of theological principles to take seriously the formal claims of caesaropapism. Their attitude is indicated by Justinians's Sixth Novella, dated March 16, 535: "The greatest gifts which God has granted to men are the priesthood and the empire, the priesthood concerns things divine, the empire presides over mortals." The goal to be achieved was an agreement or "symphony" between these two institutions, and not the subjection of one to the other. As far as Byzantium was concerned, this harmony was never worked out in precise juridical terms: we have to do rather with a state of mind than a system of government, which allowed certain emperors to act arbitrarily but did not formally subject the Church to the state. The Byzantine Church was always capable, especially after the ninth century, of producing patriarchs willing to stand up to arbitrary emperors. Abuses of power for which the latter were responsible, although accepted by weak-willed prelates, were almost always condemned later on by the church authorities.

In fact, there is no basis in Christian teaching for the religious power claimed by the emperors, even indirectly. The sacral character of the imperial office under the old pagan empire could not survive in a Christian empire, except in popular fancy or as a mere survival. Nevertheless it is a fact that, because the emperor reigned over an empire at least theoretically Christian, because of the universal nature of his power, and because the Church, equally universal, had accepted his support and his protection, the Byzantine emperor was regarded as the Chosen of God, as the earthly reflection of the celestial power of Christ, and the Biblical titles applied to the Jewish kings in the Old Testament were applied to him in court ceremonies.

This whole field of relations between the emperor and the ecclesiastical herarchy, between sate and Church, remained rather vaguely defined. This vagueness and pragmatism reveal a positive fact: the awareness of the fundamental instability of the relations between the Church and the world, between the Kingdom of God and that of the fallen world, had not been wholly lost. That unsteady balance, established during the early centuries of the Christian Empire, was really only upset for the first time by the iconoclastic emperors Leo III (717-741) and Constantine V (741-775). Of all the Eastern emperors they were the only ones who formally claimed the plenitude of both powers, spiritual and temporal. Their campaign against the cult of images amounted to an attempt to establish imperial control over all the manifestations of religious life and to inaugurate in Byzantium a theocratic type of totalitarianism. Doubtless they were influenced in this respect, either consciously or unconsciously, by the example of the Moslem khalifs, for it is well known that in Islam, the people of God, there is no distinction between temporal and spiritual, between Church and state. Constantine V wished to be both "priest and king" (*basileus kai hiereus*) and to realize the fond ambition, already guardedly entertained by Justinian, of making the terrestrial Empire an exact replica of the Kingdom of Heaven.

After a crisis lasting for more than a century (725-843), the iconoclastic party in Byzantium was finally defeated. A balance was once more achieved between Church and state on an even firmer basis, later expressed by Patriarch Photius in a document called the Epanagoge, which clearly distinguishes between the rights of the emperor and those of the patriarch.[2] In spite of many extravagant

2 An English translation of this text is to be found in W. K. Medlin, *Moscow and East Rome* (Geneva, 1952), pp. 232-33.

ideas about Byzantine caesaropapism which are current, it is a fact that from the ninth century on the emperors of New Rome were no longer in a position to impose their doctrinal will on the Byzantine Church. The brief efforts in this direction by the Comneni and even more so by the Palaeologi were all brought to naught and cannot possibly be compared with the doctrinal decrees of a Zeno, a Justinian, or a Heraclius in the fifth, sixth and seventh centuries.

The true legacy of the Christian Empire founded when Constantine was converted, therefore, was not caesaropapism but the ideal of a single "Christian state." Empire and Church no longer constituted two societies but a single society, the "Christian society" (*christeponymon politeuma*) the orthodox *oikoumene* (world), in which the political and the religious powers would henceforth be regarded only as two complementary aspects of the same organized society. Confronted by the evident danger inherent in this state of affairs, namely the risk of forgetting that the Kingdom of God present in the Church still remains an entity that will be fully realized only in the future, proclaimed and anticipated by the sacraments but not identifiable with the earthly Empire, the Church, responding to the voice of conscience, reacted in various ways, particularly by placing a special emphasis on the liturgy and by the promotion of monasticism.

Before the fourth century Christian worship had been the worship of a persecuted minority. This had helped to emphasize the corporate nature of the liturgy. Only true Christians, whose who were prepared to accept the Gospel in all its fullness and in the full awareness of its meaning, were members of the Church. Christian worship was the mystery of the community meeting together. From the fourth century onward, however, it gradually became a worship dominated by the sanctuary. Was a development of this kind not inevitable once the liturgy came to be celebrated in the great basilicas which Constantine had erected throughout the Empire—in the "Great Church" of Hagia Sophia, for example, which held thousands of worshippers? Moreover, the faithful themselves felt that they now belonged to a privileged religion, to an imperial Christianity, they were no longer a group hated by the "world."

But, basically speaking, the Church did not modify either its stand toward the world or its consciousness of being "outside the world." It the new circumstances in which it found itself it could not help devising new methods for protecting the Christian mystery. Formerly the non-baptized had been forbidden to enter the *ecclesia* (church); henceforth the laity were forbidden to enter the sanctuary since many of them were only superficially baptized at best. The liturgy was gradually transformed into an "office" chanted by the clergy in the "presence" of the people. In sermons, theological works, and the symbolism of church art, from now on there would be much more emphasis on the terrifying mystery of the divine presence in the Church, on the dangers of an unworthy reception of the "communion" in the mystery, and on the role of the clergy as mediators between the people and the Mystery.

This increased emphasis upon ecclesiastical formality, which obscured but did not deny the essential traits of Christian worship, was necessary in order to maintain the sense of the Sacred in the Church over the centuries. This was particularly true at a time when confusion between the sacred and the profane was quite general. Taken over, protected, used by the Kingdom of this world, the Church had to continue to assert that its true Master was the King who was to come again one day and who wished to manifest himself now only under the sacramental veils.

Certain Christians, however, went even further. They refused outright to have anything to do with the new "Christian society": they abandoned it altogether and retired to the desert to witness there to the supernatural and eschatological nature of the Church.

It is rather odd but nevertheless a fact that the Church of the first three centuries was not acquainted with the institution of monasticism, as the word is generally understood. This is strange, because we know what close bonds there were between the early Christian community, its liturgy, organization and outlook, and contemporary Judaism, for the Apostles were all Jews. Now Judaism had a long tradition of asceticism which was experiencing a revival precisely in the time of Christ. St. John the Baptist was the most outstanding example of this tendency, and Christian monks later adopted him as their chosen model. Had the Lord himself not withdrawn into the desert to fast for forty days before beginning his ministry? The New covenant was first preached in the desert, as if to show that history was being given anew beginning and that the New City should owe nothing to the old. But Christians did not follow this precedent, because it was all too apparent to them that wherever their communities were established they were surrounded by a hostile desert. The stark contrast between the Church and the world was all too apparent for them to wish to emphasize this factor by following a particular way of life: their very existence was a prophetic announcement of the Kingdom to come.

Only after peace had been concluded between the Empire and the Church do we find thousands of Christians fleeing into the desert.[3] A few of them preferred to live completely isolated lives there, others established communities and sought to reconstruct the ideal of the first community in Jerusalem: "All the faithful held together, and shared all they had, selling their possessions and their means of livelihood, so as to distribute to all, as each had need" (Acts 2:44-45). Aware of having a prophetic mission to fulfill in the Christian world, these individuals, soon to be called "monks," practiced chastity, for was it not their role to announce the *supernatural* nature of the Kingdom of God? Now in this kingdom, "there is no marrying and giving in marriage; they are as the angels in heaven are" (Mt 22:30). They were constantly given up to prayer,

3 See on this whole subject the penetrating study of L. Bouyer, *La Vie de saint Antoine* (Éditions de Fontenelle, Abbaye de Saint-Wandrille, 1950), pp. 7-11.

either the chanting of the psalms in monastic communities or the "pure" or "monologic prayer" of the hermits. Soon monks began to take up residence in the towns, where they could make the full impact of their eschatological calling apparent to one and all in the very midst of the new society.

The monastic world was certainly not immune to temptations and deviations of all kinds, but by and large it can be said that the monks remained faithful to the doctrinal, heirarchic, and sacramental structure of the Church and in time became a permanent institution. Throughout the medieval period, both in the East and the West, the monastic ideal continued to attract the best elements in Christian society. In the East, from the sixth century, the episcopate was reserved exclusively to monks, while in the West the ideal of monastic celibacy was later extended to the clergy in general. The moral prestige of the monks, moreover, served as a kind of brake on the process of absorption and control by the state to which the Church was continually subject. Among them also the great traditions of mysticism and holiness flourished, which have nourished Orthodox spirituality throughout the ages.

The founding of a "Christian state" in the Greco-Roman world in the fourth century did not put an end to the doctrinal controversies of the early Christians. Constantine and his immediate successors had to cope with the Arian crisis and this was then followed by the christological controversies of the fifth, sixth and seventh centuries. Finally, in the eighth century, the Byzantine Empire was shaken to its very foundations by the iconoclastic controversy.

Before Constantine's time the Church had had to deal with schisms and heresies by relying entirely upon itself. Each bishop was doctrinally supreme in his own diocese and sat "on the chair of Peter." It was up to him to solve the various disputes that arose concerning the faith and to condemn heretics. Sometimes, however, disagreements between bishops or the spread of heresy made necessary a more solemn witnessing to the Christian truth. In that case synods or councils would be held. We employ the term "witness" here purposely to mark the true significance of these gatherings. The bishops were all depositaries of the same grace and all equal in office: they gathered not to add anything to the grace that each possessed in its entirety—*in solidum*, as St. Cyprian of Carthage used to say—but to witness to their unanimity in the true doctrine. That is why councils never adopted the procedure of modern parliamentary assemblies in their deliberations: it was not a question of causing the opinion of the majority to triumph, but of assisting the adoption by all of the true revealed doctrine. Heretical majorities—Arian, Monophysite, iconoclastic—sometimes succeeded in imposing themselves on "false councils." The mere fact of their being a majority therefore could not be regarded as a criterion of infallibility. The Church ultimately upheld a St. Athanasius or a St. Maximus, who, at one time, were almost alone in fighting for the truth. Nor have these "false councils" ever succeeded in bringing the institution and authority of councils into disrepute, any more than heretical bishops have succeeded in undermining the authority of the episcopate. Without ever being considered infallible individually, the bishops—separately or gathered in council—were the normal witnesses to the true teaching and it was they perforce who bore witness to the final triumph of orthodoxy over heresy. After heresy had triumphed temporarily, later councils in which an orthodox unanimity was apparent would always succeed in reaffirming the revealed Truth.

These ecclesiastical norms continued to be observed in the fourth century as in the past. However, a new factor was introduced when imperial support made possible the holding of councils more frequently and with a larger attendance. Hence, when Constantine became worried abut the spread of the Arian controversy, he decided on the summoning of an "ecumenical" council which would include all the bishops of the whole "inhabited" (ecumenical) world.

Ecumenical councils are distinguished from those which preceded Constantine by two features: they were convoked by the emperor and their decisions were held to be laws of the Empire. While the Church had entered into an agreement with the Empire, the Empire, for its part, had assumed the responsibility for protection the orthodox faith. It was natural, under the circumstances, that the emperor should be eager to have an exact definition of the faith so that he could appeal to it in his use of the political and judicial machinery of the state. This was the real purpose of ecumenical councils from the imperial point of view.

In fact, however, the Church and its Tradition never bowed completely to the imperial will. The ecumenical councils never became organs of infallibility whose decisions were accepted automatically. They rarely won the acceptance of the whole Empire at once. The first council, that of Nicaea (325), was rejected for more than half a century before it obtained general recognition and came to be regarded as *the* symbol of an ecumenical council par excellence. Again at Ephesus, in 449, a council formally declared to be ecumenical was repudiated and has gone down in history as the *Latrocinium* or "Robber Council." The Council of Chalcedon (451), held under exceptional circumstances with regard to freedom of attendance and discussion and with representatives of different theological schools present, should have been able, it would seem, to work out an acceptable synthesis of various views, but its decisions were never received by the majority of the non-Greek elements in the Eastern Empire.

The Western Christian today may find himself somewhat perplexed by this absence of a precise and definite theological criterion. If he is a Roman Catholic he is accustomed to think of Tradition as something that is recognized or can be defined by the doctrinal authority of the Roman see, or, if he is a Protestant, as something which is determined ultimately by Scripture alone. He has difficulty in seeing how the Church can continue to express itself organically in the maze of dogmatic controversies without a permanent criterion of truth. He will prefer the apparent security offered the West by the medieval papacy, or he will take refuge in the principle of *sola scriptura*. The Roman Catholic will maintain that a certain "dogmatic development" was necessary to bring some measure of order out of the initial chaos of conflicting doctrines during the early centuries and to make apparent the concept of the doctrinal authority of the Roman see which the Fathers had only recognized implicitly. The Protestant will generally reject the very basis for these dogmatic controversies, since in his view those who took part in them had already departed from written revelation. The Orthodox historian, however, sees in the ecumenical councils an obvious sign of the continual fidelity of Christ to his Church, a miraculous fidelity that no definite juridical institution can express fully. Of course our theological handbooks speak of the infallibility of ecumenical councils, but the fact remains and cannot be denied that several councils, regarded as ecumenical today, were not so recognized at the time, while others, declared to be ecumenical, were later repudiated. Russian theologians of the nineteenth century, particularly A. S. Khomiakov, made much of this "reception" of conciliar decisions by the entire Church, though they were not the first to do so. In fact, it would be wrong to see an opposition between this idea of "reception" and that of the infallibility of the councils, as is sometimes done. An ecumenical council truly representative of Christ will certainly be inspired by the Holy Spirit and will therefore be infallible. However, it belongs to the Spirit and to the Church guided by him to judge whether a gathering which declares itself or is declared to be ecumenical is actually so or not. The council is not an organ external to the body of the Church. The Church's infallibility is ultimately always the infallibility of the Spirit of Truth alone, who resides in the whole organism of the Church. This organism is subject to its own special law, the law of the Spirit, and has its own peculiar form or structure, the hierarchic organization of the Church, both being dependent upon a deliberate personal profession of the true faith, by all and at all times.

The Orthodox regard the period of the ecumenical councils as a normative period. It was then, by and large, that the dogmatic and canonical norms of the Orthodox faith were laid down, as we know them today, rather than in later ages as was the case with Western Christianity.

The Orthodox church acknowledges seven ecumenical councils:[4]

1. *The First Council of Nicaea* (325), which condemned Arius and defined the incarnate Son of God as "consubstantial" with the Father.

2. *The First Council of Constantinople* (381), which finally settled the Arian controversy. Later on this council was credited with having adopted the present Creed known as the Nicaean-Constantinopolitan Creed.

3. *The Council of Ephesus* (431), which condemned Nestorianism and declared that there were not two persons existing side by side in Christ—God and a man called Jesus—but that the divinity and humanity were united in one person (the "hypostatic union"), the Person of the Word, the Son of God incarnate. Consequently, Mary, the Mother of Jesus, is the Mother of God (*Theotokos*).

4. *The Council of Chalcedon* (451), which, while confirming the existence in Christ of a single Person, condemned the Monophysites, because the latter refused to distinguish between the concepts of Person (*hypostasis*) and Nature (*physis*). If Christ were one Person, they claimed, he could not have two natures but only one (*mono-*, "one," *physis*, "nature"). The council affirmed that the son of God must be confessed in two natures "unconfusedly,

---

4 An English translation of the canons and dogmatic decrees of the seven councils may be found in *The Nicene and Post-Nicene Fathers*, Second Series, vol. 14 (Grand Rapids, 1956).

immutably, indivisibly, inseparably, united...in one Person or 'hypostasis'." Many of the non-Greek elements in the Empire (Copts, Ethiopians, Syro-Jacobites, Armenians) left the Orthodox Church at this time and formed schismatic Monophysiste churches.

5. *The Second Council of Constantinople* (533). The Emperor Justinian was anxious to win back the Monophysites and wished to prove to them that the Council of Chalcedon had not fallen into Nestorianism and was not contrary to the doctrine proclaimed at Ephesus. Summoning a new council, he had three theologians of the fifth century (the "Three Chapters") suspected of entertaining Nestorian views condemned.

6. *The Third Council of Constantinople* (680), which condemned a bastard form of Monophysitism known as Monothelitism. According to the Monothelites (*thelesis,* "will") while Christ has two natures he has only one will, his divine will or "energy." The council maintained that the humanity is not an abstract entity in Christ but is manifested by its own will, subject freely and in all things to the divine will. Christ therefore has two wills.

7. *The Second Council of Nicaea* (787), which defined the Orthodox doctrine concerning the images (icons) which represent Christ or the saints. The Word of God was truly incarnate and became true man. He may therefore be pictorially represented, and the same is true of the saints. While sacred images ought to be venerated, the one whom they represent is the true object of the veneration. However, it is not lawful to pay to them the highest form of worship (*latreia*), which is due to God alone (the distinction between "veneration" [*proskynesis*] and "true worship" [*latreia*] has become classical in theology). The veneration of images was opposed by several Byzantine emperors, who were responsible for the iconoclastic controversy.

The work of the ecumenical councils was not limited to deciding these purely dogmatic questions, but was also concerned with the Church's constitutional and administrative organization.

During the pre-Constantinian period there were no precise juridical norms governing the relations of local churches with each other. These relations were determined ultimately by the awareness all Christians had of belonging to the one Lord and to the one Catholic Church. Church unity was manifested in a practical way: for example, when the bishop from neighboring districts convened in a city which had lost its chief pastor for the consecration of a new bishop. Occasions of this kind soon came to be used for the holding of synods, which became a regular feature in the life of the Church. In this way local churches came to be grouped into provinces, which generally coincided with the administrative divisions of the Empire. Moreover, it was inevitable that the bishops of the larger sees, the heads of sizable and wealthy communities, should preside over these synods, or councils, and although they exercised no jurisdictional power over their colleagues, the latter were nevertheless prepared to acknowledge their *de facto* authority. Their votes were often the determining factor in reaching common decisions.

The councils of the Constantinian period simply codified and gave juridical form to this state of affairs in their *canons*.

The canons of the Council of Nicaea (325) are almost all concerned with the adjustment of the government of the Church to that of the Empire, which was now of course well-disposed toward the Church: the local churches were grouped together in ecclesiastical provinces which had the same boundaries as the civil provinces, and the provincial synod, which was to meet regularly, was to be presided over by the bishop of the capital of the province, or "metropolitan." Canon 6 allows for an exception to this rule in the case of the three greater sees of Rome, Alexandria and Antioch, whose jurisdiction in any case by this time extended far beyond the limits of a single province. The Council of Nicaea officially granted them the right to approve the episcopal elections in several civil provinces. The overwhelming importance of these

cities—by far the largest in the Empire—was certainly the determining factor in this decision. Later an attempt would be made to
explain Canon 6 on the basis of the apostolic origin of the three
churches, but the objective historian cannot be unduly impressed
by this argument (to which the council never refers!) for it could
be alleged more convincingly on behalf of certain other churches,
especially Jerusalem. In spite of the honor conferred on him by
Canon 7, Nicaea still decreed that the bishop of Jerusalem should
be subject to the metropolitan of Caesarea in Palestine.

The second ecumenical council at Constantinople (381) decreed a similar exception in the case of the Church of Constantinople, because of its status as the New Rome, the capital of the
Empire, but it remained subject to the overall primacy of the
Elder Rome (Canon 3).

Still later, especially at Chalcedon (451), the Roman world was
divided into five "patriarchates"—Rome, Constantinople, Alexandria, Antioch and Jerusalem—which had the privilege of presiding over the metropolitan elections in groups of provinces,
while the metropolitans themselves continued to consecrate the
bishops under their immediate jurisdiction.[5] The Novellae of
Justinian refer to the five patriarchates as the five senses of the
Empire.

This gradual evolution of the Church's governmental structure
did not take place without certain clashes. Beginning in the fifth
century, for example, we can discern the seeds of future conflict
over the exact role which the Church of Rome was destined to
play. Whereas for the Orientals—who were always in a majority at
the ecumenical councils—the privileges of Rome, universally recognized, were based on the numerical importance of the Roman
see and also on the fact that it was located in the capital of the

---

5 Within each patriarchate, as a matter of fact, a different procedure was followed: the
bishop of Alexandria, for example, had abolished the privileges of metropolitans as
early as the fourth century and himself consecrated all the bishops of the civil
"dioceses" of Egypt, Libya and the Pentapolis.

Empire. In Rome itself there was an awareness that this interpretation could lead to the complete disappearance of the Roman primacy, for was Constantinople not the new capital and thus capable of eclipsing the glory of the old capital? On the other hand, Rome was the *only* "apostolic" Church in the West; the relics of the holy Apostles Peter and Paul had long been venerated there and there was no question at all that, for the Western Christian, Rome was the center of Christianity. By appealing to these considerations the popes, particularly St. Leo the Great (440-461), attempted to oppose the rise of the see of Constantinople, but they could not succeed in their purpose, except temporarily, for its rise was logical and in the nature of things. From the time of Patriarch John the Faster (528-595), the bishop of New Rome adopted the title of "ecumenical patriarch," which was partly of honorary significance, but which in any case was not intended to infringe upon the Roman primacy.

However this may be, it is undeniable that as a result of these differences two opposing ecclesiologies began to take shape, each with its own view of what the primacy meant which all the world acknowledged belonged to Rome. For one side this primacy was of direct apostolic and hence "divine" origin, while for the other it was only a primacy of "ecclesiastical law" and origin, the exact significance of which it was up to the councils to define and which in any case could only function with the consent of and subject to control by the other churches. The canons of the councils definitely favor this latter interpretation.[6]

It is impossible to dwell any longer on the history of the councils. We must be content with having pointed out their importance for the Orthodox Church. Later ecclesiastical writers have sometimes compared them with the Seven Pillars of Wisdom or with

---

6 For a more detailed study of the question, see our article "La Primauté romaine dans la tradition canonique jusqu'au concile de Chalcédoine," in *Istina*, no. 4 (1957), pp. 463-82; see now also the remarkable study of Prof. F. Dvornik, *The Idea of Apostolicity in Byzantium and the Legend of the Apostle Andrew* (Cambridge, MA: 1958).

the Seven Gifts of the Holy Spirit. But such symbolical explanations stressing the number seven have only a relative importance. They indicate that the Councils have indeed been venerated by tradition, but they have no real theological meaning. When the Orthodox Church says that it recognizes only these seven councils as ecumenical, it is not claiming, of course, that its authority is confined to one historical period, or that other councils or witnesses to tradition—the Church Fathers or liturgical formulas—may not also witness to the Truth. We shall see further on that certain local councils, recognized later as having universal validity, defined the Orthodox position on grace in the fourteenth century, and a similar function was performed by still other councils which met between the seventeenth and nineteenth centuries.

The seven ecumenical councils recognized as such by the Orthodox Church were held under certain definite historical circumstances, those prevailing at the time of the Christian Roman (or Byzantine) Empire. Now while it is perfectly true that the Church remains essentially the same at all times, historical circumstances vary from time to time. Consequently it would be foolish to think that we can simply reproduce the forms and procedures that governed the ancient councils. New forms and procedures will be called for in keeping with the new conditions that will prevail, and we must not suppose that this natural evolutionary process detracts in any way from the permanence of Truth in the Church. Moreover, the Roman Catholic Church commonly recognizes twenty councils as ecumenical today, but it does not pretend to claim that the later ones were held in accordance with the same forms and procedures governing the earlier ones. In fact, the word "ecumenical" is used today in such a variety of senses that it has become rather vague. What matters is not the number of councils recognized as "ecumenical," but the awareness which the Church has of itself and of the Truth. The Orthodox Church claims that it remains faithful to the ancient councils—the common heritage of Eastern and Western Christendom—and it believes itself to be the One Church to which the ancient councils bore witness.

Chapter 3

SCHISM AND ATTEMPTS AT REUNION

The schism between Byzantium and Rome was without doubt the most tragic event in the history of the Church. Christendom became divided in two halves, and this separation still endures today and has determined the destiny of both East and West to a very great extent. While the Eastern Church claimed—and still claims today—to be the only true Church of Christ, it saw its cultural and its geographical field of vision restricted: historically, it became identified with the Byzantine world. The Church of the West, as viewed by the Orthodox Church, lost the doctrinal and ecclesiological balance of primitive Christianity and this lack of balance was ultimately responsible for provoking the reaction of the sixteenth century, the Protestant Reformation.

If we wish to assess the true meaning and extent of this catastrophe, we must avoid the romantic fallacy of thinking that there was ever an "undivided Church" which lasted for some nine centuries. As a matter of fact, the Church has experienced a succession of heresies and schisms from the very earliest times. A particularly important and long-lived separation began in the fifth and sixth centuries over christological issues, when whole nations—Egypt, Ethiopia, Armenia, and large segments of the Syrian population—abandoned the communion of the orthodox "Great Church," which they referred to scornfully as the "Melkite" or "imperial" Church. The latter was thereby deprived of communion with various venerable non-Greek traditions of Christianity, those of the Semites and Copts, and found itself reduced, practically speaking, to the Greek and Latin parts of the Empire. In the ninth and tenth centuries this Greco-Roman world was in turn divided into two great branches, along the linguistic and political frontiers which then demarcated the two zones of the ancient Roman Empire.

However, these various schisms cannot be regarded merely as evidence of an inescapable tendency toward fragmentation on the part of the churches. The Greek and Latin Churches both continued to exhibit the signs of true catholicity. Neither allowed itself to be transformed into a purely national church. Both continued to direct their energies outward toward the spreading of the Gospel. While Rome was preoccupied with the conversion of the new nations of the West, the "barbarians" of the North, Byzantium could claim credit for the conversion of the Slavs and was continually active throughout its history in the attempt to win back the Monophysites to union with the Church. We have to admit, therefore, that in addition to the various linguistic, cultural, and political reasons for the separation, theological differences of a profound nature were also at work toward this end. In attempting to explain the nature of the schism we are forced to admit that both theological and non-theological factors were hopelessly mixed up together. It would be pointless to deny either the one or the other. We shall find later on, however, that theological causes are at the root of the matter because all attempts at conciliation and reunion have been frustrated by the failure to overcome these hurdles. Moreover, they still constitute today the major obstacle to the ultimate goal of ecumenism.

We have seen that from the fourth to the eighth century tension already existed in the Church between East and West over the true significance of the Roman primacy. This tension, however, was not always readily apparent, because of the flowery rhetoric and studied vagueness used by Eastern prelates when writing to the popes. The latter, for their part, avoided pressing their claim to universal jurisdiction over the whole Church, in all its implications, for the claim was contrary to the traditions and customs of the Church. The latent tension only came to the surface in the ninth century, when it developed into open hostility.

The political event which occasioned this conflict was the founding of the Carolingian Empire in the West.

History textbooks are fond of portraying Charlemagne as the great restorer, for his own benefit, of the Roman Empire in the West which had disappeared in the fifth century. It is asserted that when Charlemagne was crowned in 800 by the pope in Rome, he was occupying a throne that had long been vacant. But, as a matter of fact, many contemporaries regarded him as a usurper, for the legitimate Roman Empire with its capital at Constantinople had not ceased to exist, and its claim to rule the entire Christian Roman world had never been given up. One of the primary objectives of the reign of the Frankish king was to get Byzantium's approval for the step that had been taken in the West. When a project for the marriage of Charles and the reigning Byzantine empress fell through, the Frankish king decided to ruin Constantinople's claim to universal jurisdiction. One of the means used to achieve this end was to bring the charge of heresy against the East. The Eastern emperor could not claim to be the successor of earlier Christian *basileis* because he worshipped images and because he confessed that the Holy Spirit proceeds "from the Father by the Son" instead of "from the Father and the Son." These allegations by Charlemagne in his famous *Libri Carolini,* sent to the pope in 792, formed part of the Frankish refutation of the decrees of the second ecumenical council of Nicaea (787) and pre-pared the way for the interminable quarrel between East and West over the question of the *filioque*.[1] Several Western bishops and theo-logians—Paulinus of Aquileia, Theodulphus of Orleans, and Sma-ragdus, abbot of St. Mihiel—took up the cudgels against the Greeks at the invitation of the Frankish court at Aix-la-Chapelle. Alcuin was thus able to write to Charlemagne in 799.[2]

1 During the sixth century certain anti-Arian councils in Spain had inserted in the Nicaean-Constantinopolitan Creed the word *filioque* which was not in the original (*Credo...in Spiritum Sanctum...qui ex Patre Filioque procedit*). This new version of the Creed spread to Gaul and the Frankish lands in the eighth century. It was not accepted by the Church of Rome, which opposed the interpolation until the eleventh century. The most complete account of the question of the origins of the *filioque* remains that of H. B. Swete, *On the History of the Doctrine of the Procession of the Holy Spirit* (From the Apostolic Age to the Death of Charlemagne) (Cambridge, 1876).

2 *Letters of Alcuin, No. 174,* Monumenta Germaniae historica Epistolae, IV, Epistolae

Three persons have been at the head of the hierarchy of the world: firstly, the representative of the apostolic sublimity, the vicar of blessed Peter...secondly, the occupant of the imperial dignity which exercises secular sway in the second Rome...thirdly, the royal dignity which our Lord Jesus Christ has reserved to you in order to rule the Christian peoples...It is now on you alone that the Churches of Christ must rely, from you alone that they expect salvation...

These words are very revealing with regard to the true nature of the new empire in the West; it was dominated by the ideals of caesaropapism—it seems that the Frankish court was influenced by the example of the iconoclastic emperors of Byzantium, whose theology was taken over by Charlemagne, at least in part—and it was intended to supplant both the traditional empire (in the East) and the papacy.

Fortunately for the cause of church unity, while the Roman Church approved Charlemagne's political aims, it was decidedly opposed to his theological attack on Byzantium. Popes Hadrian I (772-795) and Leo III (795-816) defended of Council of Nicaea and formally rejected the interpolation in the Creed. We must acknowledge frankly that the Christian world is indebted to them for having preserved its unity, if only for a relatively short time. When political interests finally caused the Byzantines to extend recognition to the Carolingian Empire—though with reservations—the Western attacks on the Greeks ceased, but they left behind a certain amount of ill feeling; and because of this and because of the existence of polemical tracts, it was not long before animosity flared up again.

The most serious consequence of the creation of Charlemagne's empire was the appearance of a new type of Christianity in the West, the work of men from the "barbarian" parts of Northern Europe, who were only very vaguely acquainted with the intellectual atmosphere of the Roman-Byzantine world in which the Fathers of the Church had lived and in which the ancient councils had been held. More serious still was the fact that the learned men at Aix-la-

aevi Carolini, II (Berlin, 1895), p. 288.

Chapelle felt free to define theological issues without reference and even in opposition to the East. The *Libri Carolini* and the whole literature connected with them have no other meaning. On the other hand it must be admitted that while the Byzantines were wise enough not to pay any attention to the doctrinal attacks of Charlemagne, they were unable to adopt toward the new Carolingian learning and culture a sympathetic and charitable attitude which might have helped to smooth off its rough edges. The Emperor Michael III was indiscreet enough in 864 to refer to the Latin language as a "barbarous" and "Scythian" tongue, incapable of expressing the finer shadings of theological thought. This self-satisfaction of the Byzantines with their own culture, which could boast a Photius or a Psellus while the medieval West was scarcely able to cope with the rudiments of learning, presented them from taking the theological position of the Franks seriously

The Church of Rome alone was capable of maintaining the bridges. It was the only religious authority which the Franks respected; it had preserved enough of the Greek Traditions to be able to understand both East and West. We have seen how, when they were opposed by Charlemagne, the Roman popes had been able to perform their role as supreme judges worthily, and Photius publicly acknowledged the Church's indebtedness to Pope Leo III a century later.[3]

The open breaks between East and West in the ninth and eleventh centuries occurred when the political aims of the Frankish Empire became confused with the canonical pretensions of the popes and both found themselves united in a common opposition to the East.

From the eighth century the history of the papacy is dominated by its relations with the new Carolingian Empire. At first, in the eighth century and then again particularly in the tenth and eleventh centuries, the bishops of Rome were hardly more than mere tools in the hands of the Western emperors, whose outlook was thoroughly

---

3 In his *Mystagogia*, written against the *filioque*, Photius mentions with approval the opposition of this pope to its insertion in the Creed.

caesaropapist. However, a few great popes managed to assert themselves and react against this tendency, Nicholas I in the ninth century, and especially the great theoretician of the medieval papacy, Gregory VII (1073-1081), who was preceded by the vigorous but short-lived Leo IX (1049-1054) and Nicholas II (1059-1061). This papal reaction, which ultimately led to the triumph of the papacy over the Empire, was inspired by a new consciousness of the meaning of the Roman primacy. The see of Rome must become something more than a mere patriarchate of the West, something more than one apostolic see among others, if a Henry IV were to be forced to go to Canossa. Its traditional primacy of honor and authority must be transformed into a real power of jurisdiction, universal in scope and absolute in nature.

Antipapalist writers have often seen in this development a sign that the popes had succumbed to a wicked desire for domination. But this is to read the signs incorrectly and miss the essential point. The great reforming popes were sincerely attempting to restore the Church and free it from excessive lay control. They fought the evil of simony and raised the standard of clerical morality. The result of their efforts was the birth of a Christian Europe and a new civilization. However, these great pontiffs, almost all of whom were of Northern European origin and closely identified with the Cluniac reform movement, were the heirs of that Carolingian civilization which, as we have seen, had dared to reach definitions by itself in opposition to the East and had developed without being influenced to any extent by the Greek Fathers. Basically Latin and Western in outlook, this civilization was shared by both Roman popes and Western emperors. This is why, ultimately, the controversy between the *Sacerdotium* and the *Imperium* appeared to be more of a political than a religious quarrel. The popes turned the emperor's own arms against him, they adopted his methods and identified themselves with his ambition to destroy the prestige of the old but legitimate Roman Empire and Constantinople. The Orthodox historian therefore will not question the sincerely of the reforming popes or their zeal for the welfare of the Church. He will simply feel obliged to question the theological and ecclesiological basis of a theory of power which appears to him as alien to the spirit of the Gospel. He will refuse to regard the development of the medieval papacy as something absolute and will attribute to this development, at least in part, those secularizing, reformist, and anti-clerical tendencies which will begin to appear in the West later on.

When reforming the Western Church the popes tried to extend their reforms to the East but failed. This failure would serve more than anything else to strengthen the unity of Western Christendom and make it monolithic and self-contained.

Nicholas I (858-867) was without question the greatest of the reforming popes of the early Middle Ages. In the West he was confronted by the three kingdoms into which the Carolingian Empire had become divided, and in the East by the Byzantine Empire which was experiencing a violent quarrel between two factions in the Church. Appeal from both sides was made to his tribunal, in accordance with tradition. But whereas his predecessors in the time of Charlemagne were called upon to arbitrate *between* the two Christendoms, he was obligated to deal with quarrels within each side. This gave him the opportunity to press those reforms which he deemed necessary, on the one side as well as the other.

We cannot linger here over the crisis brought on by the divorce of Lothar II. Skillfully utilizing the rivalry between the latter and his uncles, Charles the Bald and Louis the German, Nicholas succeeded in annulling the sentences of several councils of the Frankish episcopate, in judging the archbishops of Cologne and Trier at Rome, and finally in compelling the royal power to yield. He attempted also, in the course of a violent quarrel with Hicmar, the archbishop of Reims, to limit the authority of the metropolitans in the West, which had been decreed, as we have seen, by the

First Council of Nicaea, and to establish a system which would have subjected the entire Western episcopate directly to the Roman see. In support of its new policy the latter now began to appeal—in good faith, of course—to the celebrated False Decretals, which were compiled about this time and which aimed at substituting for the old conciliar legislation an new system exalting the prerogatives of the Roman see that is, in effect, a papal monarchy.[4]

All this might have had little effect on relations with the East. Precedents could have been cited, particularly the example of Alexandria, showing that it was lawful for powerful patriarchs to gather the reins of power into their own hands. But Nicholas was clearly of the opinion that his reforms had to do with rights which the Roman see ought to claim as properly belonging to it and therefore of universal validity. It was on this point that he clashed with the Eastern Church.

Patriarch Ignatius of Constantinople had been compelled to resign his throne in 857 to Photius, the great scholar and student of antiquity, as well as theologian and politician. The imperial government was of course responsible for the change, but at Byzantium as elsewhere in the West at this time no one questioned the right of the emperor to decide who was to sit on the patriarchal throne. This right naturally entailed a certain influence by the patriarchs over political affairs. This dyarchy of emperor and patriarch was, as it were, the very foundation stone of the Byzantine theocracy. However, it would be highly inaccurate to think of this system as merely a form of caesaropapism, particularly after the defeat of the iconoclastic party. In the case of

---

4 The compiler of the Decretals (whether of Roman or Frankish origin) was interested primarily in combating the authority of strong metropolitans like Hincmar by an appeal to a great many alleged ancient papal decretals which he forged, rather than in exalting the authority of Rome, but this was the net effect of his work. The decretals were accepted as genuine and incorporated in later canonical collections. See P. Fournier and G. Le Bras, *Histoire des collections canoniques en Occident*, vol. 1, pp. 126-33 ;cf. E. Amann, *L'Époque carolingienne*, in Fliche-Martin, *Histoire de l'Église*, vol. 6 (Paris, 1947), pp. 352-66, 387.

Ignatius, moreover, things took their accustomed course and due forms were observed: Photius was elected only after his predecessor had formally resigned.[5]

However, a group of Ignatian partisans decided to keep up the struggle and persuaded the ex-patriarch to revoke his abdication. In keeping with the canons of the ancient Council of Sardica, both parties then appealed to Rome. This move on their part was tantamount to an unprecedented act of deference by the Byzantine Church toward the see of Rome, for until then the popes had never intervened directly in the purely disciplinary affairs of the powerful ecumenical patriarchate. So the legates of Nicholas I presided over a council of bishops at Constantinople which confirmed the election of Photius (861). On the very eve of the conflict, therefore, Byzantium was displaying a more deferential attitude toward Rome than it had ever done in the past.

Since Photius continued to be opposed by an Ignatian minority at Constantinople, Pope Nicholas determined to profit by the occasion and extend to the East the reforms which he was pressing in the West. If he could limit the authority of metropolitans in one half of Christendom, why could he not humble the much more important obstacle to Roman centralization in the other, namely the Byzantine patriarchate? He decided therefore to annul the Council of Constantinople and compel both Ignatius and Photius to appear before his tribunal, as he had attempted and partially achieved in the case of the archbishops of Cologne and Trier. It hardly needs to be observed that there was no precedent in the conciliar legislation then in force to justify such a procedure. The patriarchate of Byzantium remained silent and failed to reply to the papal letters.

The situation was further complicated by the activities of Byzantine and Western missionaries in Bulgaria. Most of the

---

5 The fundamental work on the Photian crisis is by F. Dvornik, *The Photian Schism, History and Legend* (Cambridge, 1948).

Slavic tribes were on the verge of adopting Christianity about this time and were hesitating between East and West in view of the political and religious pressure being exercised by the two rival empires, the Byzantine and the Frankish. The brothers St. Cyril and St. Methodius, the Apostles of the Slavs, encountered wherever they went, in Khazaria and later in Bohemia, the opposition of German missionaries eager to impose on their new converts the Latin language and ritual and the singing of the *filioque* in the mass. Now the Bulgarians were actually baptized in 863 by missionaries from Byzantium, but when the Bulgarian khan, Boris, failed to get Byzantine approval for the autonomous status of his church in 865, he decided to transfer his spiritual allegiance to the West and allow the Frankish clergy to organize his church.

Up until this time the popes had been fairly successful in acting as arbiters between the Franks and Byzantines. It was possible for them to appear to be neutral as long as the Roman see did not have direct control over the German missionaries in Slavic countries. But this is precisely what Nicholas sought to bring about by his curtailment of the autonomy of local churches and extension of Roman jurisdiction. He was bound therefore to take a stand on the minor quarrels which until then had not been regarded as within the sphere of the papacy. In the case of Bulgaria, he decided to support the Franks against the Byzantines. He even succeeded in obtaining that the new head of the Bulgarian Church should be appointed by himself and not by the Germanic emperor Louis II, though only after some difficulty. The pope was thus creating at the very gates of Constantinople a situation until then undreamed of, namely, a church of Frankish rite subject to Roman jurisdiction. This church would of course recite the *filioque* in the Creed, although this was not done at Rome itself. Nicholas was thus not only supporting the political and cultural enemies of Byzantium, but implicitly giving his blessing to this controversial interpolation in the universal creed.

In 867 Patriarch Photius accused Pope Nicholas of heresy in his famous Encyclical and broke off communion with him.

It is impossible to go into the detail of the long conflict which ensued. Before long Photius was deprived of his patriarchal throne by a dynastic revolution in Byzantium. In order to strengthen their position, the restored Ignatius and his followers needed the support of Rome. In a new council at Constantinople (869-870), under the presidency of papal legates, Photius was condemned and the Roman primacy forcibly asserted. However, this was tantamount to a mere diplomatic maneuver on the part of the Ignatian party, for they could not be expected to go on appealing to principles that were so much at variance with the age-old conceptions of the Eastern Church. While the council was being held Ignatius received word that the Bulgarians had returned to their allegiance to Byzantium. Khan Boris drove out the Franks and requested the Byzantine Church to consecrate an archbishop for his church. Ignoring the protests of the papal legates Ignatius welcomed the Bulgarian move. Only his death (877) prevented him from being excommunicated by Pope Hadrian II. It is not accurate, therefore, to describe the Ignatian party at Byzantium as a "papal" party.

Meanwhile Photius had been reconciled with Ignatius and now found himself once again on the patriarchal throne (877). Since Providence willed that the successor of popes Nicholas I and Hadrian II should break with the policy of these two popes, peace and harmony were once more restored to the Church.

All historical sources are in agreement that Pope John VIII (872-882) realized the danger to Christian unity inherent in the policy of his immediate predecessors. Like the popes of the time of Charlemagne, he acknowledged the justice of the Greek point of view with regard to the use of the native languages in the liturgy and the exclusion of the *filioque* from the Creed. He gave support to St. Methodius in the latter's trouble with Frankish missionaries in Moravia, and, most important of all, his legates at the Council

of Constantinople in 879-880, which restores Photius, condemned the famous "addition" to the Creed, together with the
rest of the Eastern Church.[6] For the rest of his life Photius
remained grateful to Pope John for his restoration of the unity of
the Church and cited him as an example to those who wished to
deny the authority of the Roman popes at Byzantium. It cannot
be denied, as a matter of act, that the decisions of the council of
879-880, which are included in every Orthodox collection of
canon law, must be regarded as the very model of the way in
which the Orthodox Church conceives of Christian unity, that is,
as a unity in faith to which the Roman primacy may indeed bear
witness, but of which it cannot itself be the source.

The tenth century and the first half of the eleventh were not
marked by any outstanding clash between East and West. During
this time the papacy was passing through one of the most profound periods of degradation in its long history, while for Byzantium, on the contrary, this was an age of glory under the
Macedonian emperors, whose conquests greatly extended the
boundaries of the Empire; an age of cultural progress, that of
Michael Psellus, and Symeon the New Theologian; the age also of
important missions to the Slavs and the Caucasus. The Byzantines
could afford to ignore the pope, the primacy, and its far-reaching
claims, because the pope was not in a position to enforce them.

Hence they paid very little attention to one event of major
importance—as things turned out, a portent of things to come. In
1014 the German emperor Henry II came to Rome to have
himself crowned by Pope Benedict VIII, and he easily persuaded
that pope, who was completely under his influence, to allow the
use of a Germanic ritual in the coronation ceremony; this meant

6 Until recently it was held that Pope John VIII later repudiated his legates and
  excommunicated Photius anew. Modern Catholic historians (F. Dvornik, *op. cit.*, cf.
  also V. Grumel, "Y eût-il un second schisme de Photius?" in *Revue des sciences
  philosophiques et théologiques*, no. 32 [1933], pp. 432-57) have proved that the
  second Photian schism is merely a "legend."

that the *filioque* would be sung in the Credo of the mass in Rome.[7] Thus it came about that, because of the laxness and indifference of the times, the frankly caesaropapist outlook of the German monarchs became responsible for the adoption by Rome of a doctrine which was rejected by the Christian East.[8] In any case, from approximately the beginning of the eleventh century there was no longer any *communio in sacris* between Byzantium and Rome.

The controversy over the *filioque* as well as other points in dispute between Rome and Constantinople could certainly have been settled, as had so many misunderstandings before this time. But the tragic thing about developments in the eleventh century was that, because they had mutually ignored each other for so long, East and West had lost the *common ground* which had formerly enabled them to come to an understanding. Whenever they attempted to restore communion—and this was done again and again in the medieval period—they were always prevented from agreeing upon a common language because of their different understanding of the nature of the Church. For one side, the see of Rome was the sole criterion of Truth; for the other, the Spirit of Truth resided in the whole Church and normally expressed himself by means of the ecumenical councils.

Once of these attempts occurred in 1053-1054, an occasion that has wrongly been considered as marking the beginning of the

7   We know this from Berno (*De officio missae*, in PL 142, col. 1060-61), who does not explicitly mention the *filioque*. However, it is known that the popes of the ninth century had forbidden the singing of the Creed in the mass (a Frankish custom) in order to avoid the appearance of approving the Frankish interpolation. Benedict VIII was no longer in a position to keep up this opposition. It is worth noting that Byzantine tradition regards Pope Sergius IV (1009-1012), the predecessor of Benedict VIII, as the first pope to profess the heresy of *filioque* and as having been excluded from the diptychs at Constantinople on that account. This vagueness of this information shows what little importance was attached to the event by contemporaries.

8   As G. Every aptly says in his book, the singing of the *filioque* in the Creed at Rome was interpreted as a sign of allegiance to the Holy Roman Empire on the part of the pope (*The Byzantine Patriarchate* [London, 1947]), p. 170).

schism.[9] It must be admitted that the protagonists on both sides were reformers of their respective churches and the spirit of their reforms was hardly likely to be conducive to reconciliation.

The patriarch of Constantinople, Michael Caerularius, had determined on a reform of the Latin churches in his own diocese and even in those throughout the entire patriarchate. These churches fasted on Saturdays, sang the Alleluia during Eastertide, and otherwise followed Latin customs which were at variance with Byzantine practice and which appeared to be controversial. So the patriarch decided that they must conform to Byzantine custom in the matters under dispute, and when they refused to do so, he ordered the churches closed. It hardly need be said that the Latins of Constantinople did not sing the *filioque* in the Creed and that is why there is little mention of this subject in the controversial literature of the eleventh century.

In the West the Cluniac reform movement and its sympathizers were pushing ahead with their projects at this time. The most important of their measures had already been widely accepted by the Germanic world, but they were encountering a still resistance on the part of the Italians. Pope Leo IX, former bishop of Toul, and his entourage, particularly Cardinal Humbert of Moyenmoutier, were strong advocates of the new reform measures and were attempting to win Italian acceptance of one of them in particular, the celibacy of the clergy. The opponents of the celibacy measure did not fail to point to the example of the Greeks, whose secular priests were regularly married. Endless controversy raged over questions that were relatively unimportant in themselves, and was carried on by persons who were no doubt well-intentioned, but who were not always so well acquainted with the true traditions of the Church.

In spite of this mutual atmosphere of distrust, the patriarch Michael Caerularius dispatched to Pope Leo IX, at the request of

9 On the events of 1054, see especially A. Michel, *Humbert und Kerullarios* (Paderborn, 1924-1930); and G. Every, *op. cit.*, pp. 153-69.

the emperor, a letter offering to re-establish communion with Rome. In reply to this invitation and also in order to regulate the outstanding disciplinary and liturgical differences between the two churches, the pope sent legates to Constantinople in 1054, headed by Cardinal Humbert. They were received with honor by the emperor, but the patriarch refused all contact with them. He charged that they had come at the insistance of Argyrus, the Byzantine governor of Italy, a person of Lombard origin and a follower of the Latin rite, whose pro-Germanic policies the patriarch disliked. Caerularius also questioned the authenticity of the papal letters which the legates had brought with them. His suspicions were perhaps justified since Leo IX was at this time a prisoner of the Normans in Italy and would thus not have been in a position, it would seem, to sign official documents.

Thwarted by the non-cooperative and even hostile attitude of the patriarch, the legates stalked into Hagia Sophia during the celebration of the liturgy, deposited their famous sentence of excommunication on the high altar, and then stalked out again, shaking the dust symbolically from their feet. The patriarch and his clergy were excommunicated for the most unlikely crimes: for having *omitted* (!) the *filioque* from the Creed and for allowing the marriage of the clergy, among others. Caerularius replied by summoning a synod and having the legates excommunicated, in spite of attempts of the emperor to smooth things over.

The events of 1054 which seemed to put a seal on the break between Rome and Constantinople did not in fact put an end to all contacts between East and West. The other Eastern patriarchs remained in communion with the Latins for some time, and at Constantinople itself the Latin churches and monasteries remained open.[10] The true and final rupture only took place as a result of the Crusades.

Even today, it is rare for Western historians to pay adequate attention to the really disastrous part played by these great expedi-

10 See particularly G. Every, *op. cit.,* pp. 153-69.

tions in worsening the relations between East and West. From the viewpoint of church unity. When they first reached the East, lands traditionally Christian but now occupied by the Moslems, the Crusaders began by acknowledging the canonical rights of the local bishops and entering into sacramental communion with them. There is much evidence, in fact, which proves that the ecclesiastical rupture was not yet regarded as finally consummated in the eleventh or throughout the twelfth century. But the Latin princes and clergy of Outremer gradually put an end to this state of affairs by replacing the Oriental clergy with Latin clergy. Most important of all, it was the infamous fourth Crusade which gave the final blow to the last vestiges of church unity still remaining. The Venetian fleet conveying the Crusaders to the Holy Land purposely veered off its course toward Constantinople, with the approval of the Crusaders themselves, and the great city "guarded by God" was captured and sacked in one of the most famous but also disgraceful events in history. The whole West was enriched by the precious relics and Byzantine treasures carried off, and a Venetian patriarch, Thomas Morosini, was installed in the throne of Photius with the approval of Pope Innocent III. To the doctrinal differences separating the Greeks and Latins there was now added a new note, national hatred, which helped to make all future attempts at reunion more unrealistic than ever.

Yet these attempts were made, and rather frequently. Almost every one of the Palaeologi, particularly Michael VIII, who won Constantinople back from the Latins and re-established the Byzantine Empire (1259-1282), carried on discussions with the popes regarding reunion. Political motives were unquestionably uppermost in their minds: first the desire to protect their empire against Latin attempts to retake it; then the hope of being able, with Latin help, to ward of the Turkish peril, which finally reduced their empire to little more than a beleaguered city. Only a new Crusade (!) could save Byzantium. But before the popes would do anything effective in the way of military help, they insisted that there must first be reunion in ecclesiastical matters. Occasionally the Byzantine emperors would resort to force in order to break down the resistance of the Byzantine Church and impose a policy of reunion against the latter's will. Thus after taking part in the Council of Lyons (1274) through representatives and accepting the union personally, Michael VIII installed on the patriarchal throne a person sharing his own views, John Bekkos, but the reunion did not survive the emperor even by one day. Regarded as an apostate, he was even refused Christian burial. The Emperor John V (1341-1391) also embraced Catholicism on a personal basis (1369), but this too was without any effect in the ecclesiastical sphere. While remaining stubbornly opposed to any politically oriented reunion, the Byzantine Church was not opposed categorically to the idea of a negotiated peace in keeping with the ancient canons and ecclesiastical custom. In order to bring this about, the Church insisted that it was necessary to hold an ecumenical council which, it was certain, would result in the triumph of Orthodoxy. For a long time the popes refused to entertain the idea of holding a council in which both sides would be represented as equals, but the idea finally triumphed, nevertheless, during the first part of the fifteenth century, when the Great Schism of the West had shaken the papacy to its very foundations. The popes were afraid that the Greeks might reach an agreement with the schismatic council of Basel and decided to authorize at last a real reunion council.

The council met first at Ferrara, then at Florence (1438-1439), and the mere fact that it was held at all constituted a kind of moral victory for the East. An important Greek delegation headed by the emperor and the patriarch of Constantinople arrived in Italy and began theological discussions with the Western theologians and prelates. This course of these discussions showed how difficult it would be to reach an agreement of basic issues, for minds were not yet prepared to revise their thinking on certain points. The problem of the *filioque,* for example, was complicated by the fact that the

Roman Church held that it had already defined this matter dogmatically and was unwilling to go back on its pervious decision. Regarding the problem of the Roman primacy, we can only say that it was hardly more than touched upon at Florence. After weeks and even months of wrangling, the Greeks finally had to face the unpalatable alternative of either yielding to the Roman point of view or breaking off the talks and attempting to cope with the Turkish threat alone. Moral and financial pressure finally conspired to force them to accept the first alternative. The majority at length yielded and signed the act of reunion. Only the metropolitan of Ephesus, Mark Eugenicos, held out and refused to follow suit. Another outstanding theologian, Scholarios, the future patriarch, left Florence before the end of the discussions.

As soon as they returned home the Greek delegates for the most part repudiated their signature, when confronted by the general disapproval of the people. When Metropolitan Isidore of Kiev reached Moscow to proclaim the reunion there, he was imprisoned and only succeeded in escaping to Rome with great difficulty. The Byzantine emperor John VIII and his successor, Constantine XI, remained faithful to the union, but they did not dare proclaim it officially in Hagia Sophia until 1452. The following year, in 1453, the Ottoman Turkish ruler Mohammed II entered New Rome as a conqueror and the Byzantine Empire ceased to exist. The first task of the new patriarch, Gennadios Scholarios, was to repudiate the Union of Florence officially.

There can be no doubt, as we have said, that the really profound reasons for the schism between East and West are of a doctrinal and theological nature, the most important issues being those concerning the Holy Spirit and the nature of the Church. Different views about doctrine have also prevented agreement from being reached on a number of minor points of a political, canonical, or liturgical nature, for, in spite of all, both sides have made sincere efforts to come to some kind of understanding. If these efforts have failed, it can only be because the really basic issues of a doctrinal nature were never discussed seriously. From the thirteenth century on, all discussions between the popes and emperors regarding reunion took place in an atmosphere dominated more by political than by religious consideration, the Byzantine Church itself remaining largely outside the picture. Moreover, those discussions showed that the West harbored completely false ideas about the existence of Byzantine caesaropapism and thought that it was sufficient to win over the emperor to gain the allegiance of the whole Church. It was with this in mind that the popes encouraged the personal conversion of Emperor John V in 1369. Even today the view is quite common that the Byzantine "schism" had its roots in caesaropapism; nevertheless it is a fact that from the eleventh century the emperors were almost consistently in favor of reunion with Rome because of the undoubted political advantages to be derived from it, and they tried to bring reunion about at all costs, even by the use of brute force. Equally consistently, since the time of Michael Caerularius, the patriarchs, or most of them at any rate, opposed their efforts in the name of the true faith. By relying so much on the emperors to bring about reunion, the popes were relying, actually, on a caesaropapism which did not in fact exist.

We must freely confess, however, that even if serious theological discussions were to take place, there can be no assurance that they would result in a speedy agreement on fundamentals. The discussions at Florence proved this, for they were serious from the doctrinal point of new regardless of the outcome. Agreement was possible only on the basis of a common tradition, but the overwhelming impact of scholastic theology, the doctrinal formulas and definitions connected with it (such as the approval of the *filioque* by the Council of Lyons in 1274), and finally the far-reaching reforms affecting the very nature of the Church in the West brought about by the great popes of the Middle Ages made conversations extremely difficult.

Chapter 4

THE GOVERNMENT, LITURGY, AND SPIRITUALITY OF THE ORTHODOX CHURCH. ORTHODOX MONASTICISM.

We have seen how the christological disputes in the fifth century resulted in the loss to the Orthodox Church of whole nations of non-Greek origin (Copts, Armenians, Syrians, Ethiopians), some of whom refused to accept the decisions of the Council of Ephesus (431) and adopted a Nestorian profession of faith, while others accepted Ephesus but refused to acknowledge Chalcedon (451) and professed a faith that was the very opposite of Nestorianism, namely, Monophysitism. Both the former and the latter looked upon the Church of the Empire with undisguised suspicion, regarding it as a tool of the emperors. That church was now virtually conterminous with the Greek and Latin portions of the Empire.

Nevertheless, despite the losses sustained in the East, the Byzantine Church remained active in the missionary field like its sister church in the West. Most of the Slavic peoples were converted from Constantinople and received their Bible, liturgy, canon law, and spirituality from there. The Byzantine method of spreading the Gospel involved translating both the Scriptures and the liturgy into the language spoken by the people of the country and then establishing new churches modeled in all respects on the "Great Church" at Constantinople. This method differed fundamentally from that pursued in the West, where missionaries were at pains to impose Latin as the common liturgical tongue; it sufficed, however, to preserve a unity of cult among the newly converted nations. This liturgical unity soon became uniform throughout the East in any case, for the peoples of non-Greek origin who had kept the ancient liturgies of Antioch and Alexandria abandoned the Orthodox Church for the most part, as we have seen. However, it is important to realize that this liturgical centralization was not a matter of principle with the Byzantines, for the Orthodox Church has always admitted the legitimacy of various rites, but the cultural and political prestige of Constantinople was so great in the medieval period that liturgical uniformity often came about of its own accord: the provinces naturally tended to imitate the magnificent and imposing ritual of the Queen City on the Bosporus. Thus it happened that the non-Greek Churches of Syria, Egypt, and Palestine, which remained Orthodox, sooner or later adopted the Melkite or imperial rite of the capital. The Byzantine liturgy was also adopted by the Georgian Church, a distant outpost of Chalcedonian Orthodoxy, founded in the fourth century and long subject to the influence of Antioch.

Thus, many if not all of the Slavs too came to adopt the Byzantine form of Christianity. The Bulgarians (863) and Russians (988), each in turn, were baptized en masse, following the example set by their ruling princes, Boris and Vladimir. The conversion of the Serbs, from the ninth century onwards, was more gradual, as was that of the Walachians, Latin colonists who had settled in the region of the lower Danube and would later be known as Romanians. Byzantine missionaries also penetrated into Bohemia in the ninth century—where the archbishopric founded by St. Methodius was later taken over by the German and conformed to the Latin rite—and in the tenth century converted the Alans, a people residing north of the Caucasus. Thus the spiritual influence of Byzantium came to extend from the Caspian Sea to the Alps. It was not seriously affected by the decline and fall of the Byzantine Empire, and this general area constituted what may be called the Orthodox world, until the modern Diaspora of Orthodoxy to other parts of the globe.

In accordance with the twenty-eighth canon of the Council of Chalcedon, the patriarch of Constantinople had the right to consecrate new bishops for the missionary churches. He also attempted to keep them as long as possible under his direct control, an aim that was sometimes difficult to realize. When the Slavs became Christians they were content to enter the ranks of "civilized peoples" and adopt Byzantine customs but they were not happy about the continuance of Greek control. From Byzantium they took over the Byzantine theory of the state according to which there was only one Christian emperor on earth, that of Constantinople, the protector of the universal Church and the chosen of God. The Bulgarians and Serbs, each in turn, attempted to conquer the imperial crown for their own rulers, but both failed before the stout walls of Constantinople. They consoled themselves for their inability to achieve this political goal by creating national churches for themselves. Constantinople was forced to recognize the situation and grant them the right to elect their own bishops, but as soon as conditions again became favorable the Byzantines would withdraw this right and re-establish their direct control. This right of the national churches to chose their own bishops will later be known as "autocephaly."

Thus, in addition to the four traditional patriarchates of the East, Constantinople, Alexandria, Antioch, Jerusalem—of which only the first had any real authority—from the ninth to the fifteenth century, during the Middle Ages, there was created a whole series of Slavic autocephalous churches (Greek *auto-*, "self," *kephale*, "head"), whose heads were metropolitans or archbishops but sometimes also received the title of "patriarch." Byzantine canon law has always been sufficiently flexible to allow for considerable fluctuations in the course of its history: unity of faith rather than unity of organization has been regarded as the ultimate bond uniting the churches.

This system, the basic features of which are still in effect, was tantamount to an organic development of the principles of church government as laid down by the first ecumenical councils. We may remember that in the time of Justinian (527-565) the Church was thought of as constituting a Pentarchy. The five patriarchs were invested with a kind of collective primacy in the Church and consecrated the metropolitans in their respective areas. Within the Pentarchy there was an honorary order of precedence which accorded the first place to the bishop of Rome, who was then followed by bishops of Constantinople, Alexandria, Antioch, and Jerusalem. Since the schism between East and West has resulted in the breaking off of communion with the first see, in the Orthodox Church today the patriarch of New Rome is regarded as having inherited the Roman primacy. It hardly needs to be stressed that its precedence of sees and transfer of primacy were not regarded as a matter of "divine right," since all bishops are equal with respect to the sacramental functions of their office. However, the myth of an ideal theocracy and a single Christendom, as formulated in the time of Justinian, remained firmly rooted in the Byzantine consciousness. This is why the Byzantines continued to venerate the memory of the early popes and were always ready to restore the Roman primacy, provided Orthodoxy were restored in the West. This is the way Symeon, a fifteenth-century archbishop of Thessalonica, a theologian, a commentator on the liturgical rites, speaks of the possibility of reunion: "There is no point in quarreling with the Latins over the Roman primacy. Only let them show that he [the bishop of Rome] adheres to the faith of Peter and that of the successors of Peter, and he will then receive the privileges of Peter, he will be the first, the coryphaeus and head of all; he will be the supreme pontiff."[1] Canonical unity thus depends upon unity of faith, and the latter must be evident by itself and not determined by some external criterion.

The survival of the pentarchic conception did not prevent the Eastern patriarchs, with the exception of that of Constantinople,

---

1 *Dialogus contra haereses*, PG 155, col. 120B.

from being shorn, in the course of the Middle Ages, of most of their former splendor and power. The Moslem conquests reduced the size of their flocks and isolated them from the rest of Christendom. Henceforth the Church of Constantinople became the real center of the Orthodox world. The ancient canons conferring on her the right of appeal from the entire Church, the decline of the other patriarchates, the missionary conquests of the Byzantine Church, and the prestige of the "Great Church" of Hagia Sophia: all contributed to endow her with an authority without parallel. The political decline of the Byzantine Empire also helped to enhance the prestige of the ecumenical patriarchate, for the latter retained power in the spiritual sphere comparable to that which was slipping from the hands of the emperor.[2] In the fourteenth century we find the patriarchs actively interfering in the religious as well as the political affairs of Eastern Europe, settling domestic quarrels for the Russian feudal princes, negotiating with the king of Poland over the status of his Orthodox subjects, and frustrating all attempts at reunion with Rome. But in exercising this authority they never claimed to be infallible. History reveals moreover that there were far too many heretical patriarchs for any such claim to be taken seriously. As late as 1347, for example, John Calecas was deposed for having supported the teaching of a condemned monk, Akindynos.

This centralized control over the Byzantine world achieved by the ecumenical patriarchs from the ninth century onwards has been effective in making the Orthodox Church "Byzantine," somewhat in the same way that the Catholic Church in the West was dominated by Rome and is today termed "Roman." This process of Byzantinization may be observed in both the liturgical and the devotional as well as in the canonical spheres.

The Christian liturgy has been given various forms and these in turn have gone through various transformations in the course

2 See on this subject, G. Ostrogorsky, *History of the Byzantine State* (New Brunswick, NJ: Rutgers University Press, 1957), pp. 577-78.

of history, in both East and West, in response to new conditions and in accordance with the peculiar genius of different peoples. The Church of Constantinople, for example, did not have any liturgical tradition of its own prior to the fourth century, but it gradually created a new rite which was greatly influenced by Antioch. This new Byzantine rite already possessed all the essential features which it now has[3] by the ninth century, at the time when it was carried to the far corners of the Byzantine world and became *the* liturgy of numerous peoples. It is celebrated today in many different languages and is regarded as a powerful bond uniting diverse nationalities who feel that it is an expression of their one Orthodox faith. The custom of translating it into a language understood by the people has helped to root the liturgy in the minds of the faithful, who look upon their participation in the common prayer of the Church as an important sign of belonging to the Body of Christ. This is not a question of mere ritualism, but an appreciation of the corporate significance of the Gospel message combined with the realization that the new life in Christ is indeed manifested by and communicated in the sacramental nature of Christian worship. This is why the Orthodox layman pays particular attention to the form and manner in which the liturgy is celebrated. He never regarded it, as does his brother in the West who is accustomed to a liturgy celebrated in a language which he does not understand, as an act involving only the priest, but feels responsible himself for all that is done in the house of God. This awareness as to what is taking place, it can readily be appreciated, makes it difficult to carry out reforms, whether good or bad in nature. Actual schisms have resulted from attempts to change the liturgy in minor respects. This close control which the Church exercises over its own liturgy causes it to view as suspect rites with which it has not been closely in touch since the Middle Ages, especially Western variations—wrongly so,

---

3 Later changes, particularly by Patriarch Philotheus in the fourteenth century, were
   concerned only with minor points and the rubrics.

however. It is also true that this genuinely living liturgy, which is firmly rooted in the language of each country and has often been instrumental in forming that language itself, can often serve to keep the faith alive Under the Turkish and Mongol yokes the Christians of the East were strengthened in their faith by the celebration of the liturgy, and so it is in Russia today, where the liturgy remains the only means at the disposal of the Church for communicating to the faithful the truths of religion in the midst of a Marxist state. The revival of Christianity in Russia shows once more that the school of the liturgy can be a very potent influence.

It is not possible here to linger over the details of the Byzantine liturgy.[4] Various liturgical cycles, daily weekly, annual, and paschal, correspond in large part to similar cycles in other traditional liturgies, but in contrast to the rather austere Latin liturgy these cycles are much richer and more elaborate. The Psalter for the daily office (vespers, compline, nocturn or midnight prayer, matins, prime, terce, sext, none) are supplemented by a great many different kinds of hymns which vary according to the seasons or feast day. These hymns are collected in three books which are used at different times of the year:

1. The *Triodion* and the *Pentekostarion* contain the variable portions of the liturgy and office for Lent and Eastertide. Many of the hymns are from the pen of St. Theodore the Studite (beginning of the ninth century).

2. The *Octoechus* (Greek *Oktoechos*, "book of eight tones") includes the cycles of eight weeks which begins with the first Sunday after Pentecost and is then repeated throughout the year

4 The most comprehensive set of translations is to be found in the *Book of the Divine Prayers and Services of the Catholic Orthodox Church of Christ*, published by the Syrian Antiochene Archdiocese of America. For a general introduction to the Byzantine rite, see S. Salaville, *Eastern Liturgies* (London, 1938); and also Nicholas Cabasilas, *A Commentary on the Divine Liturgy*, tr. by J. M. Hussey (London 1960). This fourteenth-century commentary on the Byzantine Eucharistic service is very important for gaining an insight into the meaning and spirit of the Eastern liturgy.

until the following Lent. Each week has a different tone (*echoi*). The *Octoechus* establishes a link between each day in the year and Easter, the Feast of Feasts, since the main theme of the book is the Resurrection; it is traditionally ascribed to St. John of Damascus (eighth century).

3. The *Menaion* or *Menaia* (Greek *men*, "month"), finally, corresponds to the sanctoral of the Latin liturgy and contains the variable portions for the feasts of saints and other feasts throughout the year which are not connected with the paschal cycle.

Every day, therefore, has its own office composed of an invariable portion consisting generally of excerpts from the Bible, a variable series of hymns from the *Octoechus* or *Triodion* (sometimes during Lent the two are used together) or *Pentekostarion*, and finally portions of the *Menaion*. Only monasteries, of course, are in a position to celebrate the offices in their entirety, according to the rubrics in the Typikon, which goes back to the fourteenth and fifteenth centuries and describes the way in which the various cycles are to be combined. The Byzantine office is essentially a monastic office and parishes have to adapt it to their needs as best they can.[5] This is one sign of the strong influence which monasticism has traditionally had on the Orthodox Church.

The custom of celebrating the eucharistic liturgy on a daily basis was of relatively late origin, both in the East and in the West. However, it has never become widespread in the East, hence the Orthodox Church is not familiar with any obligation of priest to celebrate daily—the liturgy is not regarded as their private affair but as an act involving the whole Church—and the liturgy has retained some of its meaning as a "common work," a solemnity involving the whole community which normally takes place only on Sundays and feast days. But while Orthodoxy does not attach any particular importance to the frequency with which mass is celebrated,[6] is has

5 The ecumenical patriarchate published an abridged *Typikon* about fifty years ago for the use of parish churches. This is used by Orthodox churches whose liturgical language is Greek. [The Latin office is also essentially a monastic office—Translator]

6 There is no rule either ordering or forbidding the daily celebration of the liturgy. Only in monasteries and large parish churches is it customary to have daily liturgies.

inherited from Byzantium a spirituality strongly oriented toward the sacramental life. Both as a memorial and as an anticipation of the world to come, the Eucharist is the place where the Church identifies itself with the Kingdom of God. This is the essential meaning of the celebration held on "the eighth day" of the week, the Lord's Day.

The Byzantine rite has preserved a number of the countless variations which once characterized the liturgy of the ancient Church: for example, it has two eucharistic liturgies which are used on different occasions, that of St. John Chrysostom and that of St. Basil. A third type of liturgy, celebrated at Jerusalem and occasionally elsewhere, is traditionally attributed to St. James the brother of the Lord.[7] During Lent it is customary not to celebrate the liturgy except on Saturdays and Sundays, in accordance with the canons of ancient councils; the fast is intended to impress on Christians the meaning of the fallen state in which they now are until the Parousia, despite the assurance of salvation which is even now within their grasp. Lent is therefore a period of expectation interrupted only by the dominical liturgies and terminating in the triumphal paschal liturgy, the anticipation of the Second Coming of Christ. On certain days during Lent, however, it is customary to celebrate a form of vespers when communion is distributed which has been reserved from the preceding Sunday. This is called the Liturgy of the Presanctified, a form of service traditionally ascribed to St. Gregory the Great, the pope of Rome.[8]

7 We cannot go into the question of the authenticity of these liturgies here; in any case whether they are to be attributed to this or that person is a question of relatively minor importance because the liturgy has always been regarded as the liturgy of the Church and not that of any particular person as such. Liturgists seem to agree today that the hand of St. Basil can be seen in the canon which bears his name. But St. John Chrysostom certainly never compiled the liturgy which now bears his name and which is of a later date. Both liturgies have undergone modifications, even after the fourteenth century. The Liturgy of St James also appears to belong to the Byzantine type and therefore cannot have had any connection with the brother of the Lord.

8 The Sixth Ecumenical Council (Quinisext, Canon 52) forbids the celebration of the liturgies during Lent, and prescribes the celebration of the "Presanctified."

Like all traditional eucharistic prayers the Byzantine canon has
the form of a solemn thanksgiving which the bishop or priest
offers to God the Father. Because the Church is the Body of
Christ, the Son of God, it is privileged to address itself directly to
the Father in commemorating the redemptive work of the Son
and in invoking the descent of the Holy Spirit "on us and on these
Gifts here present" (Liturgy of St. John Chrysostom) so that they
may be changed into the Body and Blood of the Lord. this
trinitarian character of the canon, which reaches its culminating
point in the solemn invocation of the Spirit (*epiclesis*), is regarded
as essential by the Orthodox Church, and the lack of this feature
in the present Roman mass since the early Middle Ages is held to
be a grave defect. It is the Spirit, actually, who reveals the grace of
redemption in the Church after the ascension of Christ: "When
the truth-giving Spirit, who proceeds from the Father, has come
to befriend you, he whom I will send to you from the Father side,
he will bear witness of what I was" (John 15:26).

Orthodox teaching always has emphasized the reality of the sacramental change (*metabole*) in the Eucharist by which the bread and
wine are transformed into the Body and Blood of Christ. However,
neither the liturgy or the Fathers nor any authentic Orthodox text
prior to the sixteenth century uses the term "transubstantiation"
(Greek *metousiosis*) to describe this mystery. This term is employed in
later Orthodox confessions of faith intended to define the teaching of
the Church with respect to Protestant opinions on this matter, but
here is always the reservation that the term is only one of several that
could be employed and does not imply that the Church intends to
adopt the Aristotelian philosophical theory of form and matter.[9]

Besides the Eucharist, the Church also acknowledges the existence of six other sacraments, without, however, holding that the
number seven has the same absolute character assigned to it by

9 See especially the *Confession of Dositheus* (1672), art. 17, in P. Schallf, *The Creeds of
   Christendom*, vol. II (New York, 1889), p. 431.

Western post-Tridentine theology. No Orthodox council, as a matter of fact, has ever defined the exact number of the sacraments. The number seven was first mentioned in the East only in the thirteenth century, at the time of the "Latinizing" (*latinophronos*) emperor Michael Palaeologus VIII. Several Byzantine theologians such as Symeon of Thessalonica (fifteenth century) formally accept the number seven for the sacraments, but others in the fifteenth and sixteenth centuries hold that certain other sacred rites ought to be regarded as sacraments, particularly the assumption of the monastic habit and the blessing of the waters at Epiphany. St. Gregory Palamas refers to baptism and the Eucharist as "recapitulating" (summing up) by themselves "all the works of the God-Man,"[10] and thus without denying the efficacy of other sacraments, establishes a certain hierarchy among them. This apparent lack of a precise terminology is an indication that Byzantine theologians regarded the Christian Mystery as a unique mystery expressed in different ways by the various sacramental acts. And there was no doubt that among all these acts the Eucharist was the Mystery of Mysteries, to use an expression of Pseudo-Dionysius. The doctrine of Seven Sacraments is frankly misleading if the impression is given that Unction of the Sick is equally important as the Eucharist or baptism, or that redemptive grace is not imparted by sacramental acts such as the Blessing of the Waters. It is a convenient tool, however, for catechetical purposes and this is why it has been adopted in textbooks and manuals. (We must now say a word briefly about each of these sacraments.)

Baptism is conferred on infants in the form of a triple immersion in the water as the names of the three Persons of the Trinity are invoked.

Confirmation is generally conferred along with baptism in one rite. The Orthodox Church feels that the process of Christian initiation, involving baptism, confirmation and communion in

10 See our *Introduction à l'étude de Grégoire Palamas* (Paris: Éditions du Seuil, 1959), p. 395.

the Holy Mysteries, constitutes an inseparable whole, which ought to be conferred on each new Christian as such, whether child or adult. This belief that baptism and confirmation belong together is at the basis of the Orthodox custom of conferring them at one and the same time.[11] It is customary for Orthodox priests to confer both sacraments, whereas in the West confirmation is normally reserved to bishops.[12] Orthodox confirmation consists of an anointing with the Holy Chrism, which has been specially blessed by the bishop;[13] hence the term Chrismation customarily applied to it in the East.

The sacrament of *Holy Orders* includes the three traditional orders: the episcopate, priesthood, and diaconate; and two minor orders: subdiaconate and lectorate. Ever since the sixth century (Justinian's law, later confirmed by the council *in Trullo*) it has been the rule to choose the episcopate exclusively from the celibate monastic clergy. married men, on the contrary, may be ordained as deacons or priests.[14]

The *Marriage* rite is an impressive ceremony called "Crowning." The Lord's precept regarding the integrity and uniqueness of marriage is held to be of an absolute nature, and very strict regulations are in effect so far as the clergy are concerned; for example, it is impossible for anyone who has contracted a marriage with a widow to be ordained priest. Divorce, however, is allowed in certain cases where the grace of the sacrament has manifestly been deprived of its efficacy, whether by the fault of one of the spouses (adultery), or because of some material impediment to the fulfillment of the conjugal bond.

11 Confirmation is only conferred apart from baptism in certain special cases when heterodox persons are reconciled with the Church.

12 The bishops were the normal ministers of both baptism and confirmation in the early Church.

13 According to the present discipline only important episcopal sees have the right to prepare and bless the Holy Chrism (involving an elaborate ritual), which is then distributed to the various dioceses and parishes.

14 Marriage after ordination and second marriages of widowed priests are strictly forbidden.

Penance has generally become an act of a private nature today, as in the West. It essentially involves the reconciliation of a sinner with the Church through a remission of his sins, and it is also a "healing of the soul" or confession. The various formulas for absolution in use are of the deprecative kind; that is, the priest prays for the pardon of the sinner, the actual forgiveness coming from God, not from the priest. However, a seventeenth-century metropolitan of Kiev, Peter Moghila, did not hesitate to adopt a formula of Latin inspiration in the Slavic ritual which he published, in which is it the priest who absolves in the first person (*ego absolvo te*). This is the formula actually used by the Russian Church today.

Thus the liturgical life forms the very basis of Orthodox piety. It is the realization and expression of the mystery of the divine presence in the Church and proclaims the truths of the faith. It also governs to a large extent the moral behavior of the faithful, sometimes inviting them to do penance and fast, at other times summoning them to glorify the Creator and share in the messianic banquet. It governs their lives by associating each evening and morning, each day of the week, each season of the year, and also every important event in the life of man such as birth, marriage, sickness, and death with the great events of Revelation, and by communicating to him on such occasions the unique grace of Redemption.

Inasmuch as this liturgical life is essentially a corporate form of worship, the building where the gatherings of the faithful are regularly held acquires a special importance and significance. Here too, Byzantium has been remarkably successful in the course of its long history in creating a form of art admirably suited to express the dogmas of the faith pictorially and to give expression to religious feeling. This artistic expression assumed such an important place in the life of the Church that it brought on the iconoclastic controversy in the eighth and ninth centuries. Only an art intimately connected with dogma and religious feeling could either have aroused such fierce opposition or inspired so many valiant defenders. As a result of this controversy the Church came to define the dogmatic significance of the veneration which it paid to images. This is what the decisions of the seventh ecumenical council (the Second Council of Nicaea in 787) were about. "We define," proclaimed the Father of the council,

> that the holy images, whether in color, mosaic, or some other material, should be exposed in the holy churches of God, on the sacred vessels and liturgical vestments, on the walls and furnishings, and in houses and along the roads, namely, the image of our Lord God and Savior Jesus Christ, that of our Lady, the immaculate and holy Mother of God, those of the venerable angels and those of all holy men. Whenever these representations are contemplated, they will cause those who look at them to commemorate and love their prototypes. We define also that they should be kissed and that they are an object of veneration and honor (*timetike proskynesis*), but not of real worship (*latreia*), which is reserved for Him who is the Subject of our faith and is proper for the Divine Nature alone. . . The honor rendered to the image is in effect transmitted to the prototype; he who venerates the image, venerates in it the reality for which it stands.

The distinction established by the council between the "worship" or "adoration" (*latreia*) which is due to God alone, and the "veneration" (*proskynesis*) due to images of Christ and the saint, was intended to refute the charges of idolatry leveled against the Orthodox by the iconoclasts. It is also equally valid today in the dialogue with Protestants concerning the exact meaning of icons in the Orthodox Church. The words "worship" and "adoration" are frequently used for the veneration which the Orthodox Church pays to sacred images, whereas they ought only to be employed in circumstances which make it quite clear that they do not stand for the Greek *latreia*, in accordance with the rulings of the council. It needs to be stressed, however, that the Orthodox Church regards the veneration of icons as something dogmatically wholesome and sound. This is ultimately because of the reality of the Incarnation of the Word. The defenders of images from St. John of Damascus to Patriarch Nicephorus never tire of repeating that the Son of God really became man: the Invisible, Unknowable, and indescribable became visible, knowable, and describable in flesh which was really His own. However, this flesh is deified, that is, it has itself become the source of grace. The images which represent it therefore should reflect this divine character. That is why Byzantine art, with its strong emphasis upon the conventional and traditional, is peculiarly suited to be a Christian art. Like all the dogmatic controversies during the early centuries, the quarrel over iconoclasm was also connected with christology. The iconoclasts refused, in effect, to admit the full reality of the Incarnation and upheld the notion of a wholly transcendent God. Their Orthodox opponents, while stressing the human nature of Christ, did not forget the fact that this nature was deified, that it belongs properly to the one hypostasis of the Word, and that the images of Christ, therefore, as well as those of the Virgin Mary and the saints, who have shared in Christ's deification, should be regarded as holy and as worthy of veneration.

Holy icons therefore form an essential part of Orthodox worship and piety. Some of them have been regarded as miraculous and this exceptional status has been recognized as such by the Church, which has instituted special feasts commemorating them. Just as the portraits of famous persons or those dear to us serve to remind us of these persons as individuals, sometimes in a very realistic and compelling way, so certain icons can cause a direct contact between the prototype and the faithful, stimulating the latter to make acts of faith and ultimately helping to manifest the whole divine power.

These various aspects of Orthodox piety and spirituality, which still characterize it, had their stoutest defenders in the medieval period among the monks. We have seen that Christian monasticism was a creation of the third and fourth centuries as an antidote to the new situation of relative ease in which the Church found itself under the Empire. A select group preferred to flee to the desert and show in this way that the Kingdom of God is a future Kingdom that is to come and that the Church cannot find any permanent refuge here below. The continual attraction of the monastic way of life throughout Byzantine history proves that this eschatological awareness never slackened. Byzantine monasticism even became the support of the Church when the latter was hard pressed by willful emperors and helped to prevent it from being transformed into an imperial (state) Church. Byzantine society was grateful to the monks for the important role which they performed, and that is why, in essence, candidates for the episcopate were chosen from the monasteries, why the Byzantine *lex orandi* was modeled on that of the monks and was given its final shape by them, and why it was the monks were able to win such a brilliant moral victory over the iconoclasts and thus restore Orthodoxy in Byzantium.

Orthodox monasticism has assumed various forms in its long history, from the simple anchorites who first appeared in the deserts of Egypt and Palestine to the great monastic communities which lived under the *Rules* of a St. Pachomius or a St. Basil.

The life of a hermit (also still called *hesychast* in the East, from *hesychia*, "quiet," "spiritual repose") is a life of continual, "monologic" prayer: "Let the remembrance of Jesus be present with each breath," wrote St. John Climacus in the seventh century; "you will then know the value of solitude."[15] As a citizen of the heavenly Kingdom the monk is in constant communion with his Lord, by repeating continually and without any interruption, whether during his work or sleep, a short prayer in which the Name of Jesus is invoked. Sometimes it is the *Kyrie eleison*, at other times "Lord Jesus Christ, Son of God, have mercy on me." sometimes he will also interpret the words of St. John Climacus literally and repeat

---

15 *Ladder of Paradise, Twenty-seventh Step*, tr. by Lazarus Moore (London, 1959), p. 246.

the prayer rhythmically as he breathes. He will seek the Kingdom of God "within himself," for baptism and the Eucharist confer on every Christian the privilege of being able to live in Christ and possess in their hearts the gifts of the Holy Spirit. The hesychasts will give rise to great Orthodox mystics, such as St. Maximus the Confessor (seventh century), St. Symeon the New Theologian (eleventh century), and St. Gregory the Sinaite (fourteenth century). In the fourteenth century, led by the great theologian, St. Gregory Palamas, archbishop of Thessalonica, the hesychasts will be the foremost defenders of Orthodoxy against the ravages of a philosophical school which denies the possibility of any real communion with God here below. This controversy offered Palamas the opportunity to obtain conciliar approval (1341, 1347, 1351) for theological formulas expressing the complete reality of communion with God, which is available to all Christians who are members of the Church, a communion which the Greek Fathers called "deification."[16]

Besides hesychasm the Christian East was also familiar with another type of monastic life which came to be regarded as classical in the West, namely, that of the great disciplined, liturgically-oriented community. St. Pachomius and especially St. Basil of Caesarea furnished the monks of all succeeding ages with a set of norms in their famous *Rules*, which has displayed such a remarkable vitality. St. Theodore, abbot of the great monastery in Constantinople called the Stoudios, and stout defender of Orthodoxy against the iconoclasts (ninth century), was the most important codifier of the monastic rule in the Byzantine tradition. The Studite monks were subject to an abbot and apportioned their time between the church, the refectory, and work. It was in communal monasteries of this type that the forms of the Byzan-

16 Cf. J. Meyendorff, *Saint Grégoire Palamas et la mystique orthodoxe, Coll. "Maître Spirituels"* (Paris: Éditions du Seuil 1959); and *Introduction à l'étude de Grégoire Palamas, Coll. "Patristica Sorbonensia"* (Paris: Éditions du Seuil, 1959). Both of these books will in English translations.

tine liturgy and the style of Byzantine hymnography were per-
fected and achieved their final stage of development. The work of
earlier hymnographers, such as the great poet of the sixth century,
St. Romanus the Melode, was incorporated in the divine office.
Byzantine hymnography has retained this inspiration and form to
the present day, even now that it is no longer an exclusively
monastic affair but has been adopted by the whole Church.

The Byzantine Church therefore was familiar with both the
hesychastic and cenobitic (*koino-* "common," *bios*, "life") forms of
monasticism, and both continue to exist in the Orthodox Church
today. While conflicts have sometimes marred their relations,
both have been able to work harmoniously together. The great
monasteries occasionally produced mystics capable of practicing
the purest form of hesychasm while continuing to conform to the
ordinary rules of the community. St. John Climacus, for example,
was the abbot of the great monastery of Mount Sinai; hesychasm
flourished even in the Stoudios, in the tenth and eleventh centuries, in the persons of St. Symeon the Pious and St. Symeon the
New Theologian. Monastic federations or republics, such as those
of Mount Athos, Mount Olympus, or Mount St. Auxentius,
allowed for the existence of imposing communities and the hermits' cells of hesychasts side by side. Originally the monks of
Mount Athos were all anchorites; then St. Athanasius founded the
first great lavra (tenth century), and later the whole territory was
divided between federated monasteries under the authority of a
central monastic government, the Protaton. However, the various
charters in effect (which have been changed from time to time)
have always allowed for the existence of the *skiti* and *kellia* in
which hesychasts may devote themselves to "pure prayer." the
Rules of the monastic communities also provide for the practice
of the Prayer of Jesus by the monks.

Thus, while displaying a remarkable unity of purpose and
inspiration, Byzantine monasticism has been wise enough to al-

low for different ways in which individual temperaments could express themselves. Whether he lives apart or in a community, the monk is a witness and prophet of the Kingdom to come. His ministry is of the charismatic kind destined to serve the Church and the world. It is interesting to note in this respect that the Church has always refused to approve tendencies which would isolate the monks from the Church and imply that they had a mission that was *essentially* different from and superior to that of other Christians. Canonically speaking, the monasteries of the Orthodox Church are always subject to the local bishop and are therefore integrated in the life of the diocese. The Eastern Church has never recognized religious orders that were canonically "exempt" from diocesan control. It is therefore in the Church and for the Church that Byzantine monastic is called upon to perform its special mission.

The Byzantine liturgy, the inexhaustible richness of Byzantine art, the spiritual influence of monasticism, the use of a language understood by the people in the liturgy, a married secular clergy and therefore one in close touch with the faithful, a conception of the Church which allows for a large amount of responsibility for all Christians in the life of the Church; all these factors, which were given their definitive form in the Byzantine period, have enabled the Orthodox Church to build up and to maintain a remarkably coherent corporate attitude towards the Church and the faith through the centuries. From Byzantium also it has inherited certain historical characteristics of a less important nature, particularly the concept of a sacral state which explains many of the excesses of modern nationalism. It is our task now to attempt to distinguish in this heritage between the Tradition of the Church, the expression of revealed Truth, on the one hand, and mere human traditions which have naturally tended to accumulate, on the other. This distinction will sometimes be painful to make, sometimes it can only be made gradually; but in any case the necessary adjustments can only be achieved with the help of the Spirit who teaches "all truth." For it is He who, without nullifying man's free will, guides the Church toward its final destination.

Chapter 5

THE ORTHODOX CHURCH AND ISLAM. THE CONFESSIONS OF FAITH. THE SEVENTEENTH AND EIGHTEENTH CENTURIES.

Islam launched its attack against the Eastern half of Christendom during the first part of the seventh century, toward the beginning of its historical drive to conquer the world. The Byzantine emperor Heraclius (610-641) had just succeeded in winning back from the Persians large tracts of the old *orbis Romanorum,* including the Holy Land, but this task had barely been completed before the Arabs, in a new wave, soon engulfed all of Syria, Palestine, Egypt, and North Africa.

The religious picture in these areas undoubtedly contributed to the rapid expansion of Islam. The Syrian and Coptic-speaking churches were definitely anti-Greek in sentiment, and their hatred for Chalcedonian Orthodoxy, which the emperors had for so long endeavored to impose on them by force, made them welcome the new invaders with open arms. Occasionally even the Orthodox clergy, bowing before the inevitable and hopeful of being able to preserve the vital interests of the Church, adopted the same course. Thus St. Sophronius, the patriarch of Jerusalem and one of the leading opponents of Monothelitism, negotiated the surrender of the besieged Holy City to the Khalif Omar in 638. By 678, however,, the imperial armies and fleet had been able to stem the Moslem advance, and in 718 the Arab fleet was thwarted in its attempt to capture Constantinople, the "city protected by God." These Byzantine successes against the Arabs served much the same purpose in the East as the great victory of Charles Martel at Poitiers, in 732, at the other end of Christendom.

From the ecclesiastical point of view, the Arab conquest of the former Oriental provinces of the Empire meant that the ecumenical patriarch was not destined to play the leading role in the Eastern Orthodox Church. As we have seen, Photius, for example, was able to work out with Pope John VIII a kind of mutual agreement between Rome and Byzantium, dividing between them the government of the Christian world. Henceforth, the Eastern patriarchs of Alexandria, Antioch and Jerusalem were almost wholly dependent upon their colleague in the imperial capital, in fact if not in theory, and would not dare to take up a position directly contrary to his in important matters.

Finally, in the eleventh century, the Empire was confronted by a new wave of invaders from Central Asia, the Turks, who soon gained control of the khalifate and renewed the threat of a militant Islam. Recent converts to Islam, and vigorous and warlike in habit, the newcomers proved to be formidable opponents and exerted a constant pressure on the eastern frontiers, while the Crusaders from the West delivered their famous stab in the back in 1204. Nevertheless, in spite of reverses and threats, Byzantium managed to hold out against the Turks for another two and a half centuries.

This military struggle between the Cross and the Crescent, which lasted for so long, and which is still reflected in many Byzantine liturgical texts, was not the only contact between Islam and the Byzantine world during the Middle Ages. Orthodox theologians like St. John of Damascus (eighth century) and Emperor John Catacuzene (fourteenth century) were responsible for spreading at least a cursory knowledge of the Koran and its teachings by means of their refutations of Islam. The emperors of the eighth century, the very ones who won such decisive victories over the Moslems, were themselves much attracted by certain aspects of Islamic civilization. The result was the iconoclastic crisis, but also the establishment of cultural relations, direct or indirect, between Baghdad and Constantinople.[1] Important Byzantine prelates and scholars, such as Photius, Constantine the Philosopher, and Nicholas the Mystikos, were in touch with Arab scholars. Even in the realms of spirituality and mysticism it is likely that there was a certain amount of borrowing, for the Moslem concept of *dhikr*, the practice or technique or technique of repeating the divine Name rhythmically as one breathes in and out, appears to have influenced the corresponding teaching of Orthodox hesychasts in the thirteenth and fourteenth centuries.[2] It must be noted, however, that Arabic philosophy exercised virtually no influence on Byzantine thought, for the Byzantines were always able to have direct access to ancient Greek philosophy and never needed, like the Latins, to "discover" Aristotle by way of Arabic translation and commentaries.

All this exchange of knowledge undoubtedly helped to prepare the way for the survival of Christianity under the Turkish yoke. Many important Byzantine leaders foresaw the day when the Empire might fall. They knew that Christianity would be on the whole tolerated by the Ottoman rulers.[3] As later Byzantine emperors, in their desperate attempts to summon a Western Crusade to come their assistance, were forced more and more to deny the Orthodox faith and to accept Roman "innovations," an important dignitary of the court, the Grand Duke Lucas Notaras, was led to assert publicly, on the very eve of the fall of Byzantium: "Better to see the turban of the Turks reigning in our city than the Latin miter."[4] His words certainly expressed the opinion of many.

1 On the links between Islam and the iconoclastic movement, see the study of A. Grabar, *L'Iconoclasme byzantin.—Étude archéologique* (Paris, 1957).
2 On this topic, see L. Gardet, "Un problème de mystique comparée: la mention du Mon divin (*dhikr*) dans la mystique musulmane," in the *Revue thomiste*, vol. 3 (1952), pp. 642-79; vol 1 (1953), pp. 197-216. Cf. our *Introduction à l'étude de Grégoire Palamas*, pp. 201-3.
3 St. Gregory Palamas spent some time as a prisoner in Anatolia in 1354; he gives a favorable description of Christian life under the Turks there. (See our *Introduction à l'étude de Grégoire Palamas*, pp.157-62.)
4 Ducas, *Historia*, 38, Bonn ed., p. 264.

The capture and sacking of Constantinople by the armies of Mohammed II in 1453 was nevertheless one of the greatest catastrophes in the history of Christianity. In 1456 Athens also fell and the Parthenon, which for a thousand years had been a church dedicated to the Virgin Mary, was transformed into a mosque, like Hagia Sophia in Constantinople. In 1460 the Turks conquered the Byzantine Morea and in 1461 Trebizond, the last remaining outposts of the Byzantine Empire. The two Serbian Orthodox states succumbed in turn, in 1459 and 1463. This meant that the Ottoman Empire now embraced the whole of the Christian East, with the sole exception of Muscovite Russia, which, just at this time, was liberating itself from the Mongol yoke and would become the principal bulwark of Orthodoxy in the East for several centuries to come.

Under Turkish rule, however, the Church preserved its canonical organization intact and was even able to strengthen itself as a result of certain privileges granted to the ecumenical patriarch by the conqueror. Mohammed II allowed the canonical election of a new patriarch, Gennadios Scholarios, who was both the leader of the anti-unionist party and a devoted admirer of Thomas Aquinas. The sultan personally handed the new patriarch the emblems of his office, saying: "Be patriarch, preserve our friendship, and enjoy all the privileges which the patriarchs your predecessors possessed." These privileges included the inviolability of the patriarch's person, and through him, of all the bishops, exemption from all taxes, and *civil jurisdiction over all Christians in the Ottoman Empire*. According to Moslem law all Christians were regarded as forming a single nation (*millet*) and no account was taken of confessional, linguistic, or national differences. The Christians had been conquered by Islam, the people of God, but they were allowed to retain the right to rule themselves so far as their domestic affairs were concerned, in accordance with the precepts of their religion and subject to the personal jurisdiction of the patriarch alone, who thus became a kind of Christian khalif, responsible to the sultan for all Christians. Thus the Greek hierarchy found itself invested with considerable power, both civil and religious, in some respects greater than the authority it had enjoyed before the Turkish conquest. The jurisdiction of the ecumenical patriarch was virtually limitless, for it embraced not only the faithful who belonged to his own patriarchate but also those in the other Eastern patriarchates—who were theoretically his equals according to canon law—and even heterodox Christians who happened to be living in the Ottoman Empire. The Orthodox bishops greeted the ecumenical patriarch as "their sovereign, their emperor, and their patriarch."[5] From now on the latter appropriated the special insignia of the Byzantine emperors: he wore a miter in the form of the imperial crown, stood upon a rug which bore the emblem of a Roman eagle, and let his hair grow in the manner of the emperors and Byzantine officials.[6] In his role as *millet-bachi*, "head of the Christian nation," or "ethnarch" in Greek, the patriarch was now virtually the regent of an enslaved empire.

The ethnarchic system, as created by the Turks and as it has survived to this day on the island of Cyprus and in certain countries of the Levant, guaranteed the independence of the Christian Church under alien rule. It was based on an ideas that Islam shared with Judaism, namely, the complete identification of the "people of God" with a concrete sociological entity. In the one case Islam, which included all the faithful of Allah and his Prophet, and in the other all Christians. The Ottoman authorities refused to recognize the existence of any differences of nationality in the Christian *millet* and contented themselves with approving the elections of the patriarch and the bishops. Inevitably this regime had a profound effect on the lives of Christians living under Turkish rule in the Near East.

5 *Historia patriarchica*, Bonn ed., p. 177.

6 Before long these various signs of authority were adopted by the bishops too. But in Russia they were only introduced in the seventeenth century, under Patriarch Nikon, when of course they had ceased to have any political significance.

1. It shut them up in a kind of ghetto from which they did not dare to escape, even though their situation was at times relatively prosperous and even when they were able to exercise a kind of effective control over the policies of the Porte. It was quite impossible for them to pursue any kind of missionary work. Even if they had been materially able to do so, such activity would have been regarded as a political crime against the state. Only the Russian Church was free to continue the work of Byzantium in this field.

2. As ethnarch of the Christians and an official of the Turkish Empire, the patriarch and his collaborators necessarily had a share in the dreadful system of corruption by which the Empire was governed—albeit their implication was of an involuntary nature. Each new election entailed the payment of a large sum of money to the Turkish government, which was specified on each occasion by the sultan's *berat* of investiture. The sum was levied either on the patriarchal treasury—in which case the newly elect reimbursed the amount in the course of his patriarchate by means of corresponding assessments on the dioceses—or on the personal property of the new patriarch. To a lesser degree the same procedure was followed in the case of episcopal elections, which also required the *berat* of the sultan. Moreover, as the patriarchal throne was occupied rather frequently, according to the vagaries of Ottoman policies, the corruption developed into a kind of gangrenous evil. In the eighteenth century, one of the darkest periods in the annals of the Church of Constantinople, forty-eight patriarchs succeeded each other in the space of sixty-three years! Only saints could remain faithful to the ideals of their office under such conditions as these, and the survival of the Greek Church, under four centuries of Turkish rule, is no less than a miracle.

3. The patriarch's role as ethnarch of all Christian in the Turkish Empire enabled him to claim authority over other churches as well. The Bulgarian patriarchate of Trnovo was given to a Greek prelate in 1394, and then later was reduced to the status of a simple diocese of

the ecumenical patriarchate. The autocephalous status of Ohrid was suppressed in 1776 by Patriarch Samuel I, who also abolished the Serbian patriarchate of Pech. This tendency toward centralization was unfortunately also accompanied by measures regarded as particularly obnoxious by the Slavic nations, in that Greek bishops would be appointed to Slavic sees and then proceed to suppress the use of Slavonic as a liturgical language. All oppositions to such measures on the part of the local clergy was virtually impossible, for the patriarch exercised absolute civil as well as religious control over them in the name of the sultan. Nationalism, that bane of modern Orthodoxy, began to flourish everywhere under the Turkish regime. There was Greek nationalism which identified Orthodoxy with Hellenism and the Greek longing for independence, and Slavic nationalism which forced the restoration of autocephalous churches in the nineteenth century by means of threats of revolt and in an atmosphere of mutual distrust that can hardly be described as very Christian in spirit. Domestic quarrels of this kind were the disgrace of Orthodoxy during the dark years of the Turkish yoke. However, they did not prevent a number of new Christian martyrs from shedding their blood for Christ during outbreaks of anti-Christian fanaticism. The most famous of these was the ecumenical patriarch Gregory V, who was hanged by the Turks in 1821 on Easter Sunday from the great porte-cochère of his patriarchate in the Phanar, just after he had celebrated the solemn paschal liturgy.[7]

Owing to its liturgy and the works of the Fathers preserved in the monastic libraries, the Church managed nevertheless to get across the essential burden of its message. The communal prayer in the churches and the astonishing richness and symbolism of the Byzantine liturgical formulas enabled the Greeks and other nations in the Balkans and Near East to remain faithful to their Orthodox faith and assisted them to rally more closely than ever

7 The gate has remained closed to this day in memory of the martyrdom of St. Gregory V.

around a church that had been deprived of all schools, books, and a properly trained clergy.

Elements of Byzantine theological scholarship, however, continued to be maintained by a handful of outstanding churchmen. Some of these were self-taught; others studied in the West and frequently came under the influence of their Catholic or Protestant teachers. The ideas of the Reformation and Counter-Reformation thus made their way to the East. Deprived of a genuine Orthodox schooling, the theologians of the seventeenth and eighteenth centuries not infrequently used Roman arguments against the Protestants and Protestant arguments against the Roman Catholics. Politics also played its part in the continual seesawing back and forth of those years. The ecumenical patriarchs were not above making use of the Catholic ambassadors to the Porte (Austria, France) or their Protestant colleagues (England, Holland) in order to exert pressure on the Turkish authorities, and the foreign ambassadors were not above bringing pressure to bear to cause the dethronement or election of patriarchs.

As we have seen, the patriarchate established a kind of modus vivendi with the Turkish authorities in the fifteenth and sixteenth centuries, during the period immediately after the fall of Constantinople and before direct pressure began to be exercised in such a disgraceful manner. Councils could be held more or less regularly and the affairs of the Church settled. Some of these had to do with relations with the Latin Church. That of 1454, for example, under Patriarch Gennadios Scholarios, officially repudiated the Union of Florence; and that of 1484, attended by the three other Eastern patriarchs, published a special ritual for the reconciliation of Roman Catholics with Orthodoxy.[8] Toward the end of the

---

8 This ritual included the sacrament of Confirmation. However, in the Greek islands under Venetian rule it was not uncommon, until the eighteenth century, for Catholic and Orthodox clergy to observe communion *in sacris*. This state of affairs—which poses certain canonical problems for both sides—was due partly to the existing political situation and partly to the desire not to recognize the schism as a *fait accompli*.

sixteenth century the first important contacts took place between
Protestant theologians and the Orthodox Church. In 1573-1574
a group of Lutheran theologians at Tübingen sent to the ecumenical patriarch Jeremiah II a copy of the Augsburg Confession,
which they had translated into Greek, and asked him to express an
opinion on it. The long reply of the Greek prelate constitutes a
very important document and does credit to its author, showing
that an Orthodox theologian was capable of passing a proper
judgment on Protestantism on the basis of the Augsburg Confession *alone*. This judgment was friendly but critical. It was followed
by correspondence between the two parties, but nothing came of
these moves.[9]

Relations between Constantinople and the Western powers
assumed a less peaceful character in the seventeenth century, and
were dominated in fact by the tragic case of Cyril Loukaris. The
latter was one of the best-educated Greeks of the time, having
spend many years in Italy where he learned to write Latin with
great fluency and became familiar with the works of Thomas
Aquinas, and also kept up relations with the German humanists
Noeschel and Sylburg. First elected patriarch of Alexandria (in
1602 at the age of thirty), he then became ecumenical patriarch in
1620. As the pupil, relative, and protégé of the outstanding
Meletius Pigas, who had preceded him on the throne of Alexandria, it seemed that he was destined to have a brilliant future since
he had already won the gratitude of the Greeks for his attempts to
raise the standard of education of his coreligionists and revive the
Greek pride in their national heritage. But at Constantinople he
unfortunately came under the influence of the Reformed theology, in the person of the Dutch ambassador Cornelius Haga, who
obtained the necessary books for him from the West. In 1629
Loukaris published at Geneva, in Latin, his famous *Confession*,

---

9 On the correspondence, see the work of E. Benz, *Wittenberg und Byzanz* (Marburg,
  1949).

which completely reflects the strict Calvinist point of view. This basic purpose of Loukaris was to combat the influence of missionary zeal of Roman Catholics, but his Western training and numerous contacts with Calvinist circles had led him astray and caused him to embrace Protestantism. The *Confession* accepts, pure and simple, the Protestant doctrine of *sola scriptura*, excluded the deuterocanonical books, rejects the real presence in the Eucharist, empties the Orthodox doctrine of the priesthood and holy orders of all meaning, and deplores the veneration of icons and the invocation of saints as forms of idolatry. Protestants were under the impression that they were about to witness the complete conversion of the Eastern Church to the doctrines of the Reformation in the person of the ecumenical patriarch. It is not surprising therefore, that the *Confession* was published in four French translations, an English translation, and two German translations, beginning in 1629. In 1633 it also appeared in Greek, also at Geneva.[10]

The Catholic powers, France and Austria, were not slow to intervene, when the true state of affairs became known, and gave financial and political support to a group of Orthodox bishops who dethroned the patriarch. The latter, accused of plotting with the Russians, was arrested by the Turks and strangled. His body was thrown into the Bosporus, but was later recovered and buried on the island of Halki.

It is not difficult to imagine what a great stir was caused in the East by the publication of this *Confession*. Six councils condemned it in succession: Constantinople in 1638 (three months after the death of Loukaris), Kiev in 1640, Jassy in 1642, Constantinople in 1672, Jerusalem in 1672, and Constantinople in 1691.

Under the influence of this anti-Protestant reaction, Peter Moghila, the metropolitan of Kiev, was also induced to compile

10 The original manuscript of Loukaris is preserved by the Library of Geneva and suffices to prove that the *Confession* is indeed authentic. Ancient and recent claims to question its authenticity are nothing more than pious attempts to save the good name of the patriarch.

his famous *Orthodox Confession* (1640), which he intended for use in his own province. Orphaned at the age of eleven, the son of a hospodar of Moldavia, Moghila (Romanian Movila) studied in Poland and then became a monk, finally archimandrite of the great Lavra of the Crypts in Kiev. Here he set up a printing press and founded a school that became famous and had a lasting influence on the Orthodox world as a whole. Moghila aimed primarily at raising the educational level of the Orthodox clergy as a means of preserving Orthodoxy from the encroachments of Uniatism, which had the support of the Polish kings. The case of Cyril Loukaris was particularly embarrassing to him because it seemed to prove the contention of Roman Catholic theologians that the Orthodox Church was riddled with Protestantism and was even about to embrace Protestantism as a whole! In order to remove this blot, Moghila was determined to give Orthodoxy as precise and clear a definition as Roman Catholicism and present it along the systematic lines of the various Latin catechisms. His *Confession* therefore amounts to little more than a copious borrowing from Roman catechisms then in use, especially that of Canisius. Certain disputed points with which the theologians of Kiev did not feel themselves sufficiently competent to cope, such as purgatory and the exact moment of the consecration of the eucharistic gifts, were referred to the patriarch of Constantinople for decision. Moghila himself resolved these questions in favor of the Latin view. There can be no doubt whatever that Moghila and his Kievan associates were insufficiently grounded in genuine Orthodox tradition and displayed what can only be described as a marked inferiority complex toward the formularies of the Counter-Reformation, thereby falling into the most elementary kind of Latinism. However, the *Confession* was approved at Kiev (1640), and then amended in certain important respects by the Council at Jassy (1642), at which time it was translated into Greek by the Greek theologian Meletios Syrigos. The original Byzantine position regarding purgatory and the words of institution in the Eucharist were thus restored. It was in this new form that the *Confession* was approved by the Council of Constantinople in 1643.[11] Even in its corrected form, however, the work is the most Latin-sounding document, both in spirit and form, that the Orthodox hierarchy has ever formally approved. Nevertheless, from then on it exercised great influence over the teaching of Orthodox theology, and only toward the middle of the nineteenth century when the Church began to experience a "return to the sources" did this influence begin to decline.

Besides Peter Moghila, there was also another zealous defender of Orthodoxy who was engaged in the struggle against Protestant influence, namely, Dositheus of Jerusalem. Largely self-taught, Dositheus was eager to promote a knowledge of the Fathers in the East and published an important collection of Byzantine theological texts in Romania, since the Eastern patriarchs had no printing presses of their own. His renown as a scholar came to the attention of a French diplomat, Nointel, whom Louis XIV had appointed as his ambassador to Constantinople and who was himself a student of theology, of Jansenist tendencies. This ambassador got in touch with him as well as with several other Orthodox prelates and requested him to give his opinion on the *Confession* of Loukaris. The result was a detailed and systematic refutation of the latter work, which Dositheus had approved by a council at Jerusalem in 1672. This document, known henceforth both as the *Confession of Dositheus* and the *Acts of the Council of Jerusalem*, is the most important Orthodox dogmatic text of this period. Its authority is undisputed. In the nineteenth century the celebrated Philaret of Moscow had the greatest respect for it. To be sure, Dositheus, under the influence of Moghila, occasionally makes use of a Latinized terminology, but his basic inspiration is much more fundamentally Orthodox than that of the metropolitan of Kiev. The Calvinism of Loukaris is firmly rejected in favor

11 Schaff, *Creeds of Christendom*, vol. 2 (New York, 1889), pp. 275-400.

of the traditional sacramental realism of Orthodoxy, a doctrine of the priesthood and holy orders founded on the sacramental nature of the Church, and an Orthodox explanation of the veneration of the saints and holy images.[12]

The reaction of the Orthodox Church to the Reformation was therefore sufficiently clear, so that there could be no misunderstandings on that score. The *Confessions* of Moghila and Dositheus undoubtedly played a most important part in helping to strengthen the Orthodox position, regardless of their Latinizing tendencies. This Latinism is evidence, at least in the case of Dositheus, not of any particular sympathy for the Roman Church or for Latin scholasticism, but of the absence of an adequate theological training. But how could things possibly have been otherwise after two centuries of the Turkish yoke and in the almost complete absence of proper schools and books?

A kind of instinct of self-preservation and unlimited faithfulness to the truth taught by the Church, as preserved by the liturgy—still a living force—and by the works of the Fathers, explains the reactions of the Orthodox to the temptations from the West, whether from Catholics or Protestants, both of whom were eager to enlist the Orthodox on their side in the great controversy dividing them. There can be no doubt that this was the primary motive inspiring the Western ambassadors in Constantinople to interfere in the internal affairs of the ecumenical patriarchate. The Protestants looked upon the Eastern Church as out of date and rooted in error, but they recognized that it had a long tradition of anti-Romanism which went back far beyond Luther and Calvin. Its consent to the principles of the Reformation was therefore worth obtaining, if possible. In spite of the generally bad reputation which Greeks enjoyed in the West,

12 The *Confession of Dositheus* may be found in Schaff, *op. cit,* pp. 401-44. The most recent complete collection of Orthodox dogmatic texts is that of I. N. Karmiris (in Greek), *Ta dogmatika kai sybolika mnemeia tes orthodoxou katholikes ekklesiasv* 2 vols. (Athens, 1953).

Catholics acknowledged that the Orthodox bishops were the successors of St. John Chrysostom and St. Basil. Latin missionaries in the East therefore were constantly vacillating between an extreme condescension toward and toleration of the Orthodox, even going so far as to maintain a *communio in sacris* with them, and an aggressive proselytism which aimed not only at bringing the Greeks back to union with Rome, but at Latinizing them in the process.

The reaction of the Orthodox Church to efforts of this kind was no less categorical. A synod at Constantinople in 1755, attended by the patriarchs of Alexandria and Jerusalem as well as by the ecumenical patriarch Cyril V, took up the question of the admission of Latins into the Orthodox Church. Modifying the decisions of the Council of 1484, the synod decreed that Latin and Armenian baptisms were invalid and that converts must be rebaptized according to the Byzantine rite of triple immersion before they could be admitted to the Church. Thus the strictest regulations regarding the admission of heretics to the Church were now applied to Roman Catholics and Monophysite Armenians.[13] This decision met with opposition on the part of some bishops, but it was adopted under pressure by the Greek popula-

---

13 About this time the Russian Church, which until then had generally followed the practice of rebaptizing Latins, now decided to adopt a more liberal policy and ordered that only a profession of the Orthodox faith and penance were necessary before a Roman Catholic could be admitted to the Orthodox Church. This confusion among the Orthodox regarding the admission of converts from Roman Catholicism has its counterpart in similar situations on the part of the Catholics themselves: when Orthodox became Catholics in Hungary and Poland in the fourteenth century, they were customarily rebaptized (see our article "Le projet de concile oecuménique en 1367," in *Dumbarton Oaks Papers*, vol. 14 [1960]) although *communio in sacris* was widely practiced in the Greek island under Venetian rule until the eighteenth century (see especially W. de Vries, "Das Problem der 'communicatio in sacris cum dissidentibus' im Nahen Ostem zur Zeit der Union," in *Ostkirchlichen Studien*, no. 6 [1957], pp. 81-106). While on the Roman side these differences were ironed out in the nineteenth century, there are still variations on the Orthodox side between the more liberal Russian practice (penance) and that of the Greeks who have now returned to the canons of 1484 (Chrismation).

tion in Constantinople, which was violently anti-Latin. It remained in force in the Greek churches until the beginning of the twentieth century.

These various episodes in the life of the church under Turkish rule add nothing of great importance to our understanding of the history of Orthodox theology, but they may serve as a sort of proof of the vitality of Greek Orthodoxy and the determination of the Orthodox to retain their identity under very trying circumstances. The fanatical attitude also displayed by some Greeks in their opposition to the West can be explained, at least in part, as a natural reaction against the outrageously aggressive acts of Latin missionaries. When the latter found what a difficult task it was to convert the Moslems, they turned their attention to the Orthodox Christians living in those parts, Greeks and Arabs, and thought nothing of depriving them of the sole remaining treasure which had been preserved to them: their Orthodox faith.

However, this fanaticism tended to die down and was less evident in works produced in the nineteenth century, giving way finally to a more moderate approach made possible by the reopening of schools and the appearance of publications of all kinds. It was in this atmosphere that the Orthodox patriarchs replied to several appeals from the popes during the nineteenth century, appeals that were hardly calculated to win their sympathy. In January 1848, just after he had ascended to the papal throne, Pius IX addressed an appeal "to the Orientals" recalling them to reunion with Rome. The four Oriental patriarchs of Constantinople, Alexandria, Antioch and Jerusalem replied with an encyclical to all the Orthodox, signed also by twenty-nine metropolitans. In it they defined "papism" as a heresy and then expressed the hope that Pius IX would himself be "converted" to the true Orthodox faith and return to the true Catholic apostolic and Orthodox Church, for, as they declared, "no patriarch or council has ever been able to introduce any novelty among us, since the Body of the Church, that is, the people themselves, is the guardian of religion." This encyclical of 1848, the text of which seems to have been approved in advance by Metropolitan Philaret of Moscow, was given wide publicity and is still regarded today as an important, authoritative statement of Orthodox views on the Church.[14] The Church, which is the guardian of truth, forms a single body and no member, whether clerical or lay, is excluded from taking an active role in the common life of the whole.

To a new appeal addressed to the East by Leo XIII in his encyclical "Praeclara gratulationis" of 1894, the ecumenical patriarch Anthimos replied with another encyclical which stigmatized the dogmas of the Immaculate Conception and papal infallibility as "Roman novelties" and declared that reunion could be contemplated only on the basis of the undivided faith of the first centuries.[15]

Doctrinal fidelity and attachment to tradition: these are the two fundamental keynotes of Orthodox writers during this dark period, conditioning their thought even when an inadequate grounding in theological principles caused them to resort to the expedient of using Protestant arguments against the Catholics and Catholic arguments against Protestants. A few strove to make it possible for contemporaries to become better acquainted with the real sources of Orthodoxy, the Scriptures and the Fathers. One name in particular deserves special mention here, that of Nicodemus the Hagiorite (1748-1808), a monk of Mount Athos, who published at Venice in 1792, in collaboration with Macarius, Bishop of Corinth, an important collection of texts from the Fathers relating to prayer. The *Philocalia*, as this collection is called, has ever since been regarded as a spiritual classic by the Orthodox. The *Philocalia* was responsible for acquainting modern generations with the mystical tradition of the Greek Fathers. This

14 Original Greek text in Karmiris, *op. cit.,* pp.905-95; Russian translation, Moscow, 1849; French translation, Paris, 1850, etc.

15 Text in Karmiris, *op. cit.,* pp. 932-46 (there are also many translations in French, Russian, English and German.

work was translated into various languages, Slavonic, Russian, Romanian, and others, and helped to start a real spiritual revival in certain countries.[16] Nicodemus, recently canonized by the Orthodox Church (1955), was also the author of several other works of spirituality inspired by Western examples (Scupoli, Ignatius of Loyola), which amount virtually to adaptions of the latter for the benefit of Orthodox mysticism. He was also an advocate of frequent communion in the Greek Church. Nicodemus and his followers brought about a revival of interest in the spirituality of the Desert Fathers, the Monks of Mount Sinai, and the hesychasts of Mount Athos, the effects of which are still being felt today.

Thus, in spite of various historical disasters the Orthodox Church has managed to survive in the Near East. Its liturgical richness and its spiritual traditions have revealed their true worth under the most trying circumstances. At times the latter have seriously impeded the normal growth of the Christian cultural tradition that was heir to Byzantium and prevented it from bearing all the fruit that one might have expected under more favorable conditions. But a new period began to dawn for the Orthodox world in the nineteenth and twentieth centuries, as a result of the overthrow of the Ottoman Empire, the final liberation of the Slavic, Greek and Romanian nations in the Balkans, the achievement of independence by various Arab states, the establishment of a lay republic in Turkey, and the mass migration of Greeks from Asia Minor. Further on we shall discuss the present status of the Orthodox Church in these countries.

---

16 A partial uncritical translation (from the Russian) is to be found in Kadloubovksy and Palmer, *Early Fathers from the Philocalia*, and *Writings from the Philocalia on the Prayer of the Heart* (London, no date).

Chapter 6

THE RUSSIAN CHURCH FROM ITS BEGINNINGS TO 1917

Byzantine missionaries first made their way to Russia in the ninth century, the century which witnessed the conversion of the Slavs. They prepared the ground for the later conversions of Princess Olga (955) and St. Vladimir of Kiev (988), which were followed by the "baptism of the Russians," that is to say the establishment of Christianity as the state religion in the principality of Kiev. The translation of the Bible and the liturgical books into the Old Slavonic language had already been largely completed for the benefit of the Bulgars and the Slavs of Moravia in the time of St. Cyril and Methodius (ninth century). The Russians therefore had but to avail themselves of this precious heritage. Thus it came about that the Slavic dialect which happened to be spoken in the neighborhood of Thessalonica—which Cyril and Methodius used in their translations—became Church Slavonic or Old Slavonic, the common liturgical tongue of all the Slavs to this day.

Baptism enabled the principality of Kiev to enter full-fledged into the concert of civilized European states and the play a very important role at that time. Jaroslav, the son of Vladimir (1036-1054), built a cathedral in his capital dedicated to Hagia Sophia, the Divine Wisdom, and had it decorated by the best artists from Constantinople. He married his daughters to the ruling princes of Europe: Ann of Russia, for example, became Queen of France. However, the European destiny of Russia was rudely interrupted by the Mongol invasion (1240), which isolated the Russians from Europe for several centuries. It has been the curious fate of the Byzantine world to have had to bear the brunt of repeated attacks

93

which have seriously disrupted the course of its organic development from the time of the ecumenical councils down to the present day. Such were the Arabic, Mongol and Turkish invasions, which put an end, successively, to the spiritual influence of great centers like Alexandria, Antioch, Kiev and Constantinople.

Until the fifteenth century, the metropolitanate of Kiev, erected under Vladimir, was canonically dependent on the patriarchate of Constantinople. With only a few exceptions, the metropolitans of Kiev were all Greeks who came from Byzantium, while the rest of the episcopate and clergy were chosen locally. The ecumenical patriarchate treated Russia as one vast, firmly centralized missionary diocese. This system was at the basis of the canonical and administrative tradition which made the metropolitan of Kiev—later the patriarch of Moscow—the unique head of the Russian Church, and all other bishops directly subject to his authority. The other Oriental and Balkan patriarchates, by contrast, were always divided into metropolitanates in accordance with ancient canonical custom and have therefore never known any such patriarchal autocracy. The Russian system nevertheless had certain advantages in that it enabled the metropolitan of Kiev, appointed by Constantinople and therefore relatively neutral with respect to local politic, to act as the supreme judge of the country.

The Mongols were generally tolerant in matters of religion and allowed the Church to enjoy the privileges which it had enjoyed under the old Kievan regime. The arbitrary nature of several khans, however, who demanded that the subject Russian princes perform certain pagan rites when they were invested with authority by the Golden Horde (near Astrakhan) resulted in a number of martyrdoms: thus St. Michael of Chernigov, his friend Theodore, and St. Romanus of Ryazan were put to death for their refusal to perform these rites. However, these were isolated instances. The prevailing attitude of the Mongols toward Russian customs was one of tolerant forbearance, a fact that was not slow to be appreciated. Thus we find that a grand prince of Novgorod—the only principality not conquered by the Tartars—St. Alexander Nevsky, had no compunctions about seeking an alliance with the khan, without detriment to his religious convictions, in order to be able to oppose the invaders from the West, whose avowed aim was to effect the submission of the "schismatics." The Russian prince was obliged successively to fight Swedish Crusaders (1240) and Teutonic Knights (1242). In effect, the Western crusading spirit caused the Russians, as it later would be Byzantines, to prefer the yoke of the Asiatic to the imperialism of Roman Christianity.

Meanwhile, the Orthodox Church was free to expand and organize. It could boast, for example, of a number of remarkable missionary successes: there are numerous instances of the conversion of the Mongols to Christianity, and in 1261 it was possible to establish an episcopal see at Sarai, the capital of the Golden Horde! Missionary monasteries—Valamo and Konev on Lake Ladoga, and Solovki on the White Sea—began the work of converting the Finnish tribes of the North. Finally, in the fourteenth century, a remarkable missionary, St. Stephen of Perm, translated the Bible and the liturgy from Greek, with which he was well acquainted, into the Zyrian language. Anxious at all costs not to seem to be forcing Russian ways on his new converts, he created for them a new alphabet and steadfastly refused the political support offered him by the grand prince of Moscow. He was also the first bishop of Perm, the capital of the Zyrian nation.

Dominated by the ideals of Byzantine spirituality, the Russian Church could hardly do otherwise than to allow monasticism to play the important role which it did quite generally throughout the Christian East. At the very time when the Christian foundations of Russia were being laid, St. Theodosius established the famous Monastery or Lavra of the Crypts at Kiev. The numerous branches of this mother house served as spiritual foyers for the dissemination of the Gospel in the southern and western parts of

Russia, which would later be known as the Ukraine. In the north, St. Sergius of Radonej founded the Lavra of the Trinity (today Zagorsk), in the middle of the fourteenth century, while his disciples ranged far and wide through the northern forests. As missionaries, builders, colonizers and scholars, the monks played an important role in the religious life of the times.

Kiev, the ancient and famous capital of Russia, was sacked several times by the Tartars. Eventually reduced to the status of an abandoned village, it ceased to be the residence of the metropolitan. After a brief sojourn in Vladimir, the primatial seat was transferred to Moscow under Metropolitan Peter (1308)-1326). This was an event of great historical importance. Moscow, hitherto a rather obscure principality, became the religious capital of all the Russias. Separatist tendencies at once made themselves felt in the south and west. The princes of those areas, subject to the authority of the king of Poland and the grand duke of Lithuania, demanded the right from Constantinople to have their own metropolitan and finally won their case in the fifteenth century when Moscow became autocephalous with respect to Byzantium.

The independence or "autocephaly"[1] of the Russian Church was proclaimed as a consequence of the acceptance by the then metropolitan, Isidore, a Greek, of the decisions of the Council of Florence (1439-1440). We have already briefly touched upon the conditions under which this unionist council was held and described how its decisions were quickly repudiated by the Greek Church at large. The Metropolitan Isidore, however, was a staunch advocate of the policy of reunion. In reward for his conciliatory attitude and for the part played by him at Florence, the pope had appointed him a cardinal priest immediately after the conclusion of the council. Upon arriving in Moscow in 1441, he celebrated a solemn liturgy in the Cathedral of

---

1 According to Orthodox canon law the term "autocephaly" stands for the right, enjoyed by a group of diocese, of electing their own primate. The boundaries of the various autocephalies often coincide with the frontiers of a state, although this is not always true.

the Dormition, mentioned the pope's name in the course of the service, and proclaimed the reunion with Rome. After pondering the matter for three days, the Grand Duke Basil had Isidore arrested and imprisoned for some months in a monastery, and then allowed him to escape to Lithuania.

After much hesitation and a prolonged correspondence with Constantinople—where the Union of Florence had not yet been officially proclaimed—the Russians decided to enthrone a new metropolitan themselves. It was thus that Jonas was appointed to the see of Moscow in December 1448. Constantinople was simply informed of the *fait accompli.* The step was taken partly as a precautionary measure to forestall trouble with the ecumenical patriachate in the future, for its was widely assumed that the Union of Florence would not last long there. In fact, as soon as Constantinople fell, in 1453, the Greeks repudiated the Council of Florence. However, Moscow now had its own metropolitan and was not disposed to give up what circumstances had enable it to usurp.

These events also had their psychological aftermath, for, beginning in the fifteenth century, we find the first serious traces of a profound popular distrust of the Orthodoxy of the Greeks on the part of the Russians. Had the Greeks not betrayed the true faith at Florence, had they not been deservedly punished by God, who had handed over their empire to the Turks? Moscow was henceforth the "Third Rome." Ancient Rome was now heretical, the New Rome was groaning under the yoke of the Turks, the Third Rome alone remained intact. The theocratic ideal of a universal Christian empire thus found its last refuge in Moscow. Before long the grand dukes adopted the title of "czar" (a Slavic version of Caesar) and considered themselves henceforth as the legitimate successors of the rulers of Byzantium. In the purely ecclesiastical sphere this theory was never pushed to its logical conclusions however, for the see of Moscow, in spite of its great power and wealth, never formally claimed to supplant the ecumenical primacy of Constantinople. There were always men in Russia who saw things in a more humble and realistic and less romantic light than the partisans of the Third Rome.

Thus it came about that, in the course of the sixteenth century, the Russian clergy and indeed all of Russian society were divided by a violent quarrel over the way in which the religious future of Russia was to be envisaged. One part, headed by the learned abbot Joseph of Volock, was completely dedicated to the idea of a new Christian Muscovite empire: they were the partisans of a close alliance between Church and state in the Byzantine manner, and demanded in return that the state allow the Church and the monasteries to keep the enormous domains which they possessed and which were used for charitable, educational and social purposes. They firmly believed in the urgency of building here and now a City of God, of which Moscow was to be the center. The other party, on the contrary—whose spokesman was the austere monk of the northern forest, Nil Sorskij—preached the virtues of monastic poverty, independence with respect to the state, and canonical loyalty to Constantinople. They foresaw that a wealthy and "naturalized" Church would more easily become a prey to state control. In the end the Church finally recognized that there was an element of truth in the claims of both sides: both Joseph and Nil were canonized. However, apparent victory lay with the party of Joseph, in the sixteenth century. The Church retained its properties and allied itself with the Muscovite state. But history has shown that Nil was, to a large extent, right. The Byzantine Middle Ages were well over by the sixteenth century and the further development of the Russian Empire along the lines of a secularized modern state, which in the eighteenth century was destined completely to subject the Church to its will and confiscate its property, justified the misgivings of Nil and his party a posteriori.[2]

2 On the sixteenth-century controversies and their consequences, see also out study *Une controverse sur le rôle social de l'Église. La querelle des biens ecclésiastiques au XVIe siècle en Russie* (Chevetogne, 1956 [articles appearing in *Irénikon*, 1955 and 1956]). Cf. W. K. Medlin, *Moscow and East Rome. A Political Study of the Relations of Church and State in Muscovite Russia* (Geneva, 1952).

Having achieved an autocephalous status, the Russian Church proceeded to develop its own religious literature (lives of the saints, liturgical texts) in the course of the fifteenth and sixteenth centuries. Russian art (iconography), ever faithful to its Byzantine masters, attained a high degree of perfection with the work of Andrei Rublev. A great council, held at Moscow in 1551 (Stoglav, "Council of the Hundred Chapters"), introduced a number of reforms in the Russian Church aimed at curbing the influence of sects and the spread of Western forms of piety and religious thought. A considerable number of Russian saints were canonized. The Third Rome thus gave evidence that it intended to live up to the new title which was being attributed to her. The Russians were particularly pleased when the ecumenical patriarch Jeremias II visited their country and consecrated the first patriarch of Moscow and all the Russias, Job (1589). The new patriarchate, however, was only accorded fifth place in the hierarchy of Oriental sees and even today occupies the same place, after Constantinople, Alexandria, Antioch and Jerusalem.

The theory of the Third Rome suffered still further blows under the pontificate of the great patriarch Nikon (1652-1658). As soon as he had been elected this very authoritarian-minded prelate decided on a twofold policy for his pontificate: he intended to establish the supremacy of the spiritual over the temporal power and to reform the Russian Church in accordance with the liturgical norms then prevailing in the four other Oriental patriarchates. The close friendship between Nikon and Czar Alexis—the second of the Romanovs—enabled him to attain his first objective. For some years the Russian czar was the obedient son of the patriarch. However, Nikon was lacking in the tact and patience necessary to profit by this favorable situation, and his power did not last. His second objective resulted in a schism which separated millions of the faithful, who had taken the theory of the Third Rome seriously, from the mother church. Why, these critics asked, should minor customs (like making the sign of the cross with two fingers, singing the Alleluia twice, etc.) be reformed, when our fathers had been saved by observing them? Why accept as a criterion in these matters the corrupt Greeks whom God had punished for their infidelity? This was childish reasoning, of course, but it nevertheless contained a certain logic, all the more so in that the reforms were introduced by violence and intolerance, and certain measures—for example the requirement that the clergy wear their hair long—were not justified by the ancient practice of the Byzantine Church but were merely modern Greek customs dating from the time of the Turkish occupation. Nikon was finally deposed and condemned by a synod (1666-1667). The very Oriental patriarchs whose spokesman he had been took part in the synod and confirmed the deposition. The patriarch's reforms, however, were not abolished and the schism ("raskol") of the Old Believers lasted for centuries.[3]

The claim of Patriarch Nikon to dominate the czar haunted the mind of the young Peter the Great, who ended by imitating the impetuosity of the proud prelate but along entirely different lines. After the death of Patriarch Hadrian (1700), the czar forbade the holding of elections for a new patriarch for twenty-one years, and then in 1721 promulgated his famous *Spiritual Regulation*, compiled by Theophanes Prokopovich, bishop of Pskov, which abolished the patriarchate and placed a collegiate body at the head of the Church, the Holy Synod, consisting of bishops and two or three priests. In accordance with the new regulations, a lay procurator, appointed by the czar, was required to take part in all discussions (without formally being a member of the Synod) and gradually became the head of the administrative organization of the Church.

This system, influenced by the ecclesiastical regimes found in the Protestant states of Central Europe, did not formally regard the czar as the head of the Church (documents referred to him

3 On Nikon and the Raskol, see the monumental thesis of P. Pascal, *Avvakum et les débuts du Raskol* (Paris, 1938).

merely by the ambiguous title of "supreme judge of the present college"), but Peter subjected the Church to the state in a way that neither Byzantium nor Russia had ever dreamed of before this time. Called upon to approve the new arrangement, the other Orthodox eastern patriarchs finally gave their consent, after Dositheus of Jerusalem—whose efforts on behalf of Orthodoxy we have mentioned above—protested in vain against the whole of the czar's reforms.

Politically separate from Moscow, the provinces that later formed the Ukraine (in Russian, Ukraine signifies "frontiers") experienced an altogether different, and at times quite tragic, fate. After the election of Jonas to the see of Moscow, Isidore retained at least nominal authority over the diocese of Kiev in Polish and Lithuanian territory. He resigned in 1458. His successor was appointed by Rome and consecrated by the Uniat patriarch of Constantinople (resident in Rome). The new incumbent was Gregory Bolgarin, who for twelve years maintained the communion of the Ukrainian Church with Rome. Then, in 1470, he returned to Orthodoxy and recognized once more the authority of the ecumenical patriarch at Constantinople (under Turkish rule). The latter, after Bolgarin's death in 1472, appointed an Orthodox prelate to succeed him.

From this date the Russian dioceses of Poland and Lithuania, although canonically dependent on Constantinople, led a practically independent life and were constantly subject to pressure on the part of the Catholic kings of Poland. This pressure was exercised particularly by means of the "right of patronage" which enabled the kings and certain nobles to appoint candidates for the priesthood and the episcopate and to administer some of the property of the Church. Opposition to Latinism was fostered especially by various confraternities of Orthodox laymen, who sometimes succeeded in buying up the right of patronage over their churches, published works defending Orthodoxy, and supported Orthodox schools. Undoubtedly it was these laymen who were mainly responsible for saving the Orthodox faith in the Ukraine, and not the apathetic clergy, who were subservient to the king and corrupt.

In 1596 the metropolitan of Kiev, Michael Ragoza, and the majority of Ukrainian bishops signed an act of reunion with Rome at Brest-Litovsk. This was the origin of the "Uniat" Ukrainian Church. However, the majority of the faithful led by two bishops and an exarch of the ecumenical patriarch, Archdeacon Nicephorus, remained faithful to their Orthodoxy. When the two Orthodox bishops died (1607-1610), the faithful were without any pastors for ten years and were governed by the Uniat bishops whom the king of Poland imposed on them. In 1620, however, Theophanes, patriarch of Jerusalem, paid a visit to Kiev and re-established an Orthodox succession. At first more or less secretly, then openly, this hierarchy was finally recognized by the (Polish) state.

These events, the conditions under which the union with Rome had been imposed, excesses of all kinds, kept alive for centuries a fierce hatred among the Orthodox faithful toward the authority of Rome, which, in these parts, became identified with that of the Polish kings.

Forced to live under these difficult conditions, the Orthodox Church nevertheless had the good fortune to be governed by a number of distinguished prelates, notably the Metropolitan Peter Moghila (1632-1647). Famed for his *Confessions*, which we have mentioned above, Moghila founded a school at Kiev in which the teaching was largely according to Latin methods of instruction. He reformed the liturgy and church government, endeavoring thus to overcome the inferior position in which the Orthodox found themselves by comparison with their Latin neighbors.

Finally in 1686, as a result of Russian victories over Poland, the Ukraine was annexed to the Muscovite empire of the Romanovs and the metropolitanate of Kiev was attached to the patriarchate of

Moscow with the formal approval of the patriarch of Constantinople. Many Kievan theologians now moved to Moscow and served as invaluable assistants to Peter the Great, who was intent on introducing pro-Western reforms into Russia. They also brought along with them Latin methods and instruction and Latin ways of thought, which had a lasting effect on Russian theology.

As for the Uniats, a large part of them returned to Orthodoxy following the partition of Poland (three bishops and many faithful in 1839, at Polotzk). However, the major part of their church in Galicia, at first under Austrian, then under Polish sovereignty, remained faithful to Rome until 1946. There is evidence that the recent return of this unfortunate church to Orthodoxy was effected under conditions rather similar to if not worse than those under which it was formerly united with Rome.

The synodal period of Russian church history (1721-1917) is not viewed with a kindly eye today and is frequently cited as a classical example of the worst that can happen when a church is enslaved by the state. In actual fact, however, religion remained very much alive in Russian during this period and in many respects was even productive of exceptionally good results, so that it would be inaccurate and misleading to dismiss too summarily the rather artificial system under which it labored. Contemporaries themselves recognized the uncanonical nature of the new ecclesiastical regime, but they were powerless to do anything except tolerate it. The system of state control imposed on the Church, like a dike, left the Church's awareness of itself intact. It restricted some of the church's activities and resulted in the creation of deplorable conditions—the clergy, for example, became a social caste—but it did not corrupt church life fatally.

We shall dwell here briefly on three positive aspects of the Russian Church during this period: Russian spirituality, education, and missionary efforts.

The Christian East has always had a particular respect and even affection for the monastic life, as we have seen. The monasteries of Byzantium were the recognized centers of spiritual life in the city and Empire. In this respect, the Russians were the faithful disciples of the Greeks. During the synodal period, moreover, their loyalty to the monastic ideal was highly important because it was largely this which made possible the survival of Russian spirituality by acting as a counterweight to the process of statism, the attempt of the state to make over the Church in its own image and reduce it to the role of a mere servant. It was in the monasteries that the great Russian saints of the period made their appearance and carried on their apostolate.

In the eighteenth century, for example, a bishop of Veroneje, St. Tikhon (1724-1783), spent the remaining sixteen years of his life in the monastery of Zadonsk and there devoted himself to the contemplative life and the writing of spiritual works. Dostoevsky was inspired by his example to create a character with the same name in his *The Possessed*[4] Tikhon soon acquired a great reputation as a spiritual adviser. Under the influence of German pietism, he advocated a complete renunciation of worldly things. The excessive nature of his teaching on this point illustrates better than anything else the typical reaction of many Russian Christians to the arrogant secularism of the reforms of Peter the Great. The conflict between the new political realism and the spiritual traditions of the past came to a head only during the Russian intellectual and spiritual renaissance in the nineteenth century.

A revival of interest in patristic spirituality was heralded by the publication of a Slavic translation—the work of Paisij Velickovskij, a monk from Athos who founded the monastery of Neamt in Moldavia—of the *Philocalia* of Nicodemus (St. Petersburg, 1793). From now on the Russians possessed in their own language a collection of the important texts of the Fathers on prayer,

4 N. Gorodetzky, *St. Tikhon Zadonsky, Inspirer of Dostoevsky* (London, 1951).

asceticism and mysticism. Before long, the greatest modern Russian saint, Seraphim, had become famous in the monastery of Sarov, and the *startsi* of Optino were being chosen as the favorite spiritual advisers of the Russian intellectual élite.[5] Gogol, Dostoevsky, Alexis Khomiakov and Vladimir Soloviev all found the ultimate source of their inspiration in the Russian Church and the spiritual traditions of Orthodoxy. On the very eve of the Revolution, the conversion of noted Marxist intellectuals (Struve, Frank, Bulgakov, Berdiaev) seemed to place a seal on the reconciliation of Spirit and Matter under the sovereignty of Christ. Unfortunately, this reconciliation, achieved on the purely intellectual level, was insufficient in itself to arrest or alter the great tide of events which had been preparing for such a long time as a result of so many social and economic factors.

If these spiritual movements as a whole appeared to take place on the fringes, as it were, of the official state Church—the reforms of Peter the Great resulted in the division of Russian society into a closed caste system (nobility, clergy, peasantry)—the official Church nevertheless did contribute to the intellectual life of the country, particularly by creating a system of church-run schools which attained a remarkably high standard of excellence in the nineteenth century.

Toward the end of the seventeenth century a theological academy was founded at Moscow. This term henceforth became traditional in Russia as the designation for a graduate school of theology or what in the West would be called a major seminary. In spite of doubts about their orthodoxy, it was the Latinizing theologians of Kiev, the former pupils of Peter Moghila, who were called upon to work out the curriculum and define the methods of instruction to be used in the new school. Throughout the

5 On this movement as a whole, see especially E. Behr-Sigel, *Prière et sainteté en Russie*, (Paris, Éditions du Cerf, 1950); I. Kologrivof, *Essai sur la sainteté en Russie*, ed. *Beynaert* (Bruges, 1953); V. Zenkovsky, *A History of Russian Philosophy*, 2 vols. (New York, 1953).

eighteenth century the future higher clergy of the Russian Church studied in Latin from manuals compiled in accordance with the approved methods of Latin scholasticism. The system was only modified in 1808, but some of its features remained in effect until 1867, while its influence of course lasted much longer. Though alien in spirit, from the viewpoint of Orthodox tradition, these Latin methods nevertheless produced tangible results in the purely educational field, especially after the founding of three other academies (St. Petersburg, 1809; Kiev, 1819; Kazan, 1842) in addition to the one at Moscow. The students who attended these higher institutes were chosen from among the ablest pupils in the seminaries (secondary schools for the clergy), founded in many Russian dioceses in the course of the nineteenth century. By 1914, the Russian Church had a total of fifty-eight seminaries with 20,500 pupils, of whom only a certain portion went on to be ordained. The majority of the others became lay teachers, for the Church also controlled a part of the country's elementary school system and furnished professors of religion who taught in the secular schools. In all, there were 40,150 schools of all kinds dependent on the Church in 1914.[6]

Gradually overcoming the defects which they had when founded in the eighteenth century, the church-directed schools turned out an appreciable number of able theologians, historians and liturgists in the nineteenth and twentieth centuries, whose works—unfortunately little known in the West where only a few Slavic scholars were able to read Russian—were and still are authoritative in a number of fields. In the field of patrology, for example, special attention was paid to the translation of the original texts. More works of the Fathers and related texts have been translated into Russian than into any other European language.[7]

6 *La Documentation française* no. 1931 (Oct. 9, 1954), *Le Problème religieux en U.R.S.S.*, vol. 2, p. 5.

7 See C. Kern, *Les Traductions russes des textes patristiques, Guide bibliographique* (Chevetogne, 1957).

Thus by 1914 the Russian Church represented an imposing body of nearly a hundred million faithful, divided into sixty-seven dioceses.[8] The sixty-seven bishops in office were assisted in their work by eighty-two auxiliary bishops, 50,105 priests, 15,210 deacons. 21,330 monks and 73,299 nuns. The number of monasteries for men came to 1,025 that of convents for women to 473.[9]

During the synodal period, moreover, the Russian Church continued its missionary advance toward the East. We have seen that in the Mongol period Russian missionaries began the evangelization of several ethnic groups living in European Russia. Progress continued in the fifteenth and sixteenth centuries, facilitated by the capture of Kazan (1552) and Astrakhan (1556), and by the gradual conquest of Siberia. The missionary activity of several archbishops of Kazan (St. Gurius, St. Barsanuphius, St. Germanus) resulted in the establishment of a solid core of Christian Tartars around this city in the sixteenth century. Philotheus, metropolitan of Tobolsk (1702-1727), dispatched missionaries to the Kamchatka (1705) and to Iakutsk, in eastern Siberia (1724). He was the first to extend his missionary efforts beyond the confines of the Russian Empire by sending a mission to China (1714), where there had been a Christian Orthodox colony in the suburbs of Peking every since the year 1689, consisting of Sinicized Russian Cossacks. Toward the end of the eighteenth century, monks from the monastery of Valamo on Lake Ladoga proceeded to Alaska—then a Russian possession—and established an Aleutian-speaking mission.

In the nineteenth century the archimandrite Macarius, a Hebrew specialist and one of the most successful translators of the

8 Ever since the time of the Middle Ages, when Russia consisted of only one missionary metropolitanate dependent on the patriarchate of Constantinople, the number of Russian dioceses had traditionally been very small.

9 N. Zernov, *The Russians and Their Church* (London, 1945), p. 143; *Pamiatnaia Knizhka* (Government Annual) (1916), pp. 466-72. Cf. J. S. Curtiss, *The Russian Church and the Soviet State* (Boston, 1953), pp. 9-10 (citing the official figures for 1914).

Bible into Russian, founded a mission at Altai in western Siberia in 1830, and translated the Bible and the liturgy into the various dialects of the region. By 1903, 25,000 of the local inhabitants had become Christian and had a complete liturgy in their own language. Eastern Siberia also had its apostle in the person of John Veniaminov, who, first as a priest (1824-1840) and then as a bishop (1840-1868), labored indefatigably with a group of helpers, for the conversion of the Eskimos and the Indians of Alaska, the Aleutian Islands and the Kurile Islands, and the Yakuts of Siberia. Appointed metropolitan of Moscow in 1868, he founded in the capital an "Orthodox Missionary Society" for the purpose of centralizing all the missionary activities of the Russian Church. After thirty years of labor, the society could congratulate itself on the conversion of some 124,200 pagans to the Gospel.

The whole missionary efforts of the Russian Church was given a new direction toward the middle of the nineteenth century, when a center for missionary studies was founded at the Academy of Kazan. The heart and soul of the new center was a lay professor, I. I. Ilminsky, a remarkable linguist, who was perfectly acquainted both with the biblical languages (Hebrew, Greek), Arabic, and with the various languages of Central Asia. In order to counteract the rapid progress of Islam among the Tartars, Ilminsky and his group conceived the idea of translating the biblical and liturgical texts, not into the literary language which was very little understood by the people, but into the various spoken dialects. Thus a veritable Orthodox library was created for the benefit of the Tartars, Yakuts, Buryats, Tunlgus, Votyaks, Mordvinians, Cheremiss, Ostyak-Samarovs, and Kirghiz. By the year 1903, the liturgy of St. John Chrysostom was being celebrated in more than twenty languages in the region of Kazan. In 1899 the diocese of Samara had 128 clergy (74 priests, 17 deacons, and 37 lectors) who were able to speak Chuvask, and of this number 47 priests, 12 deacons and 20 lectors were of Chuvash origin.

Beyond the Russian frontiers the Japanese mission was by far the most important. It is still active today, as we shall see later on.[10]

Orthodox missionary activity in Asia from the fifteenth to the nineteenth centuries, on the whole—though with notable exceptions, especially in Japan—followed the colonial expansion of the Russian Empire. But this was equally true of Western missionary efforts, Catholic and Protestant, in Africa and Asia, which in general coincided with the colonial occupation of those areas by European countries. The success of the Orthodox missions, particularly in Islamic regions, is at least partly attributable to the time-honored Byzantine custom of translating the liturgy into the various local spoken languages, and partly to a certain cleverness on the part of the Russians in being able to adjust themselves to and identify themselves with the life of the subject peoples.

In any case, the story of these missions is sufficient to refute an erroneous impression regarding the dullness and ineffectiveness of Russian church history during the synodal period. While remaining outwardly a part of the governmental machinery, the Church was nevertheless still capable of producing saints and apostles who testified to the remarkable vitality of Russian Christianity during these years.

---

10 Regarding the Orthodox missions, see especially the monumental works of J. Glazik, *Die russische-orthodoxe Heidenmission seit Peter dem Grossen* (Münster-Westfalen, 1954); *Die Islammission der russisch-orthodoxen Kirche* (Münster-Westfalen, 1959), who cites many Russian sources. Cf. also E. Smirnoff, *Russian Orthodox Missions* (London, 1903), and S. Bolshakoff, *The Foreign Missions of the Russian Orthodox Church* (London, 1943).

Chapter 7

THE ORTHODOX CHURCH AND THE COMMUNIST STATE

The early decades of the twentieth century were fateful from every point of view and the Christians of Russia were destined to find themselves in the very midst of the great transformations then taking place. The part played by them in these events and above all the remarkable survival of religion in Russian prove that the Russian Church was by no means, as so readily assumed, a mere cog in the wheel of the czarist government. Throughout the nineteenth century farsighted individuals constantly looked forward to the day when the Church could be modernized by means of adequate reforms, and especially, to the imperative necessity of achieving greater independence with respect to the state. At the time of the 1905 revolution, when Nicholas II granted a constitution guaranteeing almost complete freedom of movement and speech in Russia, a wave of intellectual and social unrest broke over the Church. Russian religious publications in this period (1905-1917) are filled with passionate discussions of the reforms that were deemed necessary in the Church. The Holy Synod agreed to the holding of a national synod of the Russian Church—not since the time of Peter the Great had it even been possible to contemplate such a step—and established a Pre-Conciliar Commission charged with the responsibility of preparing the agenda. The Russian bishops were invited to suggest a program of reforms: their replies to this inquiry constitute one of the most interesting documents of the period. On the whole they were in favor of widespread reforms in the Church which would enable it to carry on its mission in a more effective way and with less control by the state. A decided majority was in favor of the re-establishment of the patriarchate.

111

Thus the Church was better prepared than is generally supposed for the events which were now about to take place. The Provisional Government of Kerensky allowed the Church to summon the council, which had been in preparation for twelve years. The body which met at Moscow in August 1917 included 265 members of the clergy and 299 laymen. Elected by indirect voting in the diocese, the council was representative of the ecclesiological tendencies prevalent in the Russian Church in the nineteenth century, and in accordance with these principles laymen were permitted to share with the episcopate responsibility for the affairs of the Church at all levels of church government. The council sat until August 1918 and drew up a new constitution for the Church, which provided for the re-establishment of the patriarchate, the election of bishops by the dioceses, and the representation of laymen on parish councils, on diocesan councils and in the higher administration of the patriarchate. On October 31, 1917—six days after the overthrow of the Provisional Government by the Bolsheviks—Tikhon, metropolitan of Moscow, was elected patriarch. Episcopal elections could not be held in all the dioceses; however, in Petrograd the popular Bishop Benjamin was elected metropolitan by the clergy and faithful in the very midst of the revolutionary turmoil. Thus, far from seeming to uphold the *ancien régime,* the Church on the one hand boldly asserted its right to independence from the state, and on the other showed that it was disposed to allow the people to elect their own ecclesiastical heads.

However, most member of the council of 1917-1918 and the majority of Russians at large lacked any clear ideas on what the proper relations between the Church and the new Russian state should be. During the brief reign of Kerensky, there was an intense longing on the part of church leaders for some form of independence, but this longing was not identified with any particular theory regarding the exact nature of future Church-state relations. The Church leaders first of all spoke out on behalf of what they regarded as the national interest, by demanding material support from the Provisional Government for the Orthodox faith as the dominant religion of the new republic, but appealing to the army to continue the war against Germany, and later, by solemnly condemning the Treaty of Brest-Litovsk, which had been concluded by Lenin. These acts clearly showed that the Church did not at first envisage the necessity of having to separate itself completely from the state and that this separation, once it had been brought about through force of circumstances, did not mean that the Church intended to remain silent with regard to the acts of the government and refrain from passing judgment on them. The Church had reformed itself internally, but its attitude toward the various phases of the Russian Revolution was determined pragmatically by the mental outlook an conscience of its rulers, especially by that of its head, Patriarch Tikhon.

The Communist Party, an intensely active and well-disciplined minority, triumphed with relative ease and unexpected suddenness in the midst of the frightful political confusion in the country at the time. The Church thus found itself confronting a government resolved to combat all religion as such, for Marx had defined religion as the "opium of the people."

The attitude of the Soviet state toward religious beliefs in general, and toward the Orthodox Church in particular, has been remarkable the same over the years, as far as theory or doctrine is concerned. Equally remarkable are the various tactics it has adopted over the same years in dealing with religious opposition.[1] It seems that this fact is to be explained not by any deliberate Machiavellianism on the part of the party leaders in the field of religious policy, but by certain misconceptions which have vitiated their analysis of the religious

1 "Marxism is materialism. As such, it is without mercy for religion," wrote Lenin (*Works*, 3rd ed. [Leningrad, 1935-1937], vol. 4, p. 70). "All religious doctrine," wrote P. Kasirin, "serves to camouflage the interests of the exploiting classes," *The Reactionary Essence of Religious Ideology* (in Russian) (Moscow, 1951), p. 29. The Soviet press still frequently regrets that "all Soviet citizens are not yet emancipated from the vestiges of former times, particularly the traces of religion." See, for example, M. Persitz, "The Legislation of the October Revolution on the Freedom of Conscience" (in Russian), in *Questions of History of Religion and Atheism*, vol. 5 (1958), p. 63.

situation in Russia. Marxist dogma, in effect, was laid down in the West and under different conditions from those prevailing in the Russia of 1918: "Christianity," wrote Engels, "has become more and more the apanage of the ruling classes and is used by them as a bridge by which to control the lower classes.[2]

According to this doctrine it was enough merely to create a classless society to bring about the disappearance of religion. But in Russia the Orthodox Church was a popular church—the ruling classes, on the contrary, had been largely secularized since the eighteenth century—and it had just provided itself with an even more "democratic" constitution in the council of 1917-1918, by accepting fundamental reforms in its structure and its administration. The anti-religious measures of the government therefore struck not at the "ruling classes" of the former regime, but at a popular clergy and the great mass of believers, who by and large did not identify their cause with the political and military counterrevolution, and did not represent, therefore, except for their religious convictions, any deep threat to the new government. In order to impose its will in this matter the government did not hesitate to have recourse to force and considerable bloodletting, and thus succeeded in transforming the Orthodox Church into a martyred church. Frightened by the consequences of its own actions, the government made several tactical retreats—it tried, for example, to win over to its side a part of the clergy, with a limited amount of success, and thus divide the Church. Finally, after many years, it arrived a kind of modus vivendi with the reunified Church, a rather unstable arrangement by the terms of which both sides, Church and state, appear to be staking all on the future.

We shall first briefly touch on the restrictive measures of the government in the field of religion, and then analyze the reaction of the church and the ensuing conflict.

---

2 See the collection entitled *Thoughts of K. Marx and F. Engels on Religion* (in Russian) (Leningrad, 1929), p. 63.

On January 20, 1918, the Council of Commissaries of the People approved the famous decree regarding the "separation of Church and State and the separation of the schools from the Church," which was promulgated on January 23.[3]

This decree forbade all participation by the Church in the life of the state and all religious instruction in public or private schools. It proclaimed complete freedom of conscience for all citizens. The freedom envisaged, however, was not the same kind as that which existed in "bourgeois" countries, for religious groups were no longer regarded as juridical persons capable of enjoying juridical rights. Such groups were deprived of the right to own property (paragraph 12); their property was declared nationalized; only places of worship (according to the autograph correction of Lenin in the original text) might be made available to them by the state, as the result of a special decision by the authorities (para. 13). Worship was not allowed except where it did not interfere with public order (para. 5), the authorities alone being the sole judge in the matter since the Church as a religious group had no juridical rights. The new government was not only separated from the Church; it placed the later completely "outside the law." The publication of the decree was accompanied by numerous antireligious disturbances, inspired and carried out by local Communist officials or by undisciplined revolutionary groups. The most notorious of these outbursts was the one that resulted in the murder of the metropolitan of Kiev, Vladimir (January 25, 1918). These governmental acts, radical and brutal by their very nature, were clearly designed to break down the resistance and organization of the Russian Church. The latter, however, remained hopeful of being able to come to some kind of an understanding with the Soviet government. On two occasions (November 4-8, 1917, March 15, 1918), a delegation from the Church council—which continued to sit in Moscow—went to the

3 An account of the history of this decree, as well as a photographic copy of the original with the autograph corrections of Lenin, has recently been published in the periodical *Questions of History of Religion and Atheism*, vol. 5 (Moscow, 1958), pp. 50-63.

Kremlin to try to reach an agreement on the relations between Church and state. But each time, while the tone of the conversations was correct no results were forthcoming. The government had decided on unilateral action.

When the great famine of 1921-1922 was raging throughout the length and breadth of the land, especially in the Volga region, Patriarch Tikhon addressed an appeal to the Russian Church (August 1921), as well as to foreign churches, to collect funds for the starving. An ecclesiastical committee was set up to centralize and distribute help. But the government was afraid of the moral prestige that might accrue to the Church if it succeeded in providing help on a massive scale, and confiscated what had already been collected. A new decree dated February 26, 1922 went even further: it ordered the confiscation of all valuable objects in the churches (metals or precious stones), declaring that they were needed to alleviate the suffering of the starving. Such valuables, in fact were already the property of the state by the decree of 1918.

By its laws and its arbitrary acts the government indicated clearly enough its intention to build in Russia a society in which there would no longer be any place for the Church. For the Christians of Russia, therefore, it was no longer merely a question of recognizing the social reforms introduced by the Soviets—the collectivization of the land, the nationalization of industry—as just or unjust, but of defending the very existence of religion in Russia and of finding the best was to do this. A part of the clergy chose the simplest path: they sided with the White armies fighting the Reds in various parts of the country. The patriarch, however, and the majority of the clergy who were in territory controlled by the Soviets could not avoid defining their attitude toward the new state of affairs in a more realistic manner. And they did so as Christians. Their witness to the truth and the moral and physical sacrifices which they were obliged to endure constitute the best guarantee for the future of religion in Russia. The figures at our disposal show, more eloquently than anything else, the enormous risk which they incurred by remaining faithful to their vocation. Between 1923 and 1926, some fifty bishops were either shot to death or died following deportation. In the years 1921-1922 the business of confiscating church valuables cost the lives of some 691 priests alone. A much greater number of priests were forced to submit to rigorous governmental measures of all kinds and were subject to various harassments, including that of being deprived of all civil rights.[4]

Three months after the October Revolution, in response to the unbelievably crude and violent initial attacks on the Church, Patriarch Tikhon launched a sentence of excommunication against the "open or disguised enemies of Christ" from his residence in Moscow:[5]

> By the authority which God has vested in me, we forbid you to approach the Mysteries of Christ; we anathematize you, provided you still bear the name of Christian and belong, by birth, to the Orthodox Church . . . As for you, faithful sons of the Church, I appeal to you to defend our holy Mother, outraged and oppressed . . . And if it becomes necessary to suffer for the cause of Christ, we appeal to you to follow the path of suffering . . . And you, my brother bishops and priests . . . organize religious groups as quickly as possible, appeal to them to form an alliance of spiritual combatants determined to oppose to physical force the power of the Spirit. We firmly believe that the enemies of the Church of Christ will be defeated and dispersed by the power of the Cross, for the promise of Him who bore the Cross is unshakable: "I will build my Church and the gates of hell shall not prevail against it."

4 The Constitution of 1918, para. 69. See M. Pol'skij, *New Martyrs of Russia* (in Russian) (Jordanville, NY: 1949), pp. 168-80; cf. N. Timascheff, *Religion in Soviet Russia* (London, 1943), p. 89; A. A. Bogolepov, *The Church under Communist Power* (in Russian) (Munich, 1958), pp. 16-17. It is obvious that the figures cited by these émigré authors cannot be controlled materially, the sole criterion being their probability. However, the latter is beyond question for the period we are studying. The ecclesiastical trials and deportations were frequently and fully reported in the Soviet press.

5 Complete English translation in P. Anderson, *Church and State in Modern Russia* (New York, 1944), pp. 65-68.

In spite of the passionate nature of this appeal, the patriarch refrained from expressly mentioning the government among the "enemies of Christ"—hoping no doubt that the latter would not carry to extremes the violence unleashed by the revolutionary spirit—and did not call upon the faithful to resist the governmental measures by force, but only by "spiritual" means. Thus while the head of the Church made no pretense of remaining "outside politics"—in March 1918 he condemned the Treaty of Brest-Litovsk—he nevertheless refrained from pronouncing any judgment on the social reforms of the new regime. From this moment, under his guidance, the Church refused to identify itself with the old regime and made it clear that it intended to exercise its own right to proclaim the Gospel to the Russian people. In October 1918, Tikhon addressed a new message directly to Lenin:[6]

> It does not pertain to us to judge the early power; all power permitted by God shall have our blessing bestowed on it, if it truly shows itself the "servant of God, for the good of the governed" (Rom 13:4) . . . As for you, we address to you this admonition: celebrate the anniversary of your assumption of power by releasing prisoners, by ceasing to shed blood, by abandoning violence and placing restrictions on the faith; cease to destroy, in order to organize order and justice, give the people the respite they are longing for . . . Otherwise, all the just blood that you have shed will cry out against you and you will perish by the sword, you who have taken the sword. (Mt 22:52)

This letter to Lenin did not mean that the patriarch was now contemplating supporting the counterrevolutionary forces. In a new appeal issued in September 1919 he called upon the faithful to refrain from any act which might arouse the suspicions of the Soviet authorities and to obey all the regulations provided they were not opposed to the faith and true piety. Several other bishops issued similar appeals to their flocks. Thus, when Metropolitan Benjamin learned in Petrograd that a plan was afoot to profane the relics of St. Alexander Nevsky, he sent a delegation to Zi-

6 This appeal of the patriarch may be found in all books devoted to the Russian Church after 1917.

noviev, the president of the local soviet, asking him to revoke the order, and solemnly promised to suspend any cleric under his jurisdiction at once if any gave assistance to the Whites.[7]

This attitude, revealing that the Church was prepared to be critical and obdurate on moral issues but politically loyal, won it a certain amount of respect. In the midst of the unbelievable turmoil into which Russia had been plunged—revolutionary excesses of all kinds, civil war was on several fronts, foreign intervention—the Orthodox Church appeared as a solid bastion and haven of hope, materially shaken, but spiritually purified by the martyrdom of many of its sons. The most serious blow which it had to face during these years was the confiscation of valuable objects.

As we have seen, the government had forbidden the Church to organize relief for the starving in its own name and then decreed in February 1922 the confiscation of all valuable objects in the churches. The patriarch thereupon issued a circular letter permitting the church authorities to hand over nonconsecrated objects (the ornaments on icons, ex-votos, candelabra, and the like), but forbidding the surrender of items used in the liturgical services (sacred vessels, sacerdotal vestments). As an alternative, he proposed that the faithful organize a drive and pay the authorities the equivalent of the objects that could not be handed over. He would certainly have gone even further, if he could have been sure of exercising the least control over the actual use of the confiscated objects. The patriarch's circular resulted in a wave of persecutory acts of unusual violence, and provided the government with a valuable propaganda weapon to use against the clergy. The patriarch and bishops, it was maintained, were refusing to come to the relief of the starving! In many towns there were violent clashes between the governmental authorities and the faithful. For the first time, the government dared to try some of the church leaders

---

7 Mentoined by *Isvestia*, Sept. 20, 1919, cited in J. S. Curtiss, *The Russian Church and the Soviet State* (Boston, 1953), p. 339.

publicly. In Moscow, forty-four persons—priests and lay-men—were dragged before the courts and eleven were con-demned to death. In Petrograd Metropolitan Benjamin himself, in spite of his repeated declarations of loyalty and disposition to come to some kind of understanding over the question of valuable objects, was condemned to death and executed along with several of his assistants[8] This controversy over valuable objects had an-other outcome: it led to schism in the Church group. One group of priests publicly declared that it was opposed to carrying out the instructions of the hierarchy. Such statements were of course given wide publicity and readily received the support of the government. This was the origin of the Living Church.

Patriarch Tikhon who had come to Moscow during the trial of the "forty-four" to attempt to protect the accused by his authority, was not arrested himself until May 9, 1922. The offices of the patriarchate were then invaded by representative of the Living Church, who claimed to be the "Provisional Government of the Russian Church." Supported by the government, the schismatics were soon able to claim the allegiance of part of the clergy and even of some of the bishops. To an already deplorable and tragic situation there was now added a new element, that of schism. The ecclesiastical revolution[9] was led by a group of secular priests, members of the so-called "white" clergy, as opposed to the "black" or regular clergy. Because the "white" clergy were married they were excluded from the episcopate according to the traditional norms of Orthodox canon law, and there was therefore a certain long-felt animosity among them toward the monks who governed the Church. The Living Church, which would soon also allow

8 Several of the present leaders of the Moscow patriarchate then formed part of the entourage of Metropolitan Benjamin. The present patriarch, Alexis, was his auxiliary and succeeded him in the government of the diocese. Metropolitan Gregory of Leningrad (†1957), then a priest, was sentenced, in the same trial, to a long term of forced labor.

9 The movement later became split into several groups, the most important of which were the Living Church and the Renovated Church.

bishops to marry, permitted priests to marry a second time, and therefore it was natural that it should derive its main strength from the circles of the married clergy. It also gained some adherents among intellectual circles, anxious at all costs to work out a modus vivendi with the government. Some of the reforms introduced by this body are not devoid of interest, notably in the liturgical field, but the whole movement was vitiated from the start by the decidedly fraudulent way in which it seized power, by the favor which it curried against the patriarch, and finally by the flagrantly uncanonical acts of which it was guilty. Before long, the moderate party of schismatics, called the Renovated Church, was given permission by the government to use the majority of churches, but it never won the widespread support of the faithful. It was the same with the other schisms, particularly that in the Ukraine, where a group of priests had unsuccessfully petitioned for the restoration of an autocephalous Ukrainian Church and then in 1921 determined to go ahead with their plans anyway in spite of the opposition of the patriarch and the bishops. Consecrating certain "bishops" themselves, they formed another schismatic group which in some cases received the support of the government, anxious as always to promote the disintegration of the Orthodox Church.

The first setback to the increasing trend toward schism occurred when the patriarch was suddenly released in June 1923, after having signed an official statement acknowledging his past "faults," specifically his condemnation of the Treaty of Brest-Litovsk, his excommunication of the communists, and his circular letter on the question of church valuables.[10] After a year's imprisonment, Tikhon thus agreed, in effect, to pass no further public judgment on the acts of the Soviet government. In appeals to the faithful he defined his new attitude as "apolitical": "Let monar-

10 The text of this statement was published by *Izvestia*, no. 141 (June 27, 1923); quoted in Curtiss, *op. cit.*, pp. 159-60, 347.

chists abroad and in the country know that I am not the enemy of the soviet government," he proclaimed.[11]

While adopting a conciliatory attitude toward the government, the patriarch nevertheless remained obdurate toward the the schismatics. As soon as he was released he formally condemned them, and certain well-known figures among the Renovated Church did solemn penance before him.[12] Tikhon died in Moscow on April 7, 1925. After his death the newspapers published his testament in which he once again called upon the faithful to recognize the new regime with a sincere conscience, to oppose its enemies, and to regain the confidence of the government, which, in turn, would then permit the religious instruction of children, the functioning of a number of theological seminaries, and the publication of books and newspapers.[13] The patriarchal Church remained faithful to this testament, without, however, having obtained even to this day all the advantages which the patriarch hoped for, notably in the fields of religious education and publications.

The next stage in the life of the Russian Church covers the period from 1927 to 1943. Patriarch Tikhon foresaw that it would probably be impossible to hold a regular election for a new patriarch and therefore designated three possible *locum tenentes* to succeed him: the metropolitans Cyril, Agathangelos, and Peter. Since the first two were imprisoned at the time of Tikhon's death, the third, Metropolitan Peter of Krutica, was recognized as *locum tenens* of the patriarchate. Eight months after his installation, on December 23, 1925, he too was arrested and exiled to Siberia, after appointing as his successor in the office of "deputy *locum tenens*" Metropolitan Sergius of Nizhni Novgorod. It was with this strange title—which many refused to recognize—that Sergius took over the direction of what remained of the patriarchal Church, and governed it from 1927 until 1943. Only a few bishops were still at liberty, while the majority of the churches were in

11 *Izvestia*, nos. 147, 149 (July 4, 6, 1923); quoted in Curtiss, *loc. cit*.
12 Among them was Sergius, then archbishop of Jaroslavl, the future patriarch.
13 *Izvestia* (April 15, 1925); quoted in Curtiss, *op. cit*, pp. 176-77, 349.

the hands of the Renovated Church. Sergius himself was arrested in December 1926. Following his release (March 30, 1927), he published a series of declarations affirming his loyalty to the government in stronger terms than ever: "We wish to be Orthodox," he proclaimed, "while at the same time recognizing the Soviet Union as our country. We wish its joys and successes to be out joys and successes and its defeats to be out defeats."[14] Moreover, he officially appealed to the NKVD (People's Commissariat for Internal Affairs) requesting it to "legalize" the existence in Moscow of a patriarchal Synod (until then the government had not even admitted that Metropolitan Sergius resided in Moscow). The latter demand appeared to many to be going too far in the way of accommodation, for government "legalization" necessarily implied an unspecified amount of government control. Many of the bishops in exile or at liberty, protested against the new attitude of Metropolitan Sergius. One group of bishops, exiled to Solovki on the White Sea, including Hilarion Troickii, a well-known theologian and former right arm of Patriarch Tikhon, sent an appeal to Sergius which also professed complete loyalty toward the state, but demanded instead an unprejudiced application of the law on the separation of Church and state guaranteeing the internal freedom of the Church.[15]

But these protests were in vain. Metropolitan Sergius acted in accordance with his conscience, in the hope of being able to reestablish some form of administrative machinery for the Church, then virtually nonexistent, and thus safeguard the embryo of a church, as it were, for the future. In spite of the humiliating declarations it was obliged to make particularly on the subject of religious persecutions, which even at the beginning of the Revolution were allegedly purely political in nature, in spite of the

---

14 The text of this statement may be found in *Le Patriarche Serge et son héritage spirituel* (in Russian) (Publications of the Moscow Patriarchate, 1947).

15 The existence of and authenticity of this message from Solovki is admitted by all. The text was circulated clandestinely in Russia and also outside the country.

obviously incorrect information it was obliged to give out regarding the existence of "religious liberty" in Russia, the patriarchal synod, established by Sergius, continued in fact to be attacked by the press and its members were often arrested and exiled. Antireligious legislation became more and more oppressive as successive modifications were made in the constitution of the Soviet Union. The constitution of 1918 had guaranteed to citizens "religious freedom" and "freedom of religious and antireligious propaganda" (para. 13). This paragraph was modified in 1929. From then on it was a question merely of "freedom of religious confession and antireligious propaganda." The Constitution of Stalin of 1936, still in force, merely confers on citizens the "freedom of religious worship and antireligious propaganda" (para. 124).

During World War II, however, the Soviet government made a sudden about-face in its tactics toward religion.

After issuing a patriotic message to the Russian people on the very day of the German invasion (June 22, 1941), Metropolitan Sergius and his church were granted a certain amount of freedom of movement and action. A few bishops were released from exile. On September 4, 1943, Sergius and two other metropolitans (Alexis of Leningrad and Nicholas of Kiev) were received by Stalin, and obtained official approval for the holding of a patriarchal election. The synod, consisting of only eighteen bishops—many of the others were still imprisoned—duly met and elected Sergius patriarch. This resurrection of the Church coincided with the prompt liquidation of the schisms of the Renovated Church, which, lacking any popular support, was in full decline. The patriarch obtained the right to use the religious edifices hitherto reserved largely to the schismatics. It was permitted, also, to proceed with the reorganization of the Church, establish theological seminaries, and publish an ecclesiastical periodical.

Whatever judgment one may feel inclined to pass on the policy of Patriarch Sergius, it is undeniable that the reappearance in Russia in 1943 of a traditional Orthodox church, faithful in all respects to Orthodox canonical norms and rites, amounted to a veritable miracle, and constituted a kind of rebuff to the anti-religious campaign and the materialist ideas with which the government had tried for so long to indoctrinate the Russian people. Wholly excluded from the schools and from the press, religion had nevertheless resisted the unprecedented assault made on it by the organs of propaganda. On the eve of the war, in its May 1941 issue, the periodical *Antireligioznik* stated that the antireligious publications issued that year by the government press included sixty-seven titles of books and pamphlets totaling 3,505,000 copies, and two periodicals and a newspaper with a total of 5,880,000 copies.[16] In addition to this, of course, all textbooks and all teaching in the schools had to be slanted in an antireligious direction.[17]

It was after surviving trials of this kind that the Russian Church was able to celebrate in 1958 the fortieth anniversary of the election of Tikhon as patriarch, in the presence of numerous foreign Orthodox prelates. To be sure, the conditions at the time of his election and the different aspects of his patriarchate were soft-pedaled or glossed over; nevertheless the Church felt that it was celebrating the memory of one who had worthily borne witness for Christ and thus prepared the way for the survival of the Orthodox faith in Russia.

But the state of course had and has no intention of abandoning its antireligious program. Its attitude was given concrete expression in the decisions of the Central committee of the Party, dated November 10, 1954, and signed by the secretary, N. Khrushchev, printed in *Pravda* on November 11, 1954. "The Communist Party," the document asserts "relying on the only truly

16 Cited by Curtiss, *op. cit.*, pp. 280-363.

17 On the effectiveness and nature of this propaganda, see especially P. B. Anderson, *People, Church and State in Modern Russia* (New York, 1944); cf. the same author's *Religious Future* (London, 1935); see also Curtiss, *op. cit.*

scientific conception of the world, the Marxist-Leninist, and on
the theoretical foundation of the latter, dialectical materialism,
cannot adopt an indifferent or neutral attitude toward religion,
since the latter is an ideology wholly alien to science." The Party,
consequently, "will assist every believer finally to get rid of his
religious errors." The text of the document then goes on to state
the classical doctrine that religion is essentially nothing but a
means employed "by the exploiters in their struggle against the
workers." Consequently, "after the victory of socialism and the
liquidation in the USSR of the exploiting classes, the social roots
of religion will find themselves cut off and the basis which served
for the support of the Church will no longer exist." The existence
of believers in Russia is therefore merely a survival from the past,
allowed by the constitution to the extent that the exercise of
religion is limited to "worship." (para. 124) and "the servants of
the Church, in the vast majority of cases, today adopt a loyal
attitude toward the Soviet authorities." Therefore, the Committee
condemns "administrative measures and harassments directed
against believers and the clergy"; these measures "cannot but be
harmful, by strengthening religious prejudice." The struggle
against religion should therefore be viewed from the purely ideological level. It should consist above all in the education of the
workers according to materialist principles. An editorial in the
periodical *Questions of Philosophy* (1959, no. 8) recently declared
that religion will gradually lose its influence over the masses "when
socialism shall become stronger, and the level of material and
cultural life rises, as technological progress is made, and as the
government is able to exercise more pressure through its attack on
religion."

We must realize therefore that the situation of the Orthodox
Church in Russia today is far from being an easy one. Obliged, in
theory, to be politically neutral, and in effect to support the
government, it does not receive anything in return for this attitude. Restricted in its activity to religious "worship," it must

nevertheless seek to oppose as best it can an active antireligious campaign directed against all religion. In the following chapter we shall attempt to analyze the present situation in Russia and speculate briefly on the prospects for the future.

The establishment, after the Second World War, of "popular democracies" in various countries of Eastern Europe with largely Orthodox populations took place under conditions totally different from those which witnessed the triumph of communism in Russia. The new rulers were able to profit by the experience of the Russians. Thus it happened that when they seized power, they were careful to avoid the violent persecutions, public trials, and other harassments which might have served as an excuse to make martyrs of the faithful. Without attempting to impose a uniform pattern for the separation of Church and state everywhere, they maintained a tight control over all the activities of the clergy, neutralizing certain prominent individuals and curtailing, wherever possible, the apostolic efforts of the Church. Faithful to the doctrine of the eventual disappearance of religion in a classless society, they preferred to rely principally on time and communist re-education of the masses to achieve their objective. Administrative measures were aimed—and still are—against all those who show too openly their opposition to the regime or official propaganda. On the whole, the Orthodox hierarchy in these countries models its attitude on that of the patriarch of Moscow. Disassociating itself from all connection with the former regimes, it is careful to express its loyalty to the new by taking part in semiofficial organizations such as the "Partisans for Peace."

At first glance, the legislative attitude of the popular democracies appears to be more favorable to religion than that of the Soviet Union. The latter, as we have seen, forbids "religious propaganda" and only allows "antireligious propaganda" (Constitution of 1936, para. 124). The Bulgarian (para. 78), Romanian (para. 84), and Hungarian (para. 54) constitutions simply mention freedom of "conscience" and of "religious worship." The Czechoslovak constitution (para. 15) is even more explicit and guarantees the freedom of "acts connected with religious profession," while the Polish constitution, by far the most liberal, admits that the Church and religious groups "may perform their religious functions" (para. 17).[18] These constitutional guarantees, however, are limited by special laws regarding religious bodies, and by the new constitutions which the latter were obliged to adopt. On the whole, such laws and constitutions are designed to permit the state to establish a tight control over all the activities of the Church. Activities such as preaching and the publication of religious works are allowed far more freely than in the USSR. However, in all the popular democracies, with the single exception of Poland, the Church is carefully excluded from the field of education of youth. It is here, ultimately, that the real battle between Christianity and the new Marxist orthodoxy will be fought. Will religious, reduced to mere "worship," gradually disappear from the new society, along with the other traces of capitalism? Only the Christians fated to live in those countries can supply the answer to this question, and the future alone will reveal the advantages or disadvantages of the present attitude of the hierarchy. In our brief discussion of the present situation in each of these countries, in the chapter that follows, we shall see that this attitude has varied considerably and that it is more flexible than is commonly supposed.

18 See A. Bogolepov (in Russian), *The Church under Communist Power* (Munich, 1958), pp. 80-81.

Chapter 8

THE ORTHODOX CHURCH TODAY[1]

It is not very easy to deal with the subject of religion in terms of pure statistics, because statistics involve numbers, and cannot adequately describe such phenomena as religious experience or religious practice. Now it is impossible to estimate the real strength of a religious group without adequate information about these fundamental factors. For more than forty years—that is, ever since the Russian Revolution—it has been impossible to give any adequate statistics for the whole of the Orthodox Church, even with respect to numbers alone. According to a very approximate estimate based on religious practice, the number of Orthodox Christians today who participate more or less regularly in the sacraments of the Church comes to roughly 100,000,000. About 50,000,000 of these are in the Soviet Union. However, it seems quite certain that the number of baptized Orthodox must be much higher, for reception of the sacrament was obligatory in Russia before the Revolution and even today there are many families who still have their children baptized but who otherwise remain aloof from the life of the Church. Therefore, it is reasonable to conclude that the above figure of 100,000,000 is not really representative of the actual strength of Orthodoxy among the various Christian confessions. The totals for Roman Catholics (450,000,000) and Protestants (250,000,000), as they are usually given, are based on baptismal records, but it is recognized that these do not reflect actual religious practice.[2]

1 See the Postscript (p. 211) for the contemporary situation.

2 Of the 450,000,000 Roman Catholics in the world (or nearer 500,000,000 according to recent statistics), some 200,000,000 are in South America, but it is admitted even by Catholic authorities that the number of practicing Catholics in Latin America does not exceed 10 percent of the nominally Catholic total population. The same situation obtains—by percentage—in certain nominally Protestant countries of Europe, particularly in Scandinavia.

129

The Orthodox Church is at present a decentralized organization, based partly on centuries-old traditions and partly on more modern conditions. It consists of a number of local or national churches, all enjoying an "autocephalous" status, that is to say, possessing the right to choose their own heads, the bishops (Greek *auto-*, "self," *kephale*, "head"). Some of these churches are contained within the boundaries of one state and are, in effect, national churches. Others, especially in the Near East, possess more traditional boundaries and include faithful belonging to several nationalities. Canonically speaking, the boundaries of all the local churches are not national but territorial in nature, and correspond to former metropolitan provinces; that is, they form groups of dioceses whose bishops meet regularly in synod and elect their own primate, who bears the title of patriarch, archbishop, or metropolitan. Bound together by observance of a common canonical tradition, these churches give expression to their communion of faith by holding general councils from time to time, as the need arises. As we have seen, councils including all or some of these autocephalous churches were frequently held, even after the close of the medieval period.

The relations of these autocephalous churches with each other are determined by a kind of hierarchy of honor, headed by the "ecumenical" patriarch of Constantinople as *primus inter pares*. The order of precedence among the three other Oriental patriarchates (Alexandria, Antioch, Jerusalem) was fixed in the fifth century. In spite of its great size and importance, the patriarchate of Moscow, established in 1589, is accorded only fifth place in this hierarchy. Other autocephalous churches are assigned a place in accordance with the date when they became ecclesiastically independent.

This system, which is theoretically nothing more than an adaptation of ancient canon law to modern conditions, undoubtedly has the great advantage of being very elastic. It permits autocephalous churches to be founded, abolished, then re-established again in the course of history without affecting the entire organization of the church. Moreover, the absence of any binding centralized authority permits the various hierarchies of the churches today to adopt different political attitudes without rupturing the doctrinal and sacramental bonds of unity. When conditions become more propitious, the leaders can once more reestablish cordial relations without too much difficulty. The disadvantages of the system, however, are equally obvious. Independent by right and in fact, the autocephalous churches are too inclined to live in isolation from each other, they are unable to take any common action effectively, and they lack a common system for the training of the clergy. The effects of nationalism, that disease which ravaged eastern Europe in the nineteenth and twentieth centuries, can be overcome in the ecclesiastical sphere only with great difficulty. The Church often comes to be regarded as nothing more than a mere adjunct of the nation, a mere instrument useful in helping to preserve the language and customs of the people. Because the missionaries from Byzantium everywhere rendered the sacred liturgy in the languages of the people and transplanted to Slavic soil not only the religion of Byzantium but the Byzantine theory of the Christian state, a fertile ground was prepared for the development of the modern, essentially secularized, form of nationalism. Everywhere in Eastern Europe the Orthodox Church has remained an essentially popular church. This is one of the important factors enabling it to survive the Turkish and Mongol yokes, and this is what holds in check today the Marxist theory of religion as an "instrument in the hands of the exploiting classes." But these very factors are also the source of a certain weakness, because they make it difficult for the Church to bear witness, *in action*, to the universal and transcendent nature of the Truth. However, the historical age in which we live has forced us to distinguish between the absolute and the relative, between Church and state, between Christ and the nation. And thus it is compelling the Orthodox world today to make a choice between mere human traditions and Revelation, and to retain only what constitutes the essential of the Christian message. From numerous signs, which will be noted in our brief survey of the present situation of the several churches, it would seem that an entirely new age appears to be dawning in Orthodox history.

1. The Ecumenical Patriarchate of Constantinople

The second and fourth ecumenical councils gave the Church of Constantinople "equal privileges" to those of the Roman Church, while reserving to the latter its traditional primacy of honor. Since the schisms between West and East the patriarch of Constantinople enjoys a primatial status in the Orthodox Church. His title is "archbishop of Constantinople-New Rome and ecumenical patriarch."[3] As diocesan bishop of Constantinople (which is know today as Istanbul) he exercises direct patriarchal authority over four metropolitan sees in Turkey, the miserable remains of the once flourishing Greek Christian communities in Asia Minor, which became mere titles when the Greek populations left as a result of the Greek-Turkish War (1922). To give him added prestige, however, the Greek Church and government agreed to leave under the patriarch's authority the dioceses of the Greek islands, and in a purely nominal way, those of northern Greece also. Moreover, the patriarchate exercises jurisdiction over a certain number of diocese of Greeks, Russians and Ukrainians belonging to the Orthodox diaspora (in Western Europe, North and South America, Australia and New Zealand) and over the Orthodox Church in Finland.[4] Since the last war his jurisdiction over the Baltic countries has been taken over by the patriarch of Moscow.

Thus the patriarchate which once exercised authority over vast stretches of the Orthodox world, as we have seen, under the

---

3 The title of ecumenical patriarch goes back at least to 588 and therefore long antedates the schism.

4 We shall have more to say in detail further on with regard to the situation of the Orthodox Church in the West.

Byzantine Empire and under the Turkish yoke which followed, has now been reduced to a very small image of its former self. The various Orthodox Churches in the Balkans obtained their autocephalous status in the nineteenth century and the Greeks in Asia Minor left the territory of the patriarchate in the twentieth. It is only through international pressure that the patriarchate has been able to survive the various trials which it has been through and has continued to maintain its headquarters in the Greek quarter of Constantinople known as the Phanar. The ecumenical patriarchate owes its prestige today, therefore, not to the fact that it exercises ecclesiastical jurisdiction over less than two million of the faithful (nearly half of whom are in America), but to the primacy of honor which it traditionally has among the various autocephalous churches.

Basically, his authority consists of the right of initiative, which the other patriarchates acknowledge as belonging to the ecumenical patriarch in matters of common concern. The ecumenical councils of Chalcedon (451) also granted him the important right to hear appeals from other churches (canon 17) and placed under his jurisdiction the missionary areas (in "barbarous" countries) which lay beyond the Roman dioceses of Thrace, Asia and Pontus (canon 28): in the fifth century this meant essentially the regions of Eastern Europe and the Caucasus. Some modern canonists tend to interpret this canon more liberally and would grant to the ecumenical patriarch jurisdiction over the entire Orthodox diaspora (which he already possesses in part),

The patriarch of Constantinople is elected by the metropolitans of the patriarchate.[5] A synod of twelve bishops assists him in running ecclesiastical affairs and appoints the bishops for vacant sees. There is a patriarchal seminary on the island of Halki, in the Princes Islands, which receives students from nearly all the Near Eastern countries.

5 Untill 1922 the patriarch, who was then also political head of the Greeks in Turkey, was elected by a somewhat larger body, including laymen.

The present occupant of the ecumenical see is His Holiness Athenagoras I, who was elected in 1948.

Also under the jurisdiction of the ecumenical patriarchate is the world-famous monastic republic of Mount Athos, an important spiritual center and remarkable survival of medieval Byzantine monasticism. Dating from the tenth century, the monasteries of Athos have survived in spite of all kinds of trials and still had 2,700 monks in 1952. In the seventeenth and eighteenth centuries Athos went through a critical period and the number of monks greatly declined. It increased again in the nineteenth century, owning particularly to a large influx of Russian novices, so that by 1913 Mount Athos had a population of 6,345. Since then, however, as a result of the generally unfavorable conditions prevailing in the Orthodox world, this number has steadily declined, and the situation is likely to remain precarious until better days return.

Isolated from the result of the world on their Chalcidic peninsula, living under conditions which have not varied essentially since the Middle Ages, the monks of Athos are grouped into twenty monasteries, distributed over the area of the peninsula, and by means of their representative govern the region. The land belongs by right to the Kingdom of Greece, but enjoys an international status. Of the twenty monasteries, seventeen are Greek (though sometimes with monks from other countries), one Russian, one Serbian and one Bulgarian. There was also, formerly, a Georgian monastery, and in the Middle Ages there were even Latin monasteries. Scattered over the peninsula of Athos there also a great many hermitages, the *skiti* and *kellia,* in which monks of various origins live in accordance with different rules. Certain *skiti* are actually large monasteries, while others are mere anchoritic cells.

As a unique example of a monastic republic which, in former days, once gave a number of great theologians and doctors of the Church, Athos can still claim to be a spiritual center for all the Orthodox. However, it suffers under certain disabilities at the present time. The monks are recruited almost exclusively from the rural Greek countryside, they are intellectually isolated (this being sometimes wrongly regarded as an ascetic virtue), and they receive almost no new vocations today from any countries other than Greece—these are the important reasons contributing to their decline. To remedy the situation, in part at least, the ecumenical patriarch established a theological school on Athos in 1953. Recently, the international situation has improved sufficiently to enable a number of new monks to arrive from Yugoslavia, but Athos should really be opened to novices from all countries, it if wishes to recover to its former glory.

2. The Patriarchate of Alexandria

At the time of the great christologial controversies in the fifth and sixth centuries, the greater number of Egyptian Christians refused to recognize the authority of the Council of Chalcedon (451) and formed the Monophysite or Coptic "Orthodox" Church, which is still the largest Christian body in Egypt. By contrast, the Orthodox constituted only a small minority and were known as Melkites (the "King's people"). They were Greek-speaking (whereas the Copts adopted the native Egyptian language for their liturgy) and were long regarded as foreigners in the land. Their numbers declined to such appoint that from the sixteenth to the eighteenth century the Orthodox patriarch of Alexandria almost never resided in Egypt but remained in Constantinople. It was only toward the beginning of the twentieth century that the Greek Orthodox population began to increase, owing to the immigration of Greeks and Syrians. However, the number of the Orthodox in Egypt has never amounted to more than 200,000. The Greek community in Egypt has a number of hospitals and schools. Owing to the present political and economic situation in Egypt, it is rapidly decreasing.

Although his flock is rather small in Egypt, the patriarch of Alexandria has jurisdiction over all the Orthodox of Africa.

Candidates for the patriarchate are elected by a council of synod of thirty-six clergy and seventy laymen, which draws up a list of three names, one of whom is then chosen by the Holy Synod. Until the beginning of 1959, there were eight metropolitans (Tripoli, Ismailia, Port Said, Tanta, Addis Ababa, Johannesburg, Khartum and Tunis). Three new sees have just been established (Accra, Central Africa and East Africa) as a result of the missionary activity of the patriarchate. The metropolitan of oriental Africa, Bishop Nicolas, was elevated to the patriarchal seat in 1968.

3. The Patriarchate of Antioch

Antioch on the Orontes was once the third largest city in the Roman Empire, after Rome and Alexandria. It is today no more than a small village on Turkish soil. The patriarch, whose jurisdiction goes back to a once glorious past, resides in Damascus. The Church over which he presides, and which includes about 400,000 faithful in Syria and Lebanon, consists of the largest group of Arabic-speaking Christians there is. Important groups are also found in Iraq and in America (more than 100,000).

From 1724 until 1899 the patriarch and all the bishops were Greek prelates, appointed because of the preponderance of Greek influence which the Phanar was able to exercise under Turkish rule. Since then, in part owning to Russian influence, Arabs have been elected to the see of Antioch. The procedure for patriarchal elections, which takes place in several states, has recently been modified to allow the laity to play a greater role. The patriarch is not assisted by a permanent synod, but the metropolitans meet once a year, after Easter, in accordance with ancient canonical custom. There are ten metropolitans sees in all (Aleppo, Sheikh Tabba, Beirut, Homs, Hama, Latakia, Zahle, Tripoli, Tyre and Sidon, and Baghdad). Three other bishops, responsible to the patriarch, govern the faithful in North and South America.

Although possessing only a few educated clergy, the Arab Orthodox in Syria and Lebanon have nevertheless experienced something of a revival since World War II, thanks to the Orthodox Youth Movement, founded by enterprising young university graduates. The movement interests itself in a variety of activities: preaching, the establishment of schools, the publication of a remarkable periodical in Arabic (*An-Nur*), sending members abroad to study theology and thus provide new ranks for the clergy, and the founding of monastic communities (Deir-el-Harf on Mount Lebanon, for example). There are thus great hopes for the future.

The patriarchal see is occupied at present by His Beatitude Theodosius VI.

4. The Patriarchate of Jerusalem

Established as an independent patriarchate by the Council of Chalcedon (451), the see of Jerusalem, especially after the Arab conquest, devoted itself primarily to protecting the Holy Places. Its present constitution is also largely oriented toward this need. A kind of monastic order, the Confraternity of the Holy Sepulcher, sees to this responsibility. The bishops and church officials are chosen from among its members. The patriarch himself is the head of the body, which consists of a hundred members, all of whom are Greeks. The faithful, by contrast, are all Arabs. The Orthodox of Jerusalem have suffered considerably as a result of recent events in Palestine and today amount to no more than about 50,000, many of whom are emigrating to Syria or Lebanon.

In addition to the patriarch, there is a Holy Synod composed of six titular archbishops (Sebaste, Mount Tabor, Diocaesarea, Philadelphia, Eleutheropolis and Tiberias). The lower clergy is entirely Arab in origin. A mixed council—including Arab laymen—was created in 1911, but friction between Greeks and Arabs is frequent, particularly when there is a patriarchal election.

The different statutes of the patriarchate have gradually made allowance for greater participation by the Arab clergy and the faithful in the affairs of the patriarchate.

The Lavra of Mar-Saba, an ancient high place of Oriental monasticism, is today inhabited by only twenty monks. It lies within the jurisdiction of the patriarchate. The Russians formerly came in droves on pilgrimage to Jerusalem and still have two convents of nuns there.

Since 1957 the see of Jerusalem has been occupied by His Beatitude Benedict I.

5. The Patriarchate of Moscow

Until the fall of 1959, it was possible to maintain that the Russian Orthodox Church had reached a relatively stable point in its relations with the state, as a result of events during the last war. However, the events of the last two years have shown that this stability is quite precarious. During the period of stability (1946-1959), it was still extremely difficult to obtain reliable information concerning the number of the faithful. The reason for this was given by Patriarch Alexis himself, in an interview grated to the Reuters Agency in 1948: "Because of the separation of Church and state, and also because of religious freedom, we do not now have at our disposal a list of all the faithful, as was formerly the case in Russia."[6] This very revealing statement means that the Church on the one hand no longer is in a position to compile accurate statistics, the latter being the monopoly of the state, and, on the other, that the drawing up of lists of the faithful, which could be used for various purposes of control, would be regarded as an infringement of the liberty of the individual faith-

6 Quoted in *Le Problème religieux in U.R.S.S.—II: Données et documents sur l'organisation actuelle des différentes églises et associations religieuses*, in *La Documentation française*, no. 1931 (Oct. 9, 1954), p. 4. This study (nos. 1624 and 1931 of the Documentation) contains very complete information on the status of religion in Russia.

ful, which he now enjoys, since religious conviction and practice are not a matter of official record. Because of this dearth of statistics, we are therefore obliged to resort to generalizations and estimates, based on sparse official information and accounts which frequently appear in the press. The estimate of roughly 25,000 parishes for the whole country, substantiated by various trustworthy sources,[7] seems to be reliable. Since witnesses unanimously report that the churches are always extraordinarily full and several of them could hold several thousand of the faithful, it does not seem unreasonable to conclude that the number of the faithful per church is about 2,000. Using this figures as a basis, we thus arrive at a total of about 50,000,000 practicing Orthodox in the Soviet Union, or about 25 percent of the population of the Soviet Union at the present time. This number could possibly be even higher.[8]

In spite of the violent persecution to which it has been subjected, and in spite of forty years of Marxist propaganda, the Orthodox Church has therefore retained the allegiance of about half its membership.[9] As, moreover, the practice of religion in

7 See especially A. Serguéenko, in *Messager du patriarchat russe en Europe occidentale*, no. 2 (1957), p. 13. G. Karpov, an official of the Soviet government, in charge of the council for the Affairs of the Orthodox Church, mentioned in 1949 the figure of 22,000 parishes (*U.S.S.R. Information Bulletin* [Washington, January 1949], pp. 54-56). The difference of 3,000 between the two figures can be explained by the existence of "prayer houses," to which A. Serguéenko also refers.

8 The city of Moscow today has a population of 6,000,000, with only 55 churches open (compared with 657 before 1917). The method we have employed to calculate the number of the faithful (2,000 per church) would only allow about 110,000 practicing Orthodox for Moscow, but this number seems to be much too small, since according to a statement of Fr. Kolchitzky, an important official of the patriarchate, 50 percent of all infants born in the capital are baptized (*Le Problème religieux en U.R.S.S.*, p. 4). In the country, the proportion would of course be even higher.

9 In 1914 there were officially 98,500,000 Orthodox in the Russian Empire. If all the infants born of Orthodox parents were instructed in the faith of the parents the normal rise in the populations would have brought the number of Orthodox today to 130 or 140 million (*Le Problème religieux en U.R.S.S.*, loc. cit.). Among non-Christian religions, Islam has the next greatest number of adherents in the USSR, with nearly 30 million (nominal).

Russia today still exposes the individual (and families) to discrimination of one kind or another—he may find it difficult to be promoted in his job or may acquire a bad political or professional reputation, factors which in large part explain why the churches are filled with so many women and old men—it is virtually certain that the hidden influence of religion is much greater still. The most serious problem confronting the Church in Russia remains that of education. While it is still capable of attracting large numbers of the faithful, it does not possess the means of instructing them in any way except through the liturgy and by sermons inside places of worship. Yet, rich as the liturgical tradition of the Orthodox Church is in suggestive imagery, this alone cannot, except to a very limited extent, make up for the complete absence of religious publications and schools other than those intended for training of the clergy.[10]

Almost totally nonexistent in 1941, the machinery of church government was reestablished in 1943 when Metropolitan Sergius was elected patriarch, and especially by the council of 1945 which, in the presence of two Oriental patriarchs (Christopher of Alexandria and Alexander of Antioch), a delegate from the ecumenical patriarch of Constantinople and several delegates from other churches, proceeded to elect the present patriarch, Alexis,[11]

10 The following table illustrates these various aspects of the present situation rather graphically, namely, the miraculous revival of the church between 1941 and 1947, but its almost complete impotence in the field of education. The table is taken—with some slight modifications—from *Le Problème religieux en U.R.S.S.*

	1914	1941	1947
Churches	54,457	4,255	22 to 25,000
Chapels	25,593	?	3,500
Priests at their posts	57,105	5,665	33,000
Monasteries and convents	1,498	38	80
Theological academies	4	none	2
Seminaries	57	none	8
Various religious schools	40,150	none	none

11 Born in 1877 in Moscow of a family of aristocratic origins, Patriarch Alexis (whose secular name is Sergei Vladimirovich Simanski) received a brilliant general education and then embraced the ecclesiastical state. In 1913 he was consecrated a bishop. He

and approved new statutes for the Orthodox Church. In contrast to the statutes of 1917-1918, the government of the Church is now centralized in the hands of the patriarch who, with a synod of six bishops, exercises almost autocratic authority, particularly in the matter of the appointment and frequent transfer of bishops from one diocese to another. Laymen, theoretically, are members of the national council which elects the patriarch, but the statutes do not specify the way in which they are to be chosen. This unusually brief document was adopted without debate. Its incomplete nature shows that the Church continues to live under conditions which it is unable to control in all respects.[12]

The Russian Church now has seventy-three dioceses inside the Soviet Union[13] and several exarchates or missions abroad. The clergy is given preliminary training in seminaries and the most promising students are then sent on to one of the two theological academies or graduate schools (Zagorsk near Moscow, and Leningrad). The exact number of students attending these institutions is only partially known. The numbers increased rapidly during the years after the war. The seminary and academy of Zagorsk jointly had 108 students in 1947, 320 in 1951-1952, and 396 in 1953.[14] In January 1961, for the first time, the *Journal of the Moscow Patriarchate,* published in Moscow, gave the number of graduating student in June 1960: forty-three students graduated from both academies and 185 from

gained some prominence because of his political activity, oriented toward the right. As auxiliary to Benjamin, metropolitan of Petrograd, when the latter was tried and condemned to death in 1922 above (cf. above p. 124), he took charge of the see. During the difficult years (1922-1941) he adhered without fail to the conciliatory policy of Sergius as metropolitan of Leningrad.

12 Complete French translation of the statutes in *Le Problème religieux U.R.S.S.*, pp. 13-15. In connection with recent antireligious policies of the state, the statutes were recently (1961) modified. They now given an increased power of control to laymen on the parish level.

13 The number of Russian dioceses has been traditionally small since the Middle Ages. There were only sixty-seven in 1914 for 100 million Orthodox. There are approximately the same number in Greece for 6 million inhabitants. *Le Problème religieux en U.R.S.S.* gives a list of the present Russian bishops and some biographic details about each.

14 *Le Problème religieux en U.R.S.S.,* p. 9.

the eight seminaries. Of the latter, 119 were ordained and received parish assignments, while sixty-six were sent to do graduate work in the academies. In hardly needs to be pointed out that the numbers are ridiculously small when compared with the needs of some fifty million faithful. This graduation took place before the recent measures aimed at restricting theological education, which will be mentioned below. Considerable difficulty has been encountered in the recruitment of competent professors, since the ranks of personnel trained in the pre-Revolutionary institutions have greatly dwindled. To judge by certain articles appearing in the *Journal of the Moscow Patriarchate* and from several personal contacts which now become possible, however, it seems that the academic level is now beginning to rise appreciably. Russian theologians still suffer a great deal from their enforced isolation from the rest of the world. They have so far been forbidden to publish any books or manuals,[15] and current theological literature can be obtained from the West only with the greatest difficulty. The publication of a Russian theological periodical, long announced, took place in 1960. Only one issue has appeared so far.

The statutes adopted in 1945 clearly refer to the control which the government intends to exercise over the religious activities of the clergy. The government's "authorization" is required before a

15 The few publications of the patriarchate are concerned with the liturgy (calendars, special liturgical offices) or are in the nature of propaganda. In the latter category must be reckoned the above-mentioned *Journal of the Moscow Patriarchate* (a monthly periodical in Russian, which always includes articles on political themes, especially on the movement of the Partisans for Peace) and several collections of the sermons of Patriarch Alexis and Metropolitan Nicholas of Krutica, in which articles or sermons of a strictly spiritual or theological nature are always accompanied by others with a definite political slant. The Bible, and the New Testament separately, were recently published in Russia for the first time in forty years, but the number of copies printed did not exceed 50,000—and most of these were sold abroad. The apostolic value of this output is therefore very slight. The patriarchate has no Slavonic press. The liturgical books used by the Church date either from before the Revolution or are imported from Czechoslovakia. Some photographic reproductions of old editions have appeared recently in Russia. No work of a theological nature or indeed on Christianity at all have been published since 1918.

synod of bishops can be summoned—such an assembly has been held as a matter of fact only twice since 1918—and a national council (comprising clergy and laity) may be summoned, curiously, "if this is externally possible" (para. 7). Paragraph 11 stipulates, moreover, that "for the USSR, the patriarch will communicate with the Council of Affairs of the Orthodox Church of the Council of Ministers of the USSR." The personal signature and seal of the patriarch (para 16), the bishops (para. 26), and parish curates (para. 48) must be registered with the civil authorities, which thus gives the latter the formal right to control the nominations to all ecclesiastical appointments. The Council of Affairs of the Orthodox Church attached to the Council of Ministers is a government office with ramifications throughout the soviet Union. All requests for the use of places of worship, which by law belong to the state, have to be made to it and may be granted under certain conditions (paras. 39, 41, etc.). Moreover, the patriarch of Moscow never fails to publish solemn declarations, signed by the patriarch and bishops, approving the position of the Soviet government on all major questions of internal politics, such as the Korean War, the problem of nuclear disarmament, French-English intervention in Suez, the Hungarian revolt, and so forth.

It would be simplifying the problem, however, to consider the patriarchate of Moscow a mere political tool in the hands of the Soviet government. Its humiliating status of subservience to the latter on all questions relating to international affairs is, in effect, the price which the Church must pay for its continued existence inside the USSR. Yet, curiously enough, far from being considered the friend of the government there, it finds itself constantly the butt of repeated attacks.

Since the fall of 1959, the government has apparently decided upon a new wave of measures hostile to the Church, in a manner which reminds one more and more of the prewar days. In December 1959, the newspapers and the radio gave wide publicity to the statement of a former Orthodox priest, Ossipov, a professor of theology at the Leningrad Academy, who left the Church and then violently attacked all religious belief and the system of theological education reestablished by the patriarchate in particular.[16] Simultaneously, new impetus was given to the antireligious campaign in various publications.

This new and direct challenge gave the patriarchate an opportunity to show that it was not a mere tool of the government. A decision of the Holy Synod was published in Moscow in the official *Journal of the Moscow Patriarchate*,[17] excommunicating Ossipov and two of his followers for having "publicly blasphemed the Name of God." The patriarch himself, invited to speak in February 1960 at a conference on disarmament in Moscow, courageously proclaimed: "The Savior himself predicted that there would be attacks against Christianity and promised that the Church will remain unshaken and that the gates of hell will not prevail against it."[18]

The government intensified its attacks on the Church. Job, the archbishop of Kazan, was publicly tried and sentenced to three years in prison for "illegal traffic in candles." Although wide publicized in the Soviet press, the trial was not mentioned in the official journal of the patriarchate. In December 1961, Andrew, archbishop of Chernigov, was sentenced to eight years in prison under a similar pretext. Finally, the government carried out a number of administrative measures calculated to have far-reaching effects, by closing two of the eight seminaries allowed to be open, and more than five hundred churches and several monasteries.

Nothing could be more paradoxical, therefore, than the present situation of the Russian Church. As the loyal ally of the

16 *Pravda*, Dec. 6, 1959, no. 340 (15099).

17 1960, no. 2, Feb., p. 27.

18 *Messager de l'exarchat du Patriarche russe en Europe Occidentale*, nos. 33-34 (January-July, 1960), pp. 8-10.

Soviet government in international affairs abroad, it is treated inside Russia as a "vestige of capitalism," and the government-controlled press is continually proclaiming that materialism is incompatible with "religious prejudices." But this paradoxical situation also applies to the Soviet government itself, for it is obliged to reconcile with Marxist principles the fact that church dignitaries are present at official receptions, and is powerless to deny that there are some fifty million practicing Christians in Russia today after forty years of "socialism." The fact that this paradoxical situation still exists is a sign of hope for the future. Externally the Church seems strong enough to be able to resist material liquidation. However, there are temptations of a subtler nature which it must face. The clergy controls rather large sums of money—the voluntary contributions of the faithful who crowd the churches—but has no means of spending them. The temptation may be simply to raise the standard of clerical life, without making any attempt to improve the effectiveness of the Church's mission. Is this not precisely the very aim of the Communist Party?—to transform the Church into an opulent vestige of the departed past, and then to compromise it in the eyes of the people. It seems that this was actually the purpose of the recent trial of the archbishops of Kazan and Chernigov.

Fortunately, there is continual evidence in the Soviet press of the purely spiritual influence which the Russian Church can still wield over large sections of the population and which gives hope that Russian Orthodoxy will be able to surmount its present difficulties.

6. The Serbian Orthodox Church

St. Sabbas, the brother of St. Stephen the "First-crowned," was consecrated as the first Serbian archbishop at Nicaea in 1220. From that time until the Turkish conquest the Serbian Church experienced a rather prosperous period within the cultural orbit of

Byzantium, while at the same time being virtually independent of the ecumenical patriarchate ecclesiastically. Its autocephalous status was only suppressed by Constantinople in 1766.

Several Serbian autocephalous churches were formed in the nineteenth century in parts of the Balkan peninsula not subject to Turkish rule. These were:

1. The *Church of Montenegro*, with a metropolitan resident at Cetinje.

2. The *Patriarchate of Karlowitz* (*Sremski Karlovci*), founded in 1848, which included all the Orthodox Serbs in the Kingdom of Hungary.

3. The *Metropolitanate of Czernowitz* (*Chernovtsy* or *Cernauti*), which included both Romanians and Serbs, and to which two dioceses in Dalmatia (Zara and Kotor or Cattaro) were added in 1873. In effect, this church had under its jurisdiction all the Orthodox in the Austro-Hungarian Empire.

4. The *Serbian Church of the Kingdom of Serbia*, autonomous since 1832, then autocephalous (1879).

5. The *Church of Bosnia-Herzegovina,* which was formed in 1878 in provinces annexed by the Austro-Hungarian Empire but never became completely autocephalous with respect to Constantinople.

These five churches were united in 1920, under a primate residing in Belgrade, to form the Serbian Church, and included all the Orthodox in the new state of Yugoslavia. The ecumenical patriarch approved the new arrangement on March 9, 1922, and recognized the head of the Church as patriarch. Before the last war the Serbian patriarch also had jurisdiction over the Romanian Banat of Temesvar and the dioceses of Mukacevo (in Czechoslovakia), as well as over certain Orthodox parishes in Hungary. Today there are a total of thirty-one dioceses on Yugoslav soil.

Until 1940 the Church possessed five seminaries and a theological faculty. Now, after the separation of Church and state, it has only two seminaries, one at Belgrade and the other at Prizren, and the faculty which has been detached from the University and is called the Patriarchal Faculty. There were about 7,500,000 faithful in 1950, with 3,101 priests and 2,864 parishes.

During the last two decades the Serbian Church has gone through a series of trials, which began in 1941 and which have not been very fully reported in the West. Patriarch Gabriel and Nicholas, the bishop of Ohrid, were arrested by the Germans as soon as the latter occupied Yugoslavia, and deported to Dachau. The Serbian faithful, whose clergy often gave support to the resistance movement, were treated with unheard-of severity, not so much by the Germans as by the fascist authorities of the state of Croatia, which was supported by the occupiers of the country. These Croatians were in large measure Roman Catholics, but it is difficult to say exactly what motives—religious, political or national—were primarily responsible for the frightful massacres that took place during the occupation. In the majority of cases, however the real excuse for the executions appears to have been the fact of belonging to the Orthodox Church. Thus the Orthodox bishop of Planski, Sabbas, was executed along with 137 of his priests (only five priests remained alive in the diocese). Bishops Plato of Banja Luka and Peter of Sarajevo were also executed along with many of their clergy. Serbian sources, corroborated by the present Yugoslav government, estimate the total number of victims at about 700,000.[19]

The moral prestige of the Serbian Orthodox Church was therefore very high at the end of the war. Patriarch Gabriel returned from Dachau to face at home a "popular democratic" form of government, one of whose first acts was to decree the separation of Church and state. The majority of bishops were outspokenly anticommunist. In this respect the Serbian hierarchy

19 See the official documents pertaining to the trial of Cardinal Stepinac. See also the book *Persecutions of the Serbian Church in Yugoslavia*, published by the Serbian Orthodox Church in the United States (Chicago, 1954).

differed decidedly from the Orthodox bishops in other Balkan countries. While anxious not to create any new martyrs—one bishop (Joannice of Montenegro) and several priests, however, were executed—the government of Tito nevertheless treated certain prelates very harshly. A series of notorious trials took place: Barnabas of Sarajevo (consecrated bishop in 1947) was condemned in 1949 to eleven years of forced labor; Joseph of Skoplié was arrested in 1950, at the time of the patriarchal election (he was the most likely candidate for the office); Arsenius of Montenegro was arrested and sentenced in July 1954. The situation seems to be somewhat improved at the present time, owing to a more conciliatory attitude on the part of the patriarchs Vincent (1954-1958) and Germanus (elected in 1959). The Holy Synod, however, has refused until now to recognize the activities of the government-sponsored Association of Priests, and opposes all efforts aimed at restricting its authority. These efforts—openly supported by the government—have to do principally with the creation of churches independent of the patriarch in the various constituent parts of the republic. A compromise solution recently put an end to a dispute of this kind relating to Macedonia: the Church there will enjoy a certain amount of ecclesiastical autonomy, but the Holy Synod in Belgrade retains canonical authority over the Macedonian Church as such.

The heroic struggle of the Serbian clergy has thus won for them an unquestioned moral prestige both in Yugoslavia and abroad. It is uncertain, however, whether they will be able to meet the challenge of the new society now being molded. In Yugoslavia, as elsewhere, the Church finds itself largely deprived of the means of assuring the religious education of the youth and the training of future clergy. Since Tito's break with the Comintern, however, Yugoslav Orthodox are now less isolated from the rest of the world than their brethren in the other communist-dominated countries. Contacts with Greece, Constantinople and the Near East have now become quite frequent, as we can see, for example, by the recent trips to those countries of Serbian prelates, particularly patriarchs Vincent and Germanus.

7. The Romanian Orthodox Church

Two autocephalous Romanian-speaking churches were established in the nineteenth century: one in Transylvania, in the Austro-Hungarian Monarchy; the other, by act of the ecumenical patriarchate in 1885, in the newly independent state of Romania. Many Romanian-speaking Orthodox were also subject to the Serbo-Romanian metropolitan of Czernowitz or Cernauti (see above). Like the Serbian patriarchate, the present Romanian Church thus was formed from a coalescence of various groups which took place in 1925, when the title of "Patriarch of the Romanian Church" was adopted by the archbishop of Bucharest.

With nearly 12,000,000 faithful, the Orthodox Church of Romania is today the largest of the autocephalous Orthodox churches after that of Russia. After being closely tied to the old monarchy—Patriarch Myron once presided over the Council of Ministers—it too has had to face the brutal shock of a change in regime. The attitude adopted by the present government authorities toward the Romanian Church differs considerably from that prevailing elsewhere. Paradoxically the new communist state has never published a decree separating church and state, but in August 1948 a law recognized the "general regime of religion" in the popular democratic Republic of Romania. This law abolished the role that the Church once played in the state and in education, but preserves the control which the state always exercised over the Church. The paradoxical situation which exists in all the communist-dominated states is thus written into the very text of the constitution in Romania. Although regarded as a lay republic, Romania possesses a constitution which mentions the Orthodox church and defines it as a "unified church with its own head." Though inspired by Marxist principles, the state pays the salaries of the clergy and supports church-run schools. Bishops must swear an oath of allegiance to the state before the Minister of Religion when they are installed ("As a servant of God, as a man and a citizen, I swear to be faithful to the People and to defend the Popular Romanian Republic against its enemies both internal and external...So help me God.")!

By acquiescing in this state of affairs the Romanian hierarchy runs the risk of appearing in the yes of its own faithful, and in those of the world at large, as a mere body of officials at the beck and call of the government, whose ultimate and avowed aim is the destruction of all "religious prejudices." In fact, however, what we know about the religious situation in Romania before 1959 seems to suggest that the Church has gained certain advantages in exchange for this formal government control—the Church had 8,326 parishes, 10,153 priests, 182 monasteries and 11,506,217 faithful, and was able to retain a part of its property. Two theological institutes were functioning, with thirty professors, one at Bucharest (290 students) and the other at Sibiu (338 students); the Church published about a dozen religious periodicals, one of which, the review *Studi Teologice,* is by far the best Orthodox theological publication appearing behind the Iron Curtain. Religious instruction may not be given, officially, to youths who are under eighteen—as in all communist countries—but this serious gap was made up partially by the existence of six "schools of cantors" where students remained for three years and received a general religious education (there were 759 in 1959). Moreover, the revival of monasticism constituted until recently one of the brightest spots for Orthodoxy in Romania. Orthodox monks in Romania in 1959 totaled more than 7,000.[20] In order to raise the

---

20 See on this subject D.I. Doens, "La Réforme législative du patriarche Justinien de Roumanie. Sa Réforme et sa Règle monastique," in the Belgian periodical *Irénikon*, vol. 27, no. 1, pp. 51-92; supplementary note in no. 3 pp. 331-51; and information in vol. 34, 1961, p. 199; for the spiritual and intellectual life in the monasteries, see *Un Moine de l'Église orthodoxe de Roumanie*, "L'Avènement philocalique dans l'Orthodoxie roumaine," in *Istina*, nos. 3 and 4 (1958).

intellectual level of these institutions, to make them veritable spiritual centers for the whole Church and thus refute the charge of the government that they were "unproductive institutions," Patriarch Justinian (elected in 1948) published a common Rule for Romanian monks, based on the traditional principles of Oriental monasticism but also incorporating certain features of the Benedictine Rule. Liturgical and private prayers, particularly the Prayer of Jesus, were accorded their accustomed place, but, on the other hand, greater emphasis was given to manual work and to intensive intellectual labor, which could serve to justify the existence of the monasteries "socially" and enable them to respond, in an original and creative way, to the challenge of the socialist regime by integrating the monasteries in the new economic life of the country. The Rule provided for the establishment of monastic seminaries, of which three were actually in existence: a seminary for monks in the monastery of Neamt, founded by the staretz Paisij Velickovskij, the translator of the *Philocalia* in the eighteenth century (38 students); and two others for nuns at Agapia and Hurezu (124 novices in all). The monastic revival has been aided by the publication of a number of spiritual works, particularly a Romanian translation of the Fathers of the Church (*Philokalia*).

Unfortunately, this entire development was brought to an end by the severe measures taken by the government beginning in July 1958. Many church leaders, including—temporarily—Patriarch Justinian himself, were arrested and several hundreds of monks and priests were reduced to the lay state. Among those condemned to a long imprisonment were several noted professor of theology, in particular Father Staniloae, the learned editor of the Romanian *Philocalia*. During the latter half of 1960 more than 4,000 Orthodox monks and nuns were reported to have been arrested.[21]

The Romanian Church at present has a total of twelve dioceses, which form three metropolitan provinces. The patriarch and a Holy

21 *Irénikon*, vol. 34 (1961), p. 199.

Synod have supreme control over all ecclesiastical affairs. Approximately 10,000 priests are now (or were) serving the faithful.

The future of the Church in Romania as well as the other countries of Eastern Europe depends largely on the effectiveness of the antireligious propaganda being aimed at the youth. The measures available to the Church for counteracting this poison are very limited indeed and are practically reduced to the personal witness that individual practicing Christians can make in the new materialist world which the government leaders are trying to build.

8. The Bulgarian Orthodox Church

The Bulgarians were baptized in the ninth century by Byzantine missionaries in the time of the great patriarch Photius and at his instigation. Ecclesiastical independence was soon attained, but again abolished when the Byzantines conquered the country in the tenth century, then re-established once more in the thirteenth century with the restoration of the patriarchate of Trnovo. Under the Turkish regime it was abolished once again in favor of the supremacy of the Phanar. The question of independence was long a sore point in the nineteenth and twentieth centuries, for the Bulgarians were governed by Greek bishops who, especially in the towns, sought to suppress the Slavonic liturgy and generally Hellenize the Church. There was great longing for ecclesiastical autonomy and feelings ran high on both sides. Several of the ecumenical patriarchs tried to satisfy the legitimate claims of the Bulgarians in the course of the nineteenth century, but they always failed because of the hopeless way in which the two populations were mixed up with each other in the Balkan area. In Constantinople itself they lived side by side, but the Bulgarians, inspired by nationalist feelings, demanded the establishment of a genuine national church without any precise territorial limits and with jurisdiction over all their compatriots, in default of which they wished to have equality between Greeks and Bulgarians in the administration of the ecumenical patriarchate. In 1860 a few Bulgarian bishops caused a schism at Constantiople. Finally, in spite of conciliatory moves by the patriarch Gregory VI, the Bulgarians obtained a "firman" (decree) from the sultan authorizing the establishment of an independent Bulgarian exarchate.

Patriarch Anthimus VI then held a synod in Constantinople in the presence of the patriarchs of Alexandria and Antioch (1872) and launched a sentence of interdict against the Bulgarian exarch, condemning at the same time the sin of "phyletism," that is to say, nationalistic rivalries and quarrels between different nationalities within the Church of Christ.

Actually, the Bulgarians were not the only ones guilty of phyletism. The wrongs were also shared by the other side, as the history of the schism shows. But formally speaking, canonical right was on the side of the Phanar. The Bulgarian Church remained under patriarchal interdict until 1945, when the ecumenical see finally recognized the autocephalous status of the Bulgarian Church *within precise territorial limits*, and after the Bulgarians had officially requested the lifting of the interdict.

The Bulgarian Church has about 6,000,000 faithful today. In 1940 there were 2,742 parishes, 2,381 priests and eleven dioceses. Until May 10, 1953 the metropolitan of Sofia bore the title of exarch, but he has now assumed the title of patriarch.

As a state church closely tied to the former regime, the Bulgarian Church could not expect any leniency when the change of regime occurred in 1944. The new government took the same measures with respect to it that were taken by the popular democracies in other countries: all religious instruction in the schools was abolished (January 1946), some of the clergy were arrested, including Bishop Cyril of Plovdiv (the present patriarch), support was given to an Association of Priests which forms part of the present "Patriotic Front," and finally the separation of Church and state was decreed (Constitution of 1947).

The exarch Stephen and the bishops followed the example of the Russian bishops and swore that they were loyal to the new state. But to avoid all possible misunderstandings, the Holy Synod forbade priests to take part in the Patriotic Front. In June 1948 it received a curricular letter from the Minister of Cults, Illiev, declaring that "since every Bulgarian ought to belong to the Patriotic Front, all pastors and priests ought to do likewise" and ordering the heads of the Church to join in the fight against anti-Communist propaganda.[22] The Holy Synod replied that it would ignore the circular. In September of the same year Exarch Stephen was obliged to resign and the Holy Synod gave the necessary permission.

The period from 1948 to 1953 was particularly difficult for the Bulgarian Church. In 1949 the government unilaterally published a law on "religious associations,"[23] establishing strict control over the various ramifications of the Church. This control is exercised particularly with respect to the laws of the Church (article 6,) religious services held out of doors (art. 7), the Church budget (art. 13), the encyclicals and other decrees of the bishops (art. 15), the training of the Clergy (art. 14), and their appointment to various posts (art. 13), and so on. In 1951 a new constitution for the Church went into effect. The hierarchy had obtained a number of benefits from its conciliatory attitude: the number of copies of religious journals allowed has increased, taxes on Church property have been eased, and above all, the Holy Synod received permission in 1955 to dissolve the Association of Priests, which the government had used until then to bring pressure to bear on the hierarchy.

For the training of the clergy the Bulgarian Church at present has at its disposal the Academy of St. Clement of Ohrid (the former theological faculty of the University of Sofia, now separated from the

22 Text in R. Tobias, *Communist-Christian Encounter in Eastern Europe* (Greenfield, IN, 1956)m p. 358.

23 English translation of the law in Tobias, *op. cit.*, pp. 371-76.

university). It is able to publish at least four religious periodicals, including an interesting theological review (the Annual of the Academy), a number of textbooks for students and even some illustrated books for children. The hierarchy faithfully follows the policy of the patriarchate of Moscow in approving the movement known as the Partisans for Peace and in issuing rubber-stamped statements on international affairs at the proper times.

9. The Church of Greece

Shortly after the achievement of Greek independence in 1833 a synod of Greek bishops proclaimed the autocephalous status of the Greek Church within the boundaries of the new state. This unilateral act was motivated particularly by the fact that the ecumenical patriarch was regarded by the Greeks as being too subject to Turkish control to be able to function effectively as the supreme head of the Greek Church in the newly independent state. After protesting in vain, the Phanar finally acquiesced in the inevitable and recognized the *fait accompli* in 1850. Since then the Greek Church has been governed by a Holy Synod, under the presidency of the archbishop of Athens. The constitution of the Church, and especially the relations between Church and state, have undergone several changes between 1850 and 1959. While the system adopted in the beginning was directly inspired by the Regulation of Peter the Great and envisaged a strict subordination of the Church to the state, the tendency since then has been to give the hierarchy much greater freedom. In 1959, however, an internal dispute among the Greek bishops caused the government to tighten its grip again. Greece therefore is today the only country where the Orthodox Church remains a state church and plays a dominant role in the life of the country.

With a total of more than 8,000,000 faithful, the Greek Church has eighty-one dioceses, forty-nine of which are in the so-called "new" provinces on northern Greece (added to the kingdom in 1913) and nominally subject to the jurisdiction of the ecumenical patriarchate. However, they are represented in the Synod at Athens. Among all the Balkan countries Greece has the greatest number of dioceses, but also the smallest in size. There were formerly 120, but this number was reduced in the nineteenth century. A further reduction has recently been decided upon. This multiplicity of dioceses goes back to the period of the primitive Church, when each important community had its own bishop. But in those days bishops were elected by the faithful and were irremovable, and there was no tendency for them to form a bureaucracy or to think of the episcopate as a career. Measures have recently been proposed aimed at eliminating these evils in the modern Greek Church.

Since the main facts about the Church in Greece are rather well known, we shall confine ourselves here to a few general remarks about the situation of religious education in the country and to the activities of the various groups engaged in an internal apostolate.

Two theological faculties, which form parts of the universities at Athens and Thessalonica, offer higher instruction in theology. Most graduates prepare for careers as teachers of religion in secondary schools and remain laymen. However, a certain number enter the ranks of the regular clergy and in this way become candidates for the higher posts in the Church. Only a small number join the ranks of the married parish clergy. parish priests are trained in minor seminaries. In general, lay theologians enjoy a more important status in Greece than in other Orthodox countries. The majority of professors of theology and many preachers are laymen. One of the most interesting features of religion in modern Greece is the extraordinary development of various missionary movements directed toward an internal apostolate in the Greek Church itself. The most important of these is the Association known as Zoe ("Life"), founded in 1911 by Father Eusebios Matthopoulos, which is a kind of monastic order of a new type.

The Association has only about 130 members, of whom only thirty-four are priests, but all—with very few exceptions—have a higher degree in theology. They practice the three traditional monastic virtues but spend only one month each year in communal life in their mother house. The rest of the time, the brothers are dispersed throughout the country, preaching, teaching, or presiding over the various missionary or catechetical efforts in which the Association is engaged. Since they have vowed to oppose any tendency toward careerism, they have steadfastly refused to accept episcopal appointments and consider themselves wholly and solely dedicated to evangelical work. They are advocates of a more meaningful performance of the liturgy (and hence favor the eucharistic canon out loud), of a more genuine participation in the sacramental life of the Church (and hence favor frequent communion), and of a deeper knowledge of the bible on the part of the faithful. Because of these attitudes, they have contributed materially to a spiritual revival in the Greek Church. The organizations which they control are numerous and varied. As examples, we may cite the Christian Union of Men of Science (an association of Christian intellectuals), the Christian Union of Students (with 2,400 members), the Women's Association *Eusebia*, the Christian Union of Teachers, and the Christian Union of Young Workers (with 2,000 regular members and 6,000 associates). Zoe even runs a school of engineering. Some idea about its extensive influence may be gained from the extraordinary number of publications which it edits (in view of the present size of the Greek population). The periodical *Zoe*—a weekly periodical of eight pages containing only articles of a religious nature—has a circulation of 170,000 copies and thus has the largest circulation of any Greek-language periodical today. The monthly review *Aktines* (the organ of the Union of Men of Science) is published in 15,000 copies. A dozen or so other periodicals—some of them illustrated for children—have a comparable wide circulation. Particular attention is paid to distributing copies of the Bible among the Greek people. The pocket edition of the New Testament published by Zoe is in its thirty-second edition and 650,000 copies have been printed.

In addition to Zoe, there are other organizations, such as the Orthodox Unions, which pursue the same objective. They owe their existence to private initiative but they carry on within the traditional framework of the Church (dioceses and parishes) and have the blessing of the hierarchy. The latter, however, tends to view with some suspicion movements that it does not directly control. It would obviously prefer that they were more closely tied in with the official machinery of church government. It realizes, however, that it would be unwise to attempt to bring this about through administrative measures. Instead, it has established, under its own auspices, an organization known at *Apostoliki Diakonia* (Apostolic Service), which performs much the same sort of work as Zoe (preaching, publications, youth work). These various Greek missionary endeavors therefore are more concerned with emulating each other than with rivalry. They are all directed toward one common objective, the preservation of the Orthodox faith among the Greek people. Their success in the field is apparent, particularly as regards the religious education of youth. Nearly 500,000 Greek children attend the 7,800 catechetical schools of the Church (of which 2,000 are controlled by Zoe). For some years now these movement have taken a keen interest in the ecumenical responsibilities of the Church. Students from Uganda, Ethiopia and Korea attend Greek institutes and seminaries, and various Greek youth movements are affiliated with *Syndesmos* (the World Association of Orthodox Youth Movements). A Committee for the Promotion of Foreign Missions has recently been formed with the approval of the hierarchy.

10. The Church of Georgia

One of the most ancient branches of the Christian Church, the Georgian Church was founded at the beginning of the fifth century by a woman apostle, St. Nino, who converted Mirian the king of Georgia to Christianity. Since Georgia lay within the ecclesiastical sphere of the patriarchate of Antioch, although remote from that capital, the Georgians long receive their bishops from there. Later they came under the jurisdiction of Constantinople. Their church achieved autocephalous status even in medieval times and was governed by its own Catholicos.[24] In 1801 Orthodox Georgia sought the help of the Russians against the Persians and found itself annexed to the empire of Alexander I. The old autocephalous status was abolished, and from 1817 the church was governed by a Russian exarch, who was a member of the Synod of St. Petersburg. At the time of the Russian Revolution, the Georgians recovered their autocephalous status, but this was not formally recognized by the patriarch of Moscow until 1943.

The Church was destined to go through a tragic period during the Revolution. Kirion, the first catholicos to be restored to the throne, was assassinated. His successor, Ambrose, was tried and sentenced to ten years' imprisonment (1923). The relative freedom gained by religion as a result of the last war also benefited the Georgian Church, but its present situation seems to be rather weak. Officially there are fifteen dioceses (as against twenty-eight in the eighteenth century), but nine of these are vacant. A new catholicos, Ephrem, has recently been elected by the national synod, following the death of his predecessor, Melchizedek. A church calendar is published at Tiflis (Tbilisi). Information with regard to the existence of a seminary is uncertain.[25] Georgia at present has 2,500,000 inhabitants, who were all Orthodox before 1917. Statistics regarding religious practice are unobtainable today.

---

24 This title was often borne by the heads of autonomous churches situated outside the borders of the Byzantine Empire.

25 See *Le Problème religieux en U.R.S.S*

11. The Church of Cyprus

The Council of Ephesus (431) proclaimed the independent status of the archbishopric of Cyprus, which until then had been dependent upon Antioch. Since that time this ancient church has had a rather turbulent history. The island was conquered by the Arabs in the seventh century, reconquered by the Byzantines, and then seized by Richard the Lion-Hearted in 1191 on his way to the Third Crusade. Cyprus remained under Latin rule for several centuries, first under the house of Lusignan (1191-1489), then under Venice (1489-1571). It was conquered by the Turks in 1571 and occupied by the British in 1878. In spite of all these different rulers, however, the Cypriots remained faithful to their Orthodox faith, though during the centuries of Latin rule they were obliged to submit to a Latin archbishop. Several massacres of the Orthodox clergy by the Turks took place after the departure of the Latins. The Turkish minority on the island, in fact, is a vestige of the former Ottoman occupation.

When the British occupied Cyprus they preserved, to a large extent, the political situation which had existed under the Turks. As we have seen, it was the Turkish custom to hand over to the Orthodox clergy both civil and religious control over their faithful, and the archbishop of Cyprus continued to be viewed as the ethnarch ("national head") of the Greek Orthodox Church under the British.

The Orthodox population of Cyprus today amounts to about 450,000 and there are some seven hundred priests. The faithful are governed by a Holy Synod consisting of the archbishop and three metropolitans (Paphos, Kition and Kyrenia), all elected by the faithful in accordance with a rather elaborate system in several stages. The present archbishop, Makarios, elected in 1950, has achieved worldwide fame as a result of his part in the Cypriot struggle for union with Greece. He has been chosen as president of the new Republic of Cyprus. The role which he has played in recent events is entirely in accordance with the traditions of the Cypriot Church, which for many centuries was the rallying point for the Greek population under so many foreign rulers.

12. The Archbishopric of Sinai

By a special privilege, the head of the monastery of St. Catherine built by Emperor Justinian I in the sixth century near the spot where Moses is said to have received the Tables of the Law, enjoys the rank of an archbishop and the monastery has the status of an autonomous church. The archbishop-abbot is elected by the chapter of monks but receives episcopal consecration and the hands of the patriarch of Jerusalem. He only has jurisdiction over the monastery and the Bedouins who live in the neighborhood. The present archbishop of Sinai, Porphyrios III, generally resides in the *metochion* (priory) of his monastery in Cairo.

The monastery of Sinai possess a very rich library of ancient Greek, Georgian and Slavic manuscripts and an interesting collection of icons.

13. The Albanian Orthodox Church

In 1944 the Albanian population consisted of 688,000 Moslem, 210,000 Orthodox and 104,184 Roman Catholics. Only after political pressure had been brought to bear did the ecumenical patriarch finally consent to recognize the autocephalous status of the Albanian Orthodox Church in 1937, a minority in the country, practically without schools or traditions of its own. Despised by the Italians, the Albanian Orthodox had still more to suffer as a result of the antireligious acts of the new communist-dominated government in 1945-1946. Two bishops were arrested toward the end of 1948, and in August 1949 the archbishop of Tirana, Christophoros, was deposed and imprisoned for "activities considered harmful to the Albanian people and the Church." His successor, Paissios, elected under dubious conditions, was recognized by the patriarch of Moscow but not by Constantiople.

14. The Polish Orthodox Church

Within the Polish frontiers, as these were defined at the end of World War I, there was a large population of 4,000,000 Byelorussian and Ukrainian Orthodox forming several dioceses which until then had been subject to the Russian Church. In 1924 these dioceses were combined by the ecumenical patriarch to form an autocephalous church. In 1939 the Polish Orthodox Church had five dioceses, 1,624 parishes and two seminaries (Vilna and Krzemieniec with a total of 500 seminarians), as well as a theological faculty at Warsaw (150 students).

In 1939 the Soviet Union occupied the part of Poland inhabited by the majority of the Orthodox, and gained still further territory as a result of World War II. Canonically, these regions were again attached to the patriarchate of Moscow, while only some 350,000 Orthodox remained on Polish soil. The situation of the latter was aggravated by the fact that the patriarch of Moscow had not recognized the act of 1924 which confirmed the autocephalous status of the Polish Church. In 1948, therefore, three Polish bishops, including the Metropolitan Dionysius, had to do penance before Patriarch Alexis and received a new autocephalous act from him. Metropolitan Dionysius was forced to retire. In 1951 a new head was provided for the church in the person of a Russian bishop, Makarios Oksiusk, the former bishop of Lvov and former professor (before 1917) of the Kiev Theological Academy. The independence of the Polish Church with respect to Moscow is therefore of a very relative nature. Metropolitan Makarios died on March 1, 1961. A successor, Timothy, archbishop of Bialystok, was canonically elected.

There are at present five Orthodox dioceses in Poland: Warsaw, Bialystok, Lodz, Wroclaw (Breslau), and Gdansk (Danzig).[26] The number of parishes is about 160.

15. *The Orthodox Church of Czechoslovakia*

Between the two world wars the Orthodox Church presented a rather heterogeneous picture in Czechoslovakia. It was composed of two originally separate groups of faithful, amounting to about 250,000 persons in all. First of all, a group of Czech Orthodox were provided with a head in 1923 by the ecumenical patriarch in the person of Bishop Sabbatios. In 1925 a more important groups of priests and faithful constituting the Czechoslovak National Church, which had separated from Rome, joined the Orthodox Church. They were provided with a head by the Serbian patriarch, who consecrated for them Bishop Gorazd. The latter therefore presided over a certain number of Orthodox faithful of the Latin rite. In 1930, 200,000 Carpatho-Russian Uniats also returned to Orthodoxy and the patriarch of Belgrade formed the diocese of Mukacevo for them. Finally, a small number of Russian parishes remained throughout this period subject to a Russian bishop who recognized the authority of Metropolitan Eulogios of Paris.

These four groups were united by the patriarch of Moscow in 1947 to form one church, the Serbian Church giving its consent to the arrangement. In 1950, finally, two dioceses of Byzantine rite in communion with Rome (Prešov and Mikailov) returned to Orthodoxy.[27] The Orthodox church in Czechoslovakia therefore

---

26 It should be remarked that two of these dioceses are on former German territory, thus implying, on the part of the Orthodox authorities, full recognition of the western frontiers of Poland. As is well known, the Vatican has to this day refused to appoint Catholic bishops to this region on the grounds that a peace treaty has not yet been signed between Poland and Germany.

27 Their union with Rome dated from 1649 and was brought about as a result of pressures exercised by the Austrian government. It must, unfortunately, be acknowledged that their return to Orthodoxy has been brought about under conditions hardly any better, if at all.

today has about 250,000 faithful. There are four dioceses (Prague, Olomouc, Prešov and Mikailov) and in 1951 its autocephalous status was confirmed by the patriarch of Moscow. Its first head, Eleutherios (who resigned in 1958), and its present head, Metropolitan John, are both Russian bishops. The independent status of the new church has recently been recognized by the patriarch of Constantinople, after the death of Sabbatios, whom the ecumenical see continued to recognize as archbishop of Prague.

An Orthodox seminary was opened at Karlovy Vary in 1948 and another is functioning, it seems, at Prešov. The Church publishes a theological review and has a Slavonic press which prints liturgical books, largely for export to Russia, where the Church has no means of publishing anything of the kind.

16. The Orthodox Church of Finland

When Finland won its independence from Russia in 1918 one of the first acts of the Finnish Orthodox—for the most part Karelians converted from paganism in the Middle Ages by the monks of Valamo on Lake Lagoda—was to remove the sigma of being called "Russians" by the vast majority of Lutheran Finns, who tended to view Orthodoxy as a "Russian faith." So under the leadership of Archbishop Germanos Aab, in 1923 the Church of Finland placed itself under the jurisdiction of the ecumenical patriarch of Constantinople. Moscow protested against this situation, but finally in 1958 recognized the autonomous status of the Finnish Church.

About 70,000 Orthodox faithful live in the midst of an overwhelming majority of some 4,000,000 Lutherans. Nevertheless, the Orthodox Church is considered to be the second state-church of Finland. The Orthodox had much to suffer when the Soviets annexed part of the country in 1939 (Finnish Karelia, annexation confirmed in 1945). Most of them in fact lived in the part of the country contiguous to Russia. They were obliged to retire to the interior of the country and are today found scattered all over Finland. Their church as two dioceses (the archbishopric of Kuopio and the bishopric of Helsinki), a seminary which has been transferred from Sortavala, in Karelia, to Helsinki, and there are plans for the creation of a theological faculty. Since the Orthodox youth are eager to promote international and ecumenical contacts and anxious to show that they belong to the Western European world, while at the same time clinging to their Orthodox traditions, it is possible that the Finnish Church is destined to play an important part in manifesting the spirit of Orthodoxy in the West.

17. The Orthodox Missions, the Orthodox in Western Europe and America

In the nineteenth and early part of the twentieth century Russian missionary activity extended far beyond the eastern limits of the Empire. The Orthodox colonies in China, Korea, Japan and Alaska are evidence of this fact to this day.

The Chinese Orthodox mission goes back to the end of the seventeenth century, when a group of Cossacks from the Russian outpost of Albazin were hired as a personal bodyguard by the Chinese emperor in Peking. Although completely Sinicized, their descendants retained their Orthodox faith and formed the nucleus of an Orthodox colony in the capital. This nucleus in turn became the basis for an important mission established at Peking in the nineteenth century, which had numerous branches and some twenty schools. However, the number of converts does not seem ever to have exceeded ten thousand. The number of Orthodox faithful in China increased after the Russian Revolution, when many refugees, including clergy, fled from Siberia. After the triumph of communism following the victories of Mao Tse-tung, the Orthodox Church, like all other Western Churches, had to rid itself of its Western personnel. The Russian clergy in charge, as representatives of the patriarch of Moscow, were not privileged in this respect and had to leave the country. In 1950 a Chinese priest, Simeon Dou, was consecrated as bishop in Tientsin in Moscow, and later transferred to Shanghai. In 1957 another Chinese priest, Basil Yo Fuan, was consecrated as bishop of Peking (Peiping). Three other dioceses remain without bishops. Two monasteries and a catechetical school are functioning in Peking.

Toward the end of the nineteenth century a Russian mission was also sent to Korea. The Orthodox faith there has managed to survive through all the recent turmoil and the mission was recently taken over by the Greek Archdiocese in the United States. It operates under the supervision of two Korean priests and has a school and a hospital.

Orthodox missionaries were even more active in Japan, thanks particularly to Father Nicholas Kasatkin, one of the most remarkable missionaries of all time. He arrived in 1861 as chaplain to the Russian consul in Hakodate but soon gave up his diplomatic tasks to devote himself exclusively to missionary work in Japan. His first efforts were directed toward translating the New Testament and essential liturgical texts into Japanese. In 1872 the first Japanese priests were ordained by a Russian bishop at Hakodate. In 1880 there were 6,099 Orthodox in Japan; by 1891 this number had climbed to 20,048 and there were twenty-two priests with 219 churches and chapels. The same year saw the completion of the imposing Orthodox cathedral of Tokyo, which remains today the most conspicuous religious edifice in the capital. The Japanese have always called it "Nicolai-Do" ("House of Nicholas"). Consecrated as bishop of Tokyo in 1880, Nicholas was extraordinarily successful in winning the confidence of the country where he was laboring on behalf of the Gospel. During the Russo-Japanese War of 1904-1905, for example, he was able to move about freely, and celebrated Te Deums for victory of the Japanese armies. Even today, the truly native character of Japanese Orthodoxy is a well-recognized phenomenon and is a sign of hope for the future.

The Japanese Orthodox Church has about 36,000 faithful, one bishop, and thirty-eight priests, all Japanese. A seminary has recently been opened with some twenty seminarians, who sometimes go abroad to complete their studies. After a period of decline between the two world wars the prospects for Japanese Orthodoxy are now beginning to brighten once again.

❖ ❖ ❖

Russian explorers discovered and occupied Alaska in 1741. Monks from Valamo (on Lake Ladoga) undertook missionary work there in 1794 and opened the first school for the Eskimos. An unusually capable missionary—John Veniaminov—labored for many long years in this arduous vineyard (1822-1852), as missionary, the author of a grammar of the Aleutian language, the translator of the Gospels and the Byzantine liturgy into the same language, and then as bishop of an immense territory embracing the Kamchatka, the Kurile Islands, Aleutian Islands and Alaska. From 1841 until 1858 there was a seminary in operation on one of the Aleutian Islands. Veniaminov was provided with an auxiliary bishop in 1858. Finally in 1868 Russia sold Alaska to the United States. The Russian mission was made an independent missionary bishopric comprising the Aleutian Islands and Alaska. In 1872 the seat of the bishop was transferred to San Francisco, and in 1905 to New York. An auxiliary bishop remained in Alaska.

❖ ❖ ❖

Such were the humble origins of American Orthodoxy. But the situation is far different today. During the latter years of the nineteenth century quite a few Uniat Catholic groups made up of emigrants from Carpatho-Russia returned to Orthodoxy and placed themselves under the jurisdiction of the Russian diocese in America. Groups of Greeks, Serbs, Albanians and Bulgarians also organized parishes under its jurisdictions. In 1904 an auxiliary bishop was provided for the Syrian and Lebanese in Brooklyn,

New York. With the blessing of the Holy Synod in Russia, Arch-bishop Tikhon (the future patriarch) authorized the publication of an English translation of the liturgy. Thus an American Ortho-dox Church began to take place.

The Russian Revolution and internal dissension in the Russian Church helped to retard the process of unification. Between 1917 and 1923 the American diocese was without any effective leader-ship (until Metropolitan Platon was appointed as the new bishop by Patriarch Tikhon) and it broke up into a number of small separate units, each national group forming its own dioceses. The steady influx of new immigrants moreover, made it extremely diffi-cult to organize and integrate the new arrivals in a single church.

Hence today, besides the original Russian diocese, the United States has a large Greek Orthodox archdiocese, an archdiocese dependent upon the Arab-speaking patriarchate of Antioch, Ser-bian, Romanian, Bulgarian and Albanian diocese. The synod of *émigré* Russian bishops under Metropolitan Vitaly likewise formed its headquarters to the United States. Some of the auto-cephalous Ukrainian clergy[28] also established parishes there. While all these groups have begun to work more closely with each other, their union alone will truly assure the future progress of Orthodoxy in America.

The total number of Orthodox in the United States is about 3,000,000. More or less numerous groups are also found in Canada and South America. All national groups in the United States, with the exception of the Greeks, are gradually adopting English more and more as the liturgical language, a factor which will help the process toward unification. Whenever an Orthodox community is able to rise above its own ethnic and nationalist

---

28 An autocephalous Ukrainian Church was established, as we have seen, during the Russian Revolution, but its status was uncanonical. At first it was without apostolic succession when no bishops would join it; then, later, apostolic succession was obtained, but under dubious circumstances. Consequently this body does not enjoy communion with the rest of the Orthodox Church.

limitations it soon reveals that it is capable of exerting a missionary influence. Thus about a third of the clergy serving in the Syrian diocese—under the jurisdiction of the patriarch of Antioch—consists of converts who have come to Orthodoxy from other Christian confessions. St. Vladimir's Seminary, in New York, receives students from all the Orthodox communities in the United States and is one of the principal centers working for the unification of American Orthodox. A Greek Orthodox theological school is active in Brookline, Massachusetts, and there are four other schools belonging to the various jurisdictions where instruction in theology is given. There are numerous religious publications in English.

Until very recently only three "major" religious confessions were officially recognized in the United States: Protestantism, Catholicism and Judaism. But by decision of most of the states the Orthodox Church has now been added to this number.

❖   ❖   ❖

Between the two world wars the number of Orthodox increased very considerably in Western Europe. A Greek exarchate, headed by the titular archbishop of Thyatire, was established at London in 1922. The bulk of Russian refugees from this time on tended to settle especially in France. In 1922 Patriarch Tikhon named Metropolitan Eulogios to look after the new parishes. When the ecclesiastical authorities in Moscow finally asked him to submit a written statement of loyalty to the Soviet state, Eulogios appealed, in 1931, to the ecumenical patriarchate and became the latter's exarch for the Russian parishes in Europe. His long faithfulness to Moscow (1922-1931) and his appeal to Constantinople got him into trouble with the *émigré* Russian bishops who had fled to Yugoslavia and established an independent Holy Synod there, but whose canonical status was not recognized by the other Orthodox Churches. As mentioned above, this synod has now transferred its headquarters to the United States and has jurisdiction over a certain number of *émigré* parishes.

Paris quickly became the chief intellectual center for the Russian emigration. Nicholas Berdiaev, Sergius Bulgakov and many other leading thinkers helped to acquaint the West with the thought, spirituality and traditions of the Christian East. The Theological Institute of St. Sergius in Paris, under the guidance of Metropolitan Eulogios and a group of capable and talented professors, has trained more than 150 Orthodox priests and has taken very active part in promoting ecumenical discussions over the years. Owing to the presence of Russian *émigrés*, but without any efforts at proselytism on their part, a number of Western Orthodox communities began to be formed in France and Germany. Both in Europe and in America, communities of Western rite have also joined the Orthodox Church and were received as such by the hierarchy. We are therefore confronted today by the gradual emergence of a Western Orthodoxy, a welcome phenomenon, which will assist the Orthodox youth who had adopted the language, culture and customs of the countries where they were born, and are to all intents and purposes as Western as their Latin brothers, to preserve their Orthodox faith. On the spiritual and intellectual side, it is also important for the Orthodox to manifest their *presence* in the great movements which are gripping Western Christianity at this time: the return to Holy Scripture and to the true Christian Tradition of the Church, the movement toward reunion, the revival of patristic studies, a greater awareness of social responsibilities, and the liturgical movement. In all these areas the Orthodox not only feels very close to his Protestant brethren but is often aware that he has much to learn from them. The principal task of Western Orthodoxy should be to show *by deeds* that these various remarkable currents and trends in Western Christianity can be given new strength and presented as a more coherent whole in the light of Orthodox truth.

We shall conclude this long section on the Orthodox Diaspora and missions by mentioning a recent development which may have important consequences for the future, namely, the appearance of a new Orthodox Church in Africa, which had thus far escaped the attention of Orthodox missionaries. In 1932 a group of Christians in Uganda left the communion of the Anglican Church and were admitted to the Orthodox Church by the patriarch of Alexandria. Under the supervision of an African-born priest, Father Spartas, this group now numbers about 20,000 faithful. Recent information indicates that this church has experienced a phenomenal growth and is receiving more and more active help from the Greek Orthodox Church. Several native seminarians from Uganda are pursuing their studies at the patriarchal college in Cairo and at the theological faculty in Athens. A new bishop has just been appointed for East Africa. It seems certain that the rapid rise of this church is due not only to the attraction of the Orthodox faith itself, but also to the fact that its missionaries are not considered to be identified with colonialism. It is greatly to be hoped that the Orthodox authorities will be able to guide the movement wisely and can profit from the great advantage of not being identified with European colonial policies of the nineteenth century.

Chapter 9

ORTHODOX FAITH AND SPIRITUALITY

We mentioned earlier the great spiritual legacy which the Orthodox Church has inherited from its medieval forebear, the Byzantine Church. This legacy embraces the prayers, hymns, and other formulas of our liturgical services, the canonical organization and discipline of the churches, our spiritual tradition, and the dogmatic system of the Orthodox faith. Yet, while it is perfectly true that the Orthodox Church claims to be the *true Church of Christ,* the one and only Catholic Church, the Orthodox theologian, nevertheless, is under a strict obligation to distinguish carefully in this heritage between that which forms part of the Church's Holy Tradition, unalterable and universally binding, received from the past, and that which is a mere relic of former times, venerable no doubt in many respects but sometimes also sadly out of date and even harmful to the mission of the Church. All modernism of the wrong kind is of course to be condemned, as exemplified recently by the Renovated Church in Russia, but also all narrow conservatism like that of the Russian Old Believers, which tends to canonize the past as such. These two tendencies, unfortunately, are always present in most local Orthodox Churches and soon make themselves felt. We need to be continually on guard against them. But this can be done only by persons who have received a sound training in theological principles, who are prepared to show a genuine respect for tradition, and who are disposed at all times and in all things to be guided by revealed Truth.

It is not possible within the limits of this book to offer the reader anything like a full systematic account of Orthodox doctrines.[1] He

---

1. The best systematic account of this kind is still that by S. Bulgakov, *The Orthodox Church* (London, 1935; reprinted: Crestwood, N.Y., SVS Press 1988)

will undoubtedly have been able to gather from the preceding pages what the main Orthodox positions are on a number of points, and further dogmatic questions will be taken up in the chapter which follows. It is our purpose here merely to give a general survey of the mysteries of the Christian faith as the Orthodox Church sees them, to describe the Orthodox attitude toward them, and finally to dwell somewhat on the Orthodox conception of man's communion with God. The Orthodox faith is expressed, jointly, by its spiritual tradition and the declared dogmas of the Church, by the lives of the saints, and by the doctrines of its teachers (the Fathers of the Church and other theologians). It is both the *lex orandi* and the *lex credendi* of the Church. According to V. Lossky:

> Eastern tradition has never clearly distinguished between mysticism and theology, between a personal experience of the divine mysteries and the dogmas declared by the Church . . . The dogma which expresses a revealed truth and appears to us like an unfathomable mystery, must be lived in such a way that, instead of assimilating the mystery to our manner of understanding it, we must, on the contrary, strive to bring about a profound change, an inner transformation of the soul, so that we will be more receptive toward the mystical experience. Far from being opposed to each other, theology and mysticism mutually support and supplement each other. One is impossible without the other. If mysticism is the application by the individual of the content of the common faith to his own experience, theology is the expression of that which can be experienced by each one for the benefit of all.[2]

The new reality made available to the world by the Incarnation of the Word and made effective in the Church through the operation of the Holy Spirit is not a mere sum of knowledge, but a New Life. It is transformation, a transfiguration of our being. We do not achieve it simply by reading the Word of God or through a knowledge of dogmas, but by dying and rising again with Christ in baptism, by receiving the seal of the Spirit in

---

2. *The Mystical Theology of the Eastern Church* (Crestwood, NY, St Vladimir's Seminary Press, 1976.)

Confirmation, by becoming members of the actual Body of Christ in the Eucharist, and finally by making progress in ever greater knowledge, until we attain the "stature of the man made in Jesus Christ" (Eph 4:13). This sacramental nature of the true life in the Spirit presupposes the existence of a visible Church with a hierarchy possessing special functions and a charisma to teach, but it also means that the *saints* are authentic witnesses of the actual presence of God in the midst of his people. By means of its hierarchic and sacramental structure, the Church expresses the *permanence* and *reality* of the union brought about, in Christ, between the human and the divine. The Ascension of Jesus does not mean the end of his presence but the glorification of human nature, which is now deified and seated on the right hand of the Father. It presupposes Pentecost and the sending of the Holy Spirit by the Father to the Church. The Spirit builds the Body of Christ in history, confers the sacraments, establishes the Church in truth, and guarantees its permanence and its infallibility. It operates through various charismas, including those of teaching and pastoring which are proper to the bishops, but it does not impose itself, magically, on the inner freedom of the individual which constitutes the very basis of the human person. Each one of us receives, through the sacraments, a seed of sanctity, but it is up to us to make it bear fruit. The Church as an "institution" is therefore not opposed to the Church as an "event," but the one presupposes the other, as grace presupposes our personal efforts to make it effective. Since the age of the Fathers the Orthodox Church has always upheld the doctrine of *synergeia*, that is, the collaboration between divine grace and the free will of man on his way toward God. We are *all* saints by grace, but we must *become* saints by our acts and in our whole being.

God, in his very Being, his Providence, his Incarnation, his presence in the Church, and his manifestation of himself at the end of time, is the unique Object whom the saints know and whom theologians seek to express by their formulas. Two aspects of the conception of God appear to be particularly important if we wish to understand Orthodox theology as a whole. These two aspects—going back of course to the Greek Fathers—are the absolute *transcendence* and the *trinitarian*, that is, the personal, *nature* of the Divine Being.

God's transcendence is a logical consequence of the Biblical account of creation *ex nihilo*. This is one of the essential traits of Biblical religion. The Bible clearly affirms that the world is not an emanation of the divine nor a reflection of a pre-existent reality, much less an extension of the Divine Being, as the result of any natural necessity. God, says St. Paul, "sends his call to that which has no being, as it if already was" (Rom 4:17). The world did not exist before the divine Fiat, but it began to exist, thus giving birth to the quantity we call "time." To be sure the Fathers spoke of "ideas" existing in the divine Mind before the creation of the world, but these ideas had only dynamic and intentional character. The appearance of created beings from nothing means that these creatures belong to an order of existence essentially different from God, an order called by the Fathers, beginning with St. Athanasius, the "natural" order, created by the *will* of God and existing by his will alone. Between God an the created world there can be no "interdependence," there can only be a total "dependence" of the creature on the Creator.

The abyss between the Absolute and the relative, the Uncreated and creatures, is a theme constantly recurring throughout the New Testament, and is what Christian theologians and mystics mean by the "transcendence" and "unknowability" of the divine Essence. Creatures can know each other, among themselves, but when it comes to knowing God they are crushed, as it were, by their total dependence on him and by their virtual nonexistence. Their only resource is to assert that God *is not* what they conceive him to be, that he is not like any creature, that no image or word can express his Being.[3] Unknown in his essence, God has however revealed himself

3. This is what is meant by the term "negative theology" or "apophatic theology," the two greatest exponents of which in the East were St. Gregory of Nyssa and the anonymous author of the fifth century who hid his real identity under the pseudonym of Dionysius the Areopagite, the disciple of St. Paul at Athens.

as Father, Son and Holy Spirit: the Son became man and the Spirit descended on the Church. The Christian God therefore is not the "unknown God" venerated by philosophers, but a living God who reveals himself and *acts*. This is the meaning of the Orthodox doctrine concerning the divine *energies* or actions, which are distinct from the unknowable essence, as formulated by St. Gregory Palamas in the fourteenth century.[4] The Old Testament has much to say about the divine intervention in the history of the Chosen People, but with Christianity we have a fullness of divine action in history: the Son of God "dispossessed himself, and took the nature of a slave, fashioned in the likeness of men, and presenting himself to us in human form; and then he lowered his own dignity, accepted an obedience which brought him death, death on the cross" (Phil 2:7-8). Henceforth the divine acts affect not only the external man, but their very Source has assumed human nature, which is now deified in Jesus Christ. We are no longer limited to acknowledging the transcendence and omnipotence of God, but we may also accept the salvation which he grants us and assimilate the divine grace which he gives us. This is what the Fathers meant by "deification": God became man that we might become God.[5] This deification is realized when we become members of the Body of Christ, but also, and especially, by the unction of the Spirit when the later touches each one of us: the "economy of the Holy Spirit" means precisely this, that we are able to enjoy communion with the one and truly deified humanity of Jesus Christ throughout history from the time of the Ascension to the final Parousia:[6] "God has sent out the Spirit of his Son into our hearts, crying out in us, Abba, Father" (Gal 4:6).

This "personal" emphasis of Orthodox theology and mysticism is intimately connected with the way in which the Fathers interpret the

---

4. See our *Study of Gregory Palamas* (London: Faith Press, 1963), and *Saint Grégoire Palamas et la mystique orthodoxe*, Coll. "Maîtres Spirituels" (Paris: Éditions du Seuil, 1959).

5. St. Athanasius of Alexandria, *The Incarnation of the Word*, 54, PG 25,192B.

6. Cf. O. Clément, *Transfigurer le temps. Notes sur le temps à la lumière de la tradition orthodoxe* (Paris: Neuchâtel, 1959.)

transcendence of God; that is, God remains unknowable in his unique essence, but he has revealed himself as a Trinity of Three Persons. The God of the Bible therefore is known to the extent that He is a living and acting Deity, the One to whom the prayers of the Church are addressed, the One who has sent His Son for the salvation of the world. This particular emphasis of the thought of the Eastern Fathers distinguished them—without opposing them, however—from the way in which their Latin brothers preferred to think of God first as a unique essence, and then only as a Trinity.[7] These two different attitudes would later give rise to two schools of Trinitarian theology. In Latin theology, the divine Persons were considered as the simple inner relations of the unique essence of the Godhead: hence, if the very existence of the Spirit is determined by its relations to the Father and the Son, the doctrine of the *filioque*—or procession of the Spirit from the Father and the Son—becomes a logical, dogmatic necessity, for the Spirit cannot be said to be distinct from the Son if he does not proceed from him.[8] Eastern theologians, on the other hand, remained faithful to the old "personalism" of the Greek Fathers. The doctrine of the *filioque* appeared to them, consequently, as semi-Sabellianism (to use and expression of Photius).[9] Consubstantial with the Father and the Son, because proceeding from the Father, the unique source of the Deity, the Spirit has his own existence and personal function in the inner life of God and in the economy of salvation: his task is to bring about the unity of the human race in the Body of Christ, but he also imparts to this unity a personal, and hence diversified, character. It is with a prayer to the Holy Spirit that all

---

7. See on this point T. de Regnon, *Études de théologie positive sur la Sainte Trinité*, vol. 1, p. 433; G. L. Prestige, *God in Patristic Thought* (London, 1952), pp. 242ff.

8. The doctrine of the *filioque* has been debated at two recent meetings of Catholic and Orthodox theologians; the minutes of the debates were published in the *Eastern Churches Quarterly*, vol. 7 (1948), suppl. issue, and in *Russie et Chrétienté*, nos. 3-4 (1950).

9. *Mystagogia*, 9, PG 102.289 A B; Sabellianism is a heresy dating from the second century attributed to a certain Sabellius, who taught that the divine Persons are simply "modes" or "aspects" of a unique God.

the liturgical services of the Orthodox Church begin, and with an invocation of his name that the eucharistic mystery is effected.

While remaining absolutely transcendent and incomprehensible, God has revealed himself in Jesus Christ, "in whom the whole plenitude of the Deity is embodied" (Col 2:9). In this way the true Life which comes from God was communicated to men, who, until then and ever since the sin of Adam, had been subject to death, a kind of hereditary, cosmic corruption, the consequence of his revolt against God.

The drama of sin, described in the first chapters of Genesis and explained by St. Paul and the ancient Fathers of the Church, provides a key to the mystery of suffering and death as found in man, both in the past and today. Adam and Eve sinned and this sin involved their death, as well as the death of all their descendants. This doctrine of original sin, which has played such an important part in Western theology ever since the time of St. Augustine, is interpreted to mean that countless generations of men have been affected by the consequences of Adam's sin, who were not responsible, it would seem, for the original fault. In their eagerness to reconcile this fact with a certain conception of the divine "justice," Western theologians have always insisted on the *joint guilt* of all men for the sin of Adam: punishment for sin could not affect all humanity unless all men had sinned "in Adam" and had therefore merited the divine wrath. This interpretation seemed to be confirmed by the Latin translation of a particular passage in the Bible—it may even have had its origin there—which speaks of the "transmission" of Adam's sin (Rom 5:12: *in quo omnes peccaverunt*). But, as a matter of fact, this is an inaccurate rendering of the original Greek.[10] The Eastern Fathers who read St. Paul in the

10. The Latin text, by translating the Greek *eph'o* as *in quo,* implies that "all have sinned in Adam." But this is impossible grammatically. The two possible translations would read: "Death passed to all men, from the fact that all have sinned"; or, "Death, on account of which all have sinned, has passed to all men." The latter version finds confirmation in several of the Greek Fathers, in the first case, St. Paul would be referring to the personal sins of men committed by them on their own responsibility and meriting punishment like that which Adam suffered; in the second case, mortality, transmitted to the whole race of Adam, would be the origin of their personal sins.

original Greek never attempted to prove the *joint guilt* of all the descendants of Adam for the sin of their ancestor: they merely observed that all men have inherited corruption and death by a process of inheritance and that all have committed sins. They preferred to interpret the state of affairs inherited from Adam as a slavery to the Devil, who exercises a usurped, unjust and deadly tyranny over mankind since the sin of man's Progenitor. On the other hand God, throughout the history of Israel, sought to steer men toward salvation by preparing them gradually to receive the Promised Messiah, the true Word of God, became incarnate of the Virgin Mary and the Holy Ghost—therefore outside the corrupt inheritance of Adam—triumphed over the Devil on the Cross, rose again on the third day, and has given back to mankind access to life.

It goes without saying that these fundamental mysteries of the Christian faith are the very essence of true doctrine and have their consequences for Christian spirituality. Doctrinal differences will necessarily entail certain variations in spiritual emphasis. Thus, the Christian East has remained a stranger to the juridical conceptions of salvation which have been dominant in the West since medieval times (the doctrines of the "merits" of Jesus Christ and indulgences) and which have so profoundly affected Western spirituality. The doctrine of original sin, moreover, as the Greek Fathers understood it, excludes the dogma of the Immaculate Conception of Mary in the form in which this was proclaimed by Pope Pius IX in 1854.[11] This dogma assumes that original sin consists of a "sin" committed "in Adam" and meriting punishment, and that the Virgin Mary could not have any share in this, for, from the moment of her conception, she was chosen and purified in view of the divine maternity. The choice that was made of her for this end is, in fact, irreconcilable with the divine anger

11. "We declare . . . that the doctrine which holds that the most blessed Virgin Mary at the first instant of her conception, by a singular grace and privilege of Almighty God, in virtue of the merits of Christ Jesus, Savior of the human race, was preserved immaculate from all stain of original sin, has been revealed by God . . . " (text in Denziger, *Enchiridion Symbolorum*, no. 1641).

associated with sin. But this reasoning no longer holds good if we adopt another interpretation of original sin. According to Orthodox tradition, slavery to the Devil, mortality, and corruption, transmitted by way of natural heredity, were the consequences of Adam's sin. The Virgin Mary was of course holy and pure from her conception, but she was born of Joachim and Anna in the same way that all other men have been born, and like them she was mortal: Adam's legacy was not passed over except in the case of her divine Son, who was born of the Holy Spirit. The Byzantine liturgy is certainly far from sparing its praise of the "Mother of God": it recognizes her exceptional role in salvation—by her *fiat* to the Archangel, Mary the New Eve, is the origin of the new human race which shares in the life of God—and also extols the corporal glorification of the *Theotokos* after her death; it sees in her the goal and perfection of all creation, ready at last to receive the Savior—but it is Jesus Christ, and not Mary, whom the Church adores as the Prince of Life, Savior and Redeemer, and it is he alone who benefited from an Immaculate Conception in her womb. Mary is the Mother of God, the one who, in the name of all mankind, received God the Redeemer.

Thus, in spite of the opposition of Orthodox theologians to the Roman dogma of the Immaculate Conception and their reservations regarding the new dogma of the Assumption of Mary—to the extent that this *could* imply that Mary did not die because of her Immaculate Conception—in spite of these differences, I say, which basically do not concern Mary herself but the doctrines of original sin and the Redemption,[12] East and West vie with each other in extolling the virtues and grace of her "whom all generations shall call blessed."

The Redemption which God granted in Jesus Christ is available to us through the Church and by means of the Church: both the whole

12. The Orthodox point of view in relation to these problems has been well stated by G. Florovsky and V. Lossky in the articles which they contributed to *The Mother of God*, ed. by E. L. Mascall (London: Dacre Press, 1949). For the doctrine of the Byzantine theologians, see our *Study of Gregory Palamas*.

corporate and personal life of each Christian is thus determined by the historical fact of the death and resurrection of Christ. We share in this resurrection in baptism and we "commemorate" it in the Eucharist. Finally, it determines our rule of prayer.

We mentioned above the very important part played by the liturgy in the life of the Orthodox Church, a living, drama-filled liturgy, which has served as a unique source of inspiration for theological thought and a last refuge for the faithful during particularly difficult periods, and has even revealed itself capable of keeping alive the essential truths of the Christian faith. Regardless of the age in which he lives or his status in life, when the Orthodox Christian enters a church he feels instinctively that he is in the presence of heaven, that the Kingdom of God is already here; he knows that Christ is there in the spiritual communion of his Body and Blood, in the Gospel read by the priest, and in the prayers of the Church.

This sacramental conception of the Christian life has been evident in Orthodox spirituality from the beginning and pervades it. Extreme tendencies toward an individualistic, personal form of piety all find themselves integrated in a coherent whole as a result of this conception, which does not regard personal forms of piety as something opposed to the corporate liturgy. This is especially true of hesychasm, a mystical movement which goes back to the Desert Fathers and which has played such an important part informing the spiritual tradition of the Christian East. It was actually in connection with the theological controversies over the question of hesychasm in the fourteenth century that the Orthodox Church came to define its doctrine on grace and its conception of the relations between God and man. These doctrinal definitions therefore gave a permanent and lasting value to a spiritual tradition, whose methods and practical features, by contrast, are only of relative significance.

It was in the deserts of Syria, Palestine and Egypt in the fourth century that we find the first hesychasts (from the Greek *hesychia*, "solitude," "contemplation"), the first exponents of continual prayer. Alone with God in their solitary habitations, the Christian hermits saw in St. Paul's commandment: "Pray without ceasing" (1 Thess 5:17) the most effective way for remaining in direct contact with the grace of Redemption. Some of them were accustomed to recite the Psalter in an endless round, thus inspiring the *lectio continua* of the Psalter in our liturgical offices. Others were devoted to a monologic or pure form of prayer consisting of the constant repetition of a short prayer stressing the Divine Name. Had not the Old Testament revealed that a more than ordinary significance was to be attached to the Divine Name? Did the Bible not teach that we must constantly "glorify the Name of the Lord" and did Christ not send his disciples to baptize people "in the Name of the Father and the Son and the Holy Spirit"? The perpetual invocation of God's Name was the most appropriate means for monks to communicate with the Divine. The form of monologic prayer often varied—sometimes it consisted of a simple *Kyrie eleison* (Lord, have mercy)—but the essence of practice was the continual repetition of a set formula.

Occasionally, the earliest doctors of hesychasm, and especially Evagrius of Pontus († c. 400), a great ascetic who had studied Origen and neo-Platonism, were inclined to envisage prayer as a means of dematerializing the self in order to attain to the world of the mind, as the "highest intellection of the intellect," as an ascension of "the immaterial toward the Immaterial." In part it was a question of mere terminology. The Greek Fathers were fond of expressing Christian truths in the language of the day and this language was permeated with the conceptions of Hellenism. But sometimes the Greek spirit also got the upper hand over Biblical doctrine, particularly in the matter of anthropology. The Bible never taught that man is a spirit imprisoned in matter, like Plato. The Word became flesh in order to save all mankind, the whole of mankind, and it should be the aim of Christian spirituality therefore to realize this salvation in its totality. Christian prayer, which Evagrius tended to conceive of as a kind of de-materialization and described without any reference to Christ, God incarnate, ought to bring the *entire man* face to face with God. Gradually these Origenist and Evagrian distortions were corrected by ecclesiastical tradition. A work by an anonymous author of the fifth century, who hid his true identity under the name of St. Macarius of Egypt, and many other works by spiritual writers of the time, were instrumental in bringing this about.

With St. Diadochus of Photice (fifth century) and St. John Climacus (†650) the "intellectual" prayer of Evagrius has been transformed into the "prayer of Jesus." Jesus henceforth will be the Divine Name incessantly invoked by ascetics, and Christ, the God become man, will be regarded as the sole mediator between the created world and the Divine. Their prayer will no longer be a flight from matter but a communion with God in soul and body. The divine grace they will seek will transfigure both the soul and the flesh, regarded as bound together in the New Life and illuminated by the uncreated divine light.

"The hesychast," wrote St. John Climacus in his *Ladder of Paradise,* "is he who strives to confine the Incorporeal into his bodily house . . . Let the remembrance of Jesus be present with each breath; then you will know the value of solitude."[13] And St. Maximus the Confessor (†662) thus describes the deification which is sought by every Christian, and especially by every hesychast:

> Man becomes God by deification, thereby he experiences a complete abandonment of all that belongs to him by nature . . . because the grace of the Spirit triumphs in him and because God alone, manifestly, acts in him. Thus God, and those who are worthy of God, henceforth have only one and the same activity in all things.[14]

The divine vision granted to mystics in deification was identified by St. Gregory of Nyssa (fourth century) and St. Maximus with

---

13. *Ladder of Paradise, Twenty-Seventh Step,* tr. by Lazarus Moore (London, 1959), pp. 237, 246.

14. *Ambigua,* PG 91.1076BC. On St. Maximus, see P. Sherwood, *The Early Ambigua of St. Maximus the Confessor* (Rome, 1955), and, by the same author, translation and commentary on works of Maximus, in *Ancient Christian Writers,* no. 21.

the vision of Moses on Mount Sinai and with the divine light that was witnessed by the Apostles on Mount Tabor when Christ was transfigured.

Later spiritual writers will place even more emphasis upon the bond between the Prayer of Jesus the mysticism of deification, and the sacramental life of the Christian community. St. Symeon the New Theologian, the great Byzantine mystic of the eleventh century, found the essential inspiration for his experience of the divine in the Eucharist: his hymns and prayers, both before and after Communion, are some of the most realistic and spiritually moving in the Byzantine *Euchologion*. In the thirteenth and fourteenth centuries the hesychast revival coincided with a new interest at Byzantium in the sacramental life of the Church. The best-known example of this tendency is Nicholas Cabasilas, whose *Life in Christ*—a comprehensive view of the spiritual life—is in the form of a commentary on the sacraments of baptism, chrismation (confirmation), and the Holy Eucharist. Thus, the Orthodox hesychasts of this period thought of the Prayer of Jesus not as a subjective and emotional way of communicating with God, but as a method by which they could make more effective, in themselves, the gifts received through the sacraments.

During this period also the practice of saying the Prayer of Jesus according to a particular method began to be widely followed. This consisted of repeating the words of the short prayer "Lord Jesus Christ, Son, of God, have mercy on me" in rhythm with one's breathing while at the same time concentrating the mind of the *region of the heart*, regarded as being the focal point for the whole psycho-physiological nature of man.

Though attacked by Barlaam the Calabrian (†1350), a philosopher of both skeptical and Platonizing tendencies, the hesychast method of prayer was defended in the fourteenth century by the great theologian and monk of Athos, who later became archbishop of Thessalonica, St. Gregory Palamas (†1359). It was the

merit of Palamas to have seen clearly the connection between the
Orthodox doctrine of God, the deification which the mystics
sought to achieve in their mystical experiences, the hesychast
method of prayer, and the sacramental life of the Church. Without attempting to construct a doctrinal *summa*, he assigned to
each one of these elements its proper place. God, essentially
unsharable and transcendent, is also a living God who communicates Himself voluntarily through His acts: He thus becomes
available not merely to knowledge, but sharable or communica-
ble, because of the hypostatic union of divinity and humanity in
Jesus Christ. Even then, however, He remains transcendent, since
this is His nature: participation in His Being or deification is only
possible to the extent that He wills it and in accordance with His
energies or acts. This participation is total in Jesus Christ, since
the Person of the Word incarnate is the source of all the divine
operations. The distinction established here between transcendent
essence and "energies" of course involves a philosophical antin-
omy, but is God subject to the limitations of our intellect? This
"deification" in Jesus Christ is available to us through baptism and
the Eucharist: the Incarnate Word communicates to us the divine
life and transforms our whole being from inside. Henceforth, "the
Kingdom of God is within us." This "within us" does not signify
necessarily "in the mind" or "in the soul," for human nature is
indivisible and shares as a whole in God. Our body therefore, as
well as our mind and soul, shares in this process through fasting,
prayer, and various acts which make up the duties of the Christian
in his search for the Kingdom of God, and it can also receive, as
of now, the first fruits of glory: does the Church not venerate the
corporeal remains of the saints after their death, and during their
life do the saints not perform miracles which attest the transfiguration already achieved?[15]

15. We have examined the doctrine of Palamas in some detail in our *Study of Gregory
Palamas*, and a more rapid sketch of the hesychast tradition, both before and after
the fourteenth century, may be found in *Saint Grégoire Palamas et la mystique*

Finally, it is the special task of Eastern Orthodox spirituality to make known to us the presence of God in history, and to make this known not only in words but also by providing living examples of God's power. God is henceforth present in the Church not only in His written Word, but in the reality of the sacraments and in the gifts of the Spirit, evident in His saints, which are available likewise to all Christians who are determined to live in accordance with their baptismal promises. The saints of the Church—from St. Paul who was "raised to the third heaven" to St. Seraphim of Sarov whose face was illumined by a divine light—are all witnesses of this New Life granted to man which transfigures matter itself. Apostles, bishops, martyrs, missionaries, monks or simple laymen: wherever God is pleased to find them, the saints are the true agents of the Kingdom of God in the world.

In the history of the Orthodox Church hesychast mysticism has proved to be the most traditional way in which this communion with God, which constitutes the very essence of the Christian life, has expressed itself. Because of its simplicity and uncomplicated nature of the Prayer of Jesus became a very popular form of spiritual devotion and was widespread not only among the monks but also among the laity. Its precise definition by great theologians saved it from degenerating into a purely individualistic form of piety. Only in the Church, in the communion of saints, is the sacramental life of the Christian community, can the mystical experience of the individual have, in reality, a truly Christian meaning. Here also is found the ultimate criterion for all spirituality. The Church does not canonize any particular form or method of devotion, but merely sanctions the holiness of those who have been able to express the reality of the Kingdom of God in their lives and in their words.

orthodoxe, Coll. *"Maîtres Spirituels,"* no. 20 (Paris, 1959). The chief work of Palamas, his *Triads for the Defense of the Holy Hesychasts,* has been edited by us with a complete translation in French, in the series *Specilegium Sacrum Lovaniense,* nos. 30-31 (Louvain, 1959), 2 vols.

Chapter 10

ORTHODOX VIEW OF THE CHURCH

Today more than ever the important topic of discussion among the various separate denominations which make up the Christian world is the nature of the church, and we can truthfully say that *inside* each one of the great confessions the ecclesiological problem is far from having been finally settled. Under Pope John XXIII, the Roman Catholic Church is now suddenly becoming aware of the fact that the incomplete and rather hastily arrived at definitions of the First Vatican Council in 1870 did not provide it with a really balanced and coherent theology of the Church. It intends, therefore, to develop its own doctrine on church unity by clarifying it. Protestants, owing to the remarkable new interest in Biblical theology and the success of the ecumenical movement, have to a large extent abandoned their former aversion to all forms of ecclesiology; without denying any of the principles of the Reformation, they are again discovering the importance of the problem of the Church from the double viewpoint of Tradition and sacramental life. The Orthodox, finally, confronted by entirely new historical situations and obliged to solve problems that were never faced by Byzantium, have been compelled to reformulate their Tradition and readjust the attitudes of the past. It is in response to this new and somewhat "fluid" situation that we shall attempt to outline here some of the essential traits of an Orthodox approach to the ecclesiological problem. The reader will probably have guessed what some of these traits are from our chapters on the history of the Church and Orthodox spirituality. We shall therefore content ourselves here with pointing out the permanent elements in the Orthodox position with regard to the great debate on ecumenism.

Curiously enough, the ecclesiological problem was never formally posed as a real issue in the medieval debate between Constantinople and Rome. It was the question of the *filioque,* and later that of purgatory and the invocation of the Holy Spirit in the liturgy, or even such questions of an altogether secondary nature as the use of unleavened bread (azymes) in the Western mass, or fasting on Saturdays, which claimed the attention of theologians and controversialists. Some modern theologians like V. Lossky emphasize that there is an intrinsic connection between the Latin doctrine of the Trinity and Roman ecclesiology, but this connection was certainly not clearly perceived or realized in the Middle Ages. In fact, as we have seen, it was the very absence of any common ecclesiological factor which led to the schism. When difficulties arose between East and West, one side appealed to the authority of Tradition and the councils, while the other appealed to the authority of the Successor of St. Peter. For a long time—until the capture of Constantinople by the Crusaders in 1204—the Byzantines did not really understand, or did not wish to understand, the new Roman attitude toward the Church, and in their discussion with Latins avoided touching on this point directly. It was only in 1204, when Innocent III appointed a Venetian, Thomas Morosini, to the see of St. John Chrysostom after the sack of Constantinople, that Byzantine theologians began to discuss seriously the origin of the power which the popes claimed to have.

Their criticism of the Roman position was concerned not so much with the person of the Apostle Peter himself or his position among the Twelve and in the primitive Church, as with the nature of his *succession.* Byzantium did not see why the Church of Rome should be able to claim the *exclusive* right to this succession, when the New Testament furnishes no information about the ministry of Peter in Rome. Could not Antioch, and particularly Jerusalem, where Peter played a key role according to the book of Acts, claim, more logically than Rome, to be the "see of Peter"? The Byzantines recognized, of course, a universal primacy in the Roman Church, but this primacy, according to them, did not have its unique origin in the fact of Peter's death in Rome, but rather in a whole collection of factors of which the chief were that Rome was a church "very great, very ancient, and known to all," as St. Irenaeus put it.[1] and because it had the tombs of the two leaders (*coryphaei*) of the Apostles, Peter and Paul, but above all, because it was the capital of the Empire. The famous Canon 28 of the ecumenical council of Chalcedon insists on this latter point.[2] In other words, the Roman primacy was not an exclusive and divine privilege, a power which was possessed by the bishop of Rome by virtue of an express commandment of the Lord, but a *de facto* authority which the Church had formally recognized by the voice of its councils. It went without saying that the pope could not, under such conditions, enjoy any privilege of infallibility. If his presence or that of his legates was considered necessary for a council to be considered "ecumenical," that is to day, truly representative of the episcopate of the whole Empire—the presence of the other great churches was also considered equally necessary—his opinion was never considered to be true *ex sese*. The Eastern churches could live for centuries outside the Roman communion without being unduly perturbed by the fact, and the sixth ecumenical council did not hesitate to condemn the memory of Pope Honorius I for having given support to the Monothelite heresy.

There could be no question therefore, in Byzantine opinion, of holding that the words of Christ, addressed to Peter: "Thou art Peter, and upon this rock I will build my Church" (Mt 16:18); "Feed my sheep" (Jn 21), etc., related exclusively to the bishops of Rome. This interpretation, generally emphasized in documents issued by the Roman Church from the third century, is not found in any Eastern or Western patristic commentary on the Scriptures, for the Fathers saw in these words, essentially, a recognition by Christ of the fact that Peter had confessed the divine nature of the Son of God on the road to Caesarea Philippi: Peter is declared to

---

1 *Against the Heresies*, 3,2.

2 See our article on "La primauté romaine dans la tradition canonique jusqu'au concile de Chalcedoine," in the periodical *Istina*, no. 4 (1957), pp. 463-82.

be the rock of the Church *to the extent* that he confesses this faith. And all those who imitate Peter and make the same confession likewise inherit the promise. It is on them, on all believers, that the Church is built. This general interpretation of the passage, which we find in Origen and many of the Fathers, received an ecclesiological corrective, however, in the Church's doctrine on the nature of the episcopate, for all bishops are invested with the special charisma to teach. Their special function is to proclaim the true faith. They are therefore *ex officio* the successors of Peter. This conception of the Petrine succession which we find clearly expressed in St. Cyprian of Carthage (third century) and which occurs again and again in the history of theology, will be taken up by Byzantine theologians.

"Well, then" writes Nilus Cabasilas in the fourteenth century,

> is the pope not a successor of Peter at all? He is, but only *as a bishop* . . . For Peter is an Apostle and the head of the Apostles, but the pope is neither an Apostle (for the Apostles did not ordain other Apostles, but pastors and teachers), nor much less the Coryphaeus (leader) of the Apostles. Peter is the teacher of the whole world, whereas the pope is the bishop of Rome. Peter could have ordained a bishop in Antioch, another in Alexandria, and another elsewhere but the bishop of Rome does not do so . . . [3]

We could multiply texts and quotations proving clearly that the controversy between East and West was due basically to profoundly different attitudes toward the Church. These differences were concerned with the nature of *authority* in the Church, and essentially with the nature of the Church itself.[4]

In the eyes of the East, the Church was above all a communion in which God is present *sacramentally*: the sacrament is, in effect, the way in which the death and resurrection of the Lord are

3 PG 149.704 C, D.

4 For the Orthodox attitude toward the Roman primacy, see *St. Vladimir's Seminary Quarterly*, vol. 4, nos. 2-3 (1960), a special issue devoted to *Primacy and Primacies in the Orthodox Church*.

"commemorated" and by which his Second Coming is pro-claimed and anticipated. Now the *fullness* of this reality—hence also the fullness of truth and fullness of the magisterium—is present in every local church, in every Christian community gathered around the eucharistic Table and having a bishop at its head, the successor of Peter and the other Apostles. For the bishop is not a successor of any particular Apostle, but of all, and it matters little whether his church has been founded by John, Paul or Peter, or whether it is of more recent and humbler origin.[5] His function is to teach in accordance with the common teaching of the apostolic college, of which Peter was the spokesman; he occupies the place of the Lord at the eucharistic Table; and he is the "image of God" in the church over which he presides, to use an expression of St. Ignatius of Antioch (about 100 AD). These episcopal functions are essentially the *same*, whether at Rome, Constantinople or Moscow, and God could not have intended to grant one Church special privileges in this respect, since he gave the plenitude of power to *all.*

The local churches, however, are not mere isolated units living in separation from each other: they are united by the *identity* of their faith and their witness to the truth. This identity is mani-fested particularly when episcopal consecrations are held, neces-sarily attended by several bishops. To give greater effectiveness to the witness of the churches and solve common problems, local councils or synods have been held from time to time since the third century, and gradually a certain order of precedence emerged among the

5 Several Fathers, particularly St. Irenaeus of Lyons, insist on the apostolic origin of certain churches in order to establish the orthodoxy of these churches as compared with the Gnostics. However, in the East, as Father F. Dvornik has recently shown in *The Idea of Apostolicity in Byzantium* (Cambridge, MA: Harvard University Press, 1958), apostolic sees never claimed to have any special authority as a result of the fact of being "apostolic": there were far too many of them in Asia Minor, Syria, Palestine and Greece for such pretensions to be taken seriously. The Church of Jerusalem, for example, until the fifth century, was subject to the metropolitan of Caesarea. In the West, on the other hand, the Church of Rome was the *only* church that could claim apostolic origin and no one disputed its prestige based on this fact.

various churches. This order includes a universal primacy—first that of Rome, then Constantinople—and also local primacies (metropolitans, today the heads of the autocephalous churches), but it is capable of further modifications, for it is not of an ontological nature, it does not restrict the fundamental identity of the local churches, and it is subject to the formal condition that the one Orthodox faith must be confessed. A heretical primate would perforce lose all rights to the primacy.

We thus see where the root of the schism between East and West lies. In the West, the papacy, as the result of a long development over the centuries, now possesses, according to the Vatican definitions of 1870, both a doctrinal infallibility and an "immediate" jurisdiction over all the faithful. The bishop of Rome therefore is the visible criterion of Truth and the unique head of the universal Church, without however possessing any sacramental powers different from those of other bishops. In the Orthodox Church, on the other hand, no power can exist by divine right outside and above the local eucharistic community, which corresponds today to what we call the diocese. The relations between bishops and the order of precedence between them are governed by the canons and are not something absolute and unchangeable. There does not exist, therefore, any visible criterion of Truth, apart from the *consensus* of the Church, the normal organ of which is the ecumenical council. But this council, as we have seen above, is not an authority *ex sese*, outside and above the local churches; it is merely the expression and witness of their accord. A council which considers itself formally "ecumenical" may even be rejected by the Church (examples: Ephesus in 449, Florence in 1438). The permanence of Truth in the Church is thus a fact of a supernatural order, similar in every respect to the nature of the sacrament. It can be detected by religious experience, but is not amenable to rational explanation or capable of being subjected to legal norms.

The unity of the Church is, above all, a unity in faith and not an administrative unity. Administrative unity can actually only be an expression of a common allegiance to the Truth. If the unity of faith could have been determined by some visible, permanent organ, the doctrinal disputes of the earliest centuries and the councils and controversies of the time of the Fathers would have no meaning. Today likewise, the reunion with the Church of the churches separated from it presupposes, necessarily and absolutely, their agreement with it in the faith.

Between Rome and the Orthodox Church, therefore, any future dialogue must necessarily hinge on the role still left in Roman ecclesiology for the local church and the episcopate. But if the pope is the final judge in doctrinal matters and exercises an "immediate" jurisdiction over each and very one of the Catholic faithful, can the bishops be anything else than his local vicars? In spite of the enormous obstacle to mutual understanding created by the Vatican Council, there appears to be hope now that a supplementary statement can be made on this point, clarifying the definitions of 1870. The Orthodox, for their part, should reflect more seriously than they have done on the possible forms which the *common* witness could and should take, and especially on the part to be played in this witness by the bishop who is *primus inter pares*. East and West are still united by too long and too common a Biblical and patristic tradition for a discussion not to be possible on this as well as on other points.

❖   ❖   ❖

On numerous occasions since the sixteenth century the Orthodox have had occasion to define their position with respect to Protestantism. However, they have sometimes done this rather ineptly without fully knowing who their correspondents were and using Roman Catholic arguments against them, as when the Calvinist *Confession* of Loukaris was condemned. Today a new fact of fundamental importance in the history of Christianity has profoundly altered the outlook of Protestantism, namely the ecumenical movement.[6]

Protestant nineteenth-century missionaries first became fully aware of the tremendous scandal being caused for non-Christians by the divisions among Christians. While preaching the same Christ, they were interpreting his teaching in different ways, were refusing to communicate from the same Table, were bitter rivals in missionary countries, and were transplanting to Africa and Asia the quarrels and prejudices of sixteenth-century Europe. It did not take the missionaries very long to become aware of these facts. This discovery led men of good will, in Europe an America, to intensify their search for Christian unity, to found world-wide interconfessional youth organizations, and finally to organize the first "ecumenical" conferences. The two trends which made up the movement—one called *Life and Work*, representing a more practical type of Christianity, the other, *Faith and Order*, more concerned with theological implications—were finally merged in the single *ecumenical movement*. Between the two world wars the movement was largely a matter of individual participation. The theologians and prelates who took part did so on their own responsibility and did not engage their churches. But in 1948, at the Amsterdam Conference, a World Council of *Churches* was formally inaugurated. Henceforth the churches themselves agreed to take part in the Council and participate in all its activities through their official representatives.

As defined by the Amsterdam Conference, the nature and goal of the Council was to be an "instrument in the service of the churches, by means of which they can bear witness together in areas requiring unity of action." It was clearly specified, moreover, that the decisions whether of the General Assembly or of any of the organs of the council were not to prejudice the individual

---

6 See R. Rouse and S. Neil, *A History of the Ecumenical Movement, 1517-1948* (London: S.P.C.K., 1954).

member churches, who were free to accept or reject them. The promoters of the movement emphasized repeatedly that it was not their intention to create a sort of super-Church or to impose a centralized organization on the member churches. Under these conditions 153 churches agrees at Amsterdam to take part in the World Council and to bear witness in this way to their common faith in "Jesus Christ, as God and Savior."

The attitude of the Orthodox Church toward the ecumenical movement from the very beginning, and then later toward the World Council of Churches, was laid down in a long series of conferences and contacts between Orthodox and Protestant theologians in the nineteenth century.[7] Orthodox representatives have regularly taken part in the great conferences since 1910, and in 1920 the ecumenical patriarch published an encyclical addressed "to the Churches of Christ throughout the world," urging them to show greater understanding for each other and to cooperate more fully in the practical sphere. Thus, paradoxically, the First See of Orthodoxy assumed the leadership of Orthodox participation in the ecumenical movement by stressing the *Life and Work* aspect of the latter rather than the usefulness of theological discussions with the West. The other Orthodox churches were much more reserved and prudent in their attitude, and remain so to this day. The majority of them, however, were represented at the ecumenical conferences of Stockholm (1925), Lausanne (1927), Oxford (1937), Edinburgh (1937), and Utrecht (1938). The Russian Church also was present—though it was not "represented"—in the person of outstanding theologians of the emigration who took a leading part in the discussions.

As a result of the Second World War, three new factors have profoundly modified the status of the problem so far as Orthodox participation in the ecumenical movement is concerned: the es-

---

7 See the remarkable well-documented study of G. Florovsky on this subject, "Orthodox Ecumenism in the 19th Century," in *St. Vladimir's Seminary Quarterly*, vol. 4, nos. 3-4.

tablishment of communist regimes in the Orthodox countries of Eastern Europe, with the single exception of Greece; the restoration of the patriarchate of Moscow; and the establishment of the World Council of Churches. Reasons both of a political and a religious nature, the relative importance of which it is difficult to assess, presented Orthodox delegates, until the New Delhi Assembly of 1961, from taking part in the sessions of the Council in sufficient numbers. While political factors may be largely responsible in the case of churches behind the Iron Curtain, which include over 90 percent of all Orthodox, this cannot be the only cause, for Protestant churches from Czechoslovakia and Hungary have never missed an opportunity to take part in the common work. The rather violent opposition among certain circles, to participation in the Council by Orthodox Churches in countries which have maintained their political ties to the West, shows that such participation involves crucial problems of a spiritual and theological nature for the Orthodox Church.

Only the churches of Constantinople, Greece and Cyprus were represented at Amsterdam in 1948 and agreed to take part in the World Council. Some months later, a conference of the churches of Russia, Serbia, Romania, Bulgaria, Poland, Albania an Czechoslovakia, in the presence of a delegate of the patriarch of Antioch who signed the acts on behalf of the two Oriental patriarchates (Antioch and Alexandria), met in Moscow and declared that the Amsterdam Conference had no other purpose than to "create a new ecumenical Church," that insufficient attention was paid to dogmatic problems in its program, while, on the contrary, political or "imperialist" interests were predominant. The churches meeting at Moscow therefore refused to send representatives.

From 1948, the ecumenical patriarchate of Constantinople was practically the only Orthodox church to take an active part in the Council. A wait-and-see attitude was adopted by the other Oriental patriarchates, which sent no delegates to the sessions until the Central Committee at Rhodes in 1959. A violent controversy raged in Greece between the adversaries and partisans of participation and the Greek hierarchy—in the main hostile to participation—decreed at the beginning of 1959 that only lay theologians who could not engage the Church would be allowed to represent the Greek Church at the ecumenical assemblies in the future. Moreover, they were forbidden to discuss purely dogmatic questions.[8]

Orthodox reservations with regard to the World Council are based primarily on the fear, conscious or otherwise, that the Orthodox Church may find itself bound by an institution which in fact does not represent it. The constitution of the Council and repeated by its leaders makes it perfectly clear that the member churches remain entirely free, doctrinally and administratively. Nevertheless, the common work of the Council is constantly going forward—is this not precisely the aim of the Council?—in the theological field, as well as in those of the missions, social work, and international affairs. But the Orthodox only take a very small part in this work, since they are represented only by a handful of delegates at the Assemblies and in the various branches of the organization of the Council. consequently they naturally feel that they are taking part in an enterprise which they do not control and which is dominated by Protestant thinking. If the Orthodox Church were in a position to make its weight felt in the work of the Council, it is likely that this situation would change considerably. But this is not the only problem.

It is undeniable that Orthodox *ecclesiology* or its attitude toward the Church means that it cannot participate in the work of the Council on the same basis as the other communions that have merged from the Reformation. Orthodox and Protestants simply do not see the same thing in the World Council of Churches.

8 At Rhodes in 1959 no bishop under the jurisdiction of the Holy Synod at Athens took part in the official discussions of the Committee.

Protestants, for whom the Church remains essentially "a communion of forgiven sinners," generally hold that the historical divisions among Christians are divisions in the *Church itself.* The unity of the Church mentioned in the Creed is not realized in any one of the Christian confessions, but all are seeking it. This is precisely what the aim of the World Council should be. Thanks to it, the Church is now drawing nearer to unity and in doing so will gradually become *more fully* the Church. It will "repent" for the sin against unity of which it has been guilty and will thus achieve greater fidelity to God's Word. Many Protestant leaders insist again and again in their discussions of the ecumenical issue that it is necessary for the "churches" to abandon their exclusive dogmatism and emphasis on doctrinal obstacles. This attitude is clearly stated in numerous documents approved by the Protestant majority in the Assemblies of the World Council. "Thus we may speak," declares the Report of Section I of the Assembly of Evanston (1954), "of the oneness of the Church on its earthly pilgrimage as a growth from its unity, as given, to its unity, as fully manifested. In this way we may think of the Church in the same way as we are able to think of the individual believer, who may be said at one and the same time to be both a justified man and a sinner (*simul justus et peccator*)..."

It is obvious that a theology of this kind which regards the Church as both "justified and a sinner" cannot be acceptable to the Orthodox Church: for the mystery of the Church consists precisely in the fact that sinners, coming together, form the *infallible Church.* They constitute the Body of Christ, the Temple of the Holy Spirit, and the Column and Foundation of Truth. No analogy can possibly be drawn between the individual member, who is a sinner, and the Church, the Body of Christ. The Protestant thesis appears to the Orthodox to amount to a negation of the full and real presence of Christ in his Church, as a repudiation of the promises which he made to his disciples: "When he will come, the Spirit of Truth, he will guide you in all truth" (Jn

16:13). This "all truth" is therefore present in the visible Church, which is one, holy, catholic, and apostolic, and from which other churches are separated. Christian unity is a unity with Christ in the Holy Spirit, and not a unity among men which has been lost at some time in the past. The unity belongs to the One Church, which cannot be divided by human controversies. Men cannot divide God and his Truth, and then later restore them to unity. They may leave them, however, and then return. It is to a return of this kind that the Orthodox Church summons all Christians: a return to the faith of the Fathers and Apostles, which she is conscious of having preserved in its fullness. From this point of view the World Council is therefore primarily a meeting place, a place for witness, for discussion, and eventually for practical collaboration. Orthodox participation does not mean that the Orthodox *Church*, as a divine reality in history, can add anything essential to what it already possesses, but it does mean that the Orthodox as *individuals*—imperfect sinners though they may be—can both help to point out to other Christians the true road to unity and also learn from them how to make better use of the divine gift which they alone possess in its entirely, by being members of the One Church.

This is the task to which the Orthodox delegates are devoting themselves in the ecumenical assemblies—few in number and inadequately prepared as they often are—and it was owing to their efforts that the Toronto Declaration was passed by the Central Committee of the Council (1950), making possible, by its negative language, the continued presence of Orthodox delegates on the Committee:

> The World Council cannot and should not be based on any particular conception of the Church. It does not prejudge the ecclesiological problem in advance . . . Membership in the World Council of Churches does not imply that a Church treats its own conception of the Church as merely relative . . . Membership does not imply that each Church must regard the other member Churches as Churches in the full sense of the word . . .

These conditions, expressed in a language that is absolutely clear, have made possible continued Orthodox participation in the ecumenical *fellowship* without having to renounce, or seem to renounce, their consciousness of being the only true Church and without having to modify their basic attitude toward the other Christian communions. This attitude, however, does not prevent the other member churches from developing an ecumenical theology on their own account. This is precisely what happened, as shown by the Report of the Evanston Assembly, which we have just been quoting. This document was worded in such a way, however, that the Orthodox delegates felt unable to support it and published a separate statement of their own on Section I:

> We believe that the return of the communions to the faith of the ancient, united and indivisible Church of the seven ecumenical councils, namely, to the pure and unchanged and common heritage of the forefathers of all divided Christians shall alone produce the desired reunion of all separated Christians for, only the unity and fellowship of Christians in a common faith shall have as a necessary result their fellowship in the sacraments and their indissoluble unity in love, as members of one and the same body of the One Church of Christ . . . We are bound to declare our profound conviction that the Holy Orthodox Church alone has preserved in full and intact "the faith once delivered unto the saints." It is not because of our human merit, but because it pleases God to preserve "his treasure in earthen vessels, that the excellency of the power may be of God" (2 Cor 4:7).

From the Orthodox point of view, therefore, Christian ecumenism cannot mean a search for unity at any price of the basis of a minimum common denominator: it is the *fullness of truth* that will unite Christians, for Christ is fullness and he can never abandon his Church. The presence of Orthodox representatives in the ecumenical movement is a direct consequence of the universal command of the Lord that we should love our brethren, particularly all those who call themselves Christians, but this love, coming from God as it does, cannot be a love without truth. The Son of God made himself *visible* in the course of history, he became man and founded on earth a *visible* communion, which was to possess sacramentally the fullness of his redemptive grace. This fullness is present in each community which professes the truth faith. In the eyes of the Orthodox, "certain fundamental elements which make up the reality of the fullness of the Church are lacking in the separated communions" (Declaration of the Orthodox Delegation at Evanston): these elements must therefore be restored. The Protestant conception of the unity and fullness of the Church as either something of an invisible nature or belonging to an eschatological future seems, to Orthodox Christians, to amount to a denial of the reality of salvation, as a repudiation of that which God himself has given us.

The Orthodox representatives have always been free to express these views clearly in the Assemblies of the World Council. But they have been present there in too few numbers, up until now, to be able to carry on an effective discussion with the Protestant majority. To be more fruitful and to be able to exercise some influence on the course of the discussion, they ought to participate more effectively and be present in greater numbers. If this is not done in the near future, it is certain that the Protestant majority in the Council, by a process of internal logic, will lead the organization more and more in a direction incompatible with Orthodox principles[9] and make their presence impossible. This issuance of separate, negative statements, and spasmodic collaboration in specialized areas, particularly those relating to material aid, do not constitute an adequate witness for the Orthodox Church. The full participation of the Moscow patriarchate and of the other Eastern European Orthodox Churches, which became a reality since New Delhi (1961), will certainly ensure a much more efficient Orthodox witness in the Council. One must simply pray and hope that political pressures and conflicts will not prevent

9 See on this subject A. Schmemann, "Orthodox Agony in the World Council," in *Christianity Today*, vol. 2 (January 8, 1958).

them from expressing the essential meaning of the Orthodox message.

Since we do not have the space to be able to deal with all aspects of Orthodox ecclesiology *systematically* and in detail, we have confined ourselves to a discussion of the Orthodox position with respect to Western Christianity and have emphasized recent developments. The reader can now see how this position differs from the others and what its peculiar features are. As opposed to Protestantism and Roman Catholicism, the Orthodox Church claims to be the true Church of Christ from which Western Christians have separated. Its claims are as exclusive and categorical as those of Rome, but they are put forth in the name of a different conception of the Church. The historic development of the papacy culminating in the proclamation of the Vatican dogma has conferred on Roman Catholicism a monolithic structure and given it a permanent criterion of Truth, which is nevertheless compatible with a great deal of doctrinal and liturgical divergence. Rome is more anxious that all Christians accept the existence of a final criterion than a particular doctrinal system. But the Orthodox Church does not claim to possess any infallible and permanent criterion of Truth or any monolithic structure: it sees unity in a communion of faith, of which the Church itself—or rather the Holy Spirit always dwelling in the Church—is the unique judge. The Spirit of Truth dwells in the communion of the faithful who are united by the bond of charity, and while he normally speaks through those who have the charisma to teach, namely, the bishops, he belongs properly to the Church as a Body. This Body is totally present everywhere that the Eucharist is celebrated, in every local church, and no authority, apart from that of the Spirit, can possibly impose itself on the people of God united in Jesus Christ. The Christian is by definition free, free with a *true* liberty which permits him to accept the Truth which God reveals to him. He is therefore also *responsible* for this Truth: he finds it and preserves it in the Church, in the communion of

the Spirit, in a reasonable obedience to the authorities of the
Church (*magisterium*), and in the unity of love with his brethren.[10]

This freedom the Orthodox enjoys in his relations with God
makes it possible for him to carry on a dialogue with all Christians, Protestants or Catholics, and to appeal to his separated
brethren to accept, not some external "criterion"—Rome or *sola
scriptura*—but the living Truth as experienced in a liturgical communion and in the Church as the Temple of the Holy Spirit. On
the other hand, the great responsibility which he feels has been
placed on his own shoulders makes him acutely aware of the
importance of all doctrinal questions. Not only will he never
consent to cast doubt on any of the dogmas of the Church, but he
even believes that any change in the rites of government of the
Church is a matter that personally concerns him, even when the
change is of a purely routine or trivial nature.

The "liberty of the children of God" is indeed a heavy burden
to bear at the present time, because it involves such a heavy
responsibility. And yet this liberty is one of the keys to Christian
ecclesiology. The Orthodox Church clings to this above all else,
and in doing so feels that it is defending the very mystery of God's
presence in the Christian communion.

---

10 This responsibility of all Christians for the truth is brought out by the Encyclical of
the Oriental patriarchs in 1848, as we have seen. The idea has been developed
particularly by Russian theologians in the nineteenth century. The most famous of
these, without question, was A. S. Khomiakov (see A. Gratieux, *A. S. Khomiakov*
[Paris: Éditions du Cerf, 1950], 2 vols.; cf. also J. S. Romanides, "Orthodox
Ecclesiology According to Alexis Khomiakov," in *The Greek Orthodox Theological
Review*, vol. 2, no. 1 [1956]). The same idea is echoed, on a different level, in
Dostoevsky's famous *Legend of the Grand Inquisitor*.

CONCLUSION

Our pages on the origin of the church in the brief account of Orthodox history and particularly the chapter on Orthodox doctrine and spirituality will help the reader to see that the essential element in the Orthodox message today is its emphasis upon a genuine "Catholic" tradition, catholicity being understood here in the broad sense with respect to truth, continuity, and fullness, rather than in a mere geographical sense.

It is a historical fact which no one can deny that the Christian East has remained aloof from the great changes which have occurred in the West as a result of papal centralization and the great Scholastic movement during the Middle Ages, the Reformation, and the Counter-Reformation. From the ninth to the fifteenth century Byzantium went on developing and living according to the great tradition of the Fathers, their theology, spirituality, and above all their sacramental conception of the Church. It deliberately refused to identify itself with any particular synthesis of philosophical thought and Revelation such as the Scholastic system, and preferred to remain faithful to patristic thought. Its theology, and particularly its doctrine on the sacraments and the Church, were never formulated in accordance with the dictates of a given philosophical system, and the constitution of the Orthodox Church was never thought of solely in terms of the laws by which a law-dominated institution was governed. Its God remained a living, acting God, the God of the Bible, the God of Abraham, Isaac, and Jacob; He was never transformed into the God of philosophers. As a matter of fact, the Church never provided itself with a complete system of canon law: the canons of those councils which it acknowledged as authentic were regarded merely as an expression of the Church's nature under certain concrete circumstances, a kind of "jurisprudence of the Holy Spirit," as it were, reflecting the eternal *order* of the Body of Christ. They were never transformed into a kind of juridical supergovernment and were never looked upon as a means by which to exercise an effective control over all members of the Church, centrally or from above, By defining the position of the Orthodox Church rather negatively and opposing it to Western Christianity in this way, it is not our intention to imply that the latter has *completely* transformed revealed doctrine into a philosophical theory or the constitution of the Church into a mere juridical system. We merely wish to point out that in its desire to bear witness to the Truth and do so effectively, the West has gone much further in these two directions than the East, and in so doing it has formulated a certain number of dogmas making any return to the past difficult. Therefore the ecumenical task of Orthodoxy, in its discussions with both Protestants and Catholics, should be to question the appropriateness of certain formulas handed down from the Latin Middle Ages and the period of the Counter-Reformation, without, however, giving the impression of wishing to deny the traditional doctrines which they are intended to express; and to urge Roman Catholics on the one hand fraternally to return to the common sources, and Protestants on the other to be more receptive to the idea of Tradition.

In order to play this role effectively, however, the Orthodox must do a bit of rethinking and reflecting themselves. If the truth which they are conscious of possessing is really Catholic truth, it must of course be valid for all men, all times, and all countries. It must be capable of supplying an answer to the very real problems raised by Western Christians during the centuries which have elapsed since the separation. It must face the challenge of the modern world. It order to make their message meaningful, the Orthodox must learn to live these problems *from inside*, not externally. It is not enough merely to conform outwardly to

Western customs or make a few liturgical adjustments; they must learn to discipline themselves spiritually; there must be an act of love as well as of humility. It is all too obvious that while the Church as a supernatural body always possesses the fullness of divine life and truth, individuals, groups, nations, and local churches fail to conform to this life and this truth in all respects. In this regard, what may be called historical Orthodoxy, that is, the various nations which formerly made up or still make up the Orthodox world, have much to ask forgiveness for. Granted their history has been a particularly tragic one. The Arab, Turkish and Mongol invasions and the recent martyrdom occasioned by the Russian Revolution have all been so many terrible disasters inter-rupting the course of development in the East. External factors of this kind largely explain, perhaps, the present weakness of Eastern Christianity. But there are also other weaknesses for which the Orthodox have only themselves to blame, in particular, the bane of excessive nationalism which has resulted in the harmful isola-tion of Orthodox churches from each other.

The future of the Orthodox Church and its spiritual influence is now clearly at stake, both in the communist-dominated coun-tries of the East and in the West, where Providence has led millions of the Orthodox and compelled them to bear witness to their faith.

In the communist-dominated countries, especially in Russia, there have been many martyrs on behalf of the faith during the terrible revolutionary period and more recently in the post-revolu-tionary years. The Russian Church has learned on the whole, rather quickly, to distinguish between the absolute values of religion and the relative values of politics, and its continued survival, a veritable miracle, may be attributed to this fact. However, if the Christians of Russia accept as normal and satisfactory the present condition of relative tranquillity and prosperity, they may be succumbing to a new an even subtler form of temptation. The Russian Church is forbidden to have anything to do with certain vital areas: it may not educate the young, it may not publish any religious works, it may not engage in missionary or charitable word, and finally it is not free to pass judgment on the policies of the government. So far, the Church has succeeded in showing that it is not the mere "vestige of capitalism" which the Soviet authorities claim that it is; however, its future depends very much on the possibility of being able to make an effective appeal to youth and thus on being able to get its message across to the coming generation.

The Orthodox presence in the West is a rather new phenomenon. Following the two world wars large numbers of emigrants from Eastern Europe sought new homes in Western Europe, and particularly in America. The social and religious consequences of this migration are not yet clearly discernible, but we may venture to say that it will certainly be regarded as of great importance in the history of Christianity. The Orthodox Church has now ceased to be an exclusively Eastern Church. This fact can readily be observed in the United States, for example, where several million of the faithful have largely adopted the language, culture, and ways of thought of their new country, while at the same time remaining faithful to the Church of their forefathers. To some extent, they have even succeeded in breathing into the latter a new missionary spirit and in imbuing it with a new zeal for organization such as it has never known before. By surmounting national difference inherited from the past by training a clergy that can cope with the new conditions in which the Church finds itself, and by their skill in reconciling a faithfulness to tradition with the needs of the modern world, the Western Orthodox can give an entirely new meaning to their witness to the faith. This is the task to which their Church calls them, a Church which claims to be the true Church of Christ, and it is by this standard that they will be judged by history, by their brothers, by other Christians, and finally by God himself.

POSTSCRIPT

Preparing the third edition of his book in English in 1981—*The Orthodox Church: Its Past and Its Role in the World Today*, Crestwood NY: SVS Press) Fr. John Meyendorff wrote an important postscript in which he included information on the Orthodox churches, amplifying what he had previously reported from the 1960's, in chapters VIII and X. Here, we too want to continue this updating by offering the reader a view of Orthodoxy from the 1980's to our decade of the 1990's, keeping the author's valuable interpretation, while not covering every detail of this period.

Without doubt, Fr. John Meyendorff was one of the finest Orthodox historians and theologians of this century. Gifted with an exceptional intellectual honesty, joined with an uncommon fairness in historical and theological judgment, what he wrote in 1981 retains its validity and deserves the reader's attention. One could have been content then in merely reproducing the postscript in this new edition, yet it is necessary to bring it up to date once more, a requirement which could burden and deter the reading of the text. Thus, we have chosen to restate the essentials of the 1981 postscript, complementing it only to the extent necessary.

Lacking Fr. John's inimitable genius for combining objectivity and right judgment, here we will try to offer, as much as possible, only a complement to his postscript, just matters of fact. Yet in pursuing the history of the Church, as in history in general, there is never simply an innocent exposition of the facts. Any relating of information always brings with it a form of judgment, at least implicitly. Fr. John's postscript will thus be presented as quotations of varying length.

The past two decades have seen substantial changes affecting not only external conditions and personnel in several Orthodox churches

211

but also important developments in Eastern Europe and America. Official contacts between Rome and the Orthodox Church have also considerably changed the ecumenical scene. Here is a list of facts and events which concern particularly chapters 7 and 10.

Constantinople: Following the death of Patriarch Athenagoras, the former metropolitan of Imbros, Demetrios, was elected ecumenical patriarch on July 18, 1972. The selection of a pious, but rather obscure candidate for the post is generally attributed to the Turkish authorities, who are fiercely opposed to the patriarchate's playing a significant international role. The number of Greeks still living in Turkey has decreased to a few thousand. The Theological School of Halki has been closed since 1975. Many commentators see the decline of the patriarchate as irreversible and suggest its relocation outside of Turkey. This solution, however, is still firmly excluded by official spokesmen of the patriarchate.

A significant monastic revival is taking place in several monasteries on Mount Athos, including Simonopetra, Philotheou, Stavronikita and Xenophontos, with many novices, often with higher education, being admitted into the communities. The total number of monks on Mount Athos again exceeds 1,000.

After Patriarch Demetrios' death on October 2, 1991, the Holy Synod of the Church of Constantinople unanimously elected, on October 22, 1991, Bishop Bartholomew (Demetrios Archondonis), then Metropolitan of Chalcedon, to the seat of the Ecumenical Patriarchate. His All-Holiness Bartholomew I, a relatively young bishop (54 years old), was educated in the theological school at Halki (again closed, but according to rumors, possibly to be again reopened by the Turkish authorities). He also studied at the Gregorian University in Rome, earning his doctorate there, at the Ecumenical Institute at Bossey in Switzerland and at the University of Munich. Patriarch Bartholomew is well known, both in the Orthodox world and in ecumenical circles and has long been active in the latter, working in the Faith and Order Commission. He was elected a member of the central committee of the World Council of Churches. He has taken very much to heart his role as primate as "first among equals," with "primacy of love and service," as he himself calls it, at the heart of Orthodoxy. Thus, he has not simply been content to visit the local Churches. In March 1993, on the Sunday of Orthodoxy, the first Sunday in Great Lent, he invited to Istanbul the patriarchs and primates of the local Churches for a great liturgical concelebration and consultation. This was a first in a history which has not been lacking in advances in the difficult process of regularizing the problems which still hinder the convocation of the Pan-Orthodox Great and Holy Council. One of the most difficult problem areas is that of an ecclesiological solution for Orthodox communities living in multi-jurisdictional situations in countries where the Orthodox have immigrated at different times. Such a solution seems to be moving in the direction of an accord among the several Churches. We should recall that Fr. John Meyendorff himself had been one of the principal architects in the search for such a solution.[1]

Patriarch Bartholomew moreover, is giving an important witness to the presence of the Orthodox community in the emerging new Europe. Hence, in April, 1994, he was invited to officially visit the European Parliament in Strasbourg, where his address had a strong impact, as well as the interviews granted to the media.

As the number of Greeks residing in Turkey continues to decrease and Muslim extremists continue to menace the Phanar, the Patriarch has fostered good relations with the Turkish authorities who have assured him protection, particularly against assassination attempts. The radiance of the patriarchate of Constantinople, grows, in the Orthodox world, in the very center of the ecumenical movement, in Europe and in the rest of the world. As for the monastic renewal on Mount Athos, it appears to be continuing, and in France several communities are tied to monasteries of the Holy Mountain.

1 See, in particular, *The Vision of Unity,* Crestwood NY: SVS Press, 1987, passim.

Alexandria: Patriarch Nicholas VI, who was elected May 10, 1968 died July 10, 1986. Upon his death, Bishop Parthenios (Aris Koinidis), former Metropolitan of Carthage, was elected on February 27, 1987, "Pope and Patriarch" of Alexandria and "of all Africa." Patriarch Parthenios is a well known and appreciated in Orthodox and other Christian circles. He has had long experience in the ecumenical movement, having been a member and vice-president of the central committee of the WCC to which he has made important contributions.

Antioch: Seriously affected by civil war and other troubles in Lebanon, the Patriarchate of Antioch has continued to be well-respected in Syria.

The present incumbent of the see, Patriarch Ignatius IV Hazim, elected on July 2, 1979, was educated at the American University of Beirut and at the Orthodox Theological Institute of St. Sergius, Paris. He possesses wide international and ecumenical experience.

Having never taken sides in the Lebanese civil war, the Orthodox Church of Antioch has always been in the first rank of humanitarian activity, caring for the wounded, sheltering orphans, and organizing schools. In the reconstruction after the war, the Church continues such humanitarian aid.

This Church, in the person of its Patriarch and certain of its bishops, notably Bishop Georges Khodr, and in its engaged lay men and women, bears an exceptional Christian witness in the face of suffering and continues to play an important role in the Council of Mid-East Churches. Bishop Georges Khodr continues to pursue, particularly in the press, a theological dialogue with Islam.

In America, the patriarchate of Antioch has received into its communion evangelical Protestant and more recently Episcopalian communities, granting these the right to celebrate the liturgy according to Western rites.

A theological school has been established at Balamand, Lebanon, opening October 14, 1990.

Jerusalem: Although not mentioned in Fr. John Meyendorff's postscript, the situation of the Church here as described in chapter VIII has not substantially changed. The current Patriarch is His Beatitude Diodoros, enthroned March 1, 1991.

Moscow: The wave of anti-religious persecutions which characterized the tenure of N. S. Khrushchev seems to have ended by 1964. However, the Church was left with less than 10,000 functioning churches and with only three seminaries, in Moscow, Leningrad and Odessa. The theological academies (graduate schools) of Moscow and Leningrad also remained open. Furthermore, in 1961, the council of bishops meeting in Zagorsk was forced to accept a modification of the legal status of the parishes. According to the new system, imposed by the government, parish priests are considered as employees of the parish committees (*dvadsatka*), which are alone in control of parish finances and are tightly supervised by local government officials for religious affairs.

After the death of Patriarch Alexis, the see of Moscow was occupied by Patriarch Pimen, elected on June 3, 1971. Tonsured a monk in 1927 with little formal education, the new patriarch spent several years in Stalin's concentration camps and later was drafted into the army during World War II. He resumed an ecclesiastical career in the late 'fifties.

The legal status of the Church was redefined in a new Decree on Religious Associations of the Presidium of the Supreme Soviet (June 23, 1975). It repeats the limitations put forward in the texts published in 1929 but increases the powers of the central government in Moscow, which now controls the "registration" of all religious associations. Clearly, the ideological principle inspiring Soviet legislation and policies towards religion remains the same as before.

In practice, however, the past two years have seen a slight softening of the governmental attitude towards the Orthodox Church. The theological schools were allowed to double their enrollment, which totals 1500 (in Moscow, Leningrad and Odessa combined). In addition, courses by correspondence are conducted in Moscow for another group of 800 young men. A theological journal of high quality is allowed to circulate in a restricted number of copies. No new churches were allowed to open, however.

One of the basic differences between the situation which existed in Stalin's days, or even in the period of Khrushchev's persecution (1959-1969), is the activity of some courageous men and women who speak out about the situation of the Church in Russia, facing severe personal risks. In 1965, seven bishops, led by Archbishop Germogen of Kaluga, protested the imposition of a statute which deprived parish priests of their authority in the parishes. Two priests wrote an "open letter" to the patriarch on the same subject. One of the two, Fr. Gleb Yakunim, remained an active spokesman for religious freedom and the rights of believers. In the fall of 1979, he was arrested together with an entire group of Orthodox "dissidents" and received a heavy prison sentence. Meanwhile, other priests have adopted a freer and more direct style of preaching. The best known among the latter is Fr. Dmitri Dudko. Arrested together with other activists in January 1980, he eventually made a public confession of guilty, regretting "antisoviet activities."

Whatever the personal, often tragic fate of individuals this and other information clearly indicates the vitality of the Orthodox Church in Russia and its appeal to an important segment of the "intelligentsia" and of youth. A certain polarization also appears between a nationalist trend, which identifies itself more readily with the present regime on the basis of Russian "roots" and patriotism, and a more searching, liberal current, which finds its inspiration in the writings of "religious philosophers" active in the years preceding the Revolution of 1917.

It is particularly regrettable that the updating of the situation of the Church of Russia could not be done by Fr. John Meyendorff himself. As we have noted, he always had a particularly pertinent and right understanding of all that occurred in Russia in the 20th century. He greeted with joy and with trembling, imposed by his prudence, the liberalization and completely new situation, without precedent in recent history, in which the Russian Church now finds itself.

The year 1988 seems to have been the decisive turning point. Actually from that year, the millennium of the Baptism of St. Vladimir and Kievan Rus', a millennium qualified as a "national celebration" by a spokesman of the Soviet government, interviewed by J.P. Elkabbach on Europe I—that the "slight softening" of the attitude of the authorities with respect to the Church of which Fr. John Meyendorff spoke in 1981 broke into broad daylight and was transformed into a veritable tidal wave of change: the restoration of church buildings, the opening of monasteries and theological schools. In 1988, likewise, there was the actual debut of "restructuring," the famous "perestroika," combined with real freedom of speech ("glasnost"). In 1986, with Gorbachev already in power, the pressure of the KGB on the Church still remained ponderous. But the situation differed from region to region. In some locations, the responsible functionaries of religious affairs did not all have the same attitude of submission to the Moscow center. The shattering of the imperial persecution of the Church began through the change in attitudes of these more independent local authorities.

Thus in 1988, the young Bishop Anthony of Stavropol in the Russian Caucasus, (sadly and prematurely deceased since then) enjoying excellent relations with the local government official for religious affairs, was ultimately successful in efforts pursued for a number of years in obtaining authorization for construction of new churches. To the question "Why should a state official support the bishop's efforts?" the same official responded: "In our society only the Church can raise ethical consciousness and the sense of participation among our people." To the observation "But isn't this a new ambiguity, a new danger of the Church's being exploited by the state?" he said: "I understand well the concern, but at present it is for the Church to keep watch over and safeguard her freedom and her fidelity to her own calling without being exploited, as formerly."

Since 1988 then, the Church of Russia finds herself in a situation without parallel in her millennium of history. Throughout this history, the Church had always been tied, in one way or

another, to the state. Since 1917, that is, throughout the entire
Soviet period, the Church has either been persecuted or exploited.
Now, for the first time, the Church finds herself in a situation
comparable to that of the Christian churches in any of the secularized countries of the West, as for example that of France. Here
and in other societies, Christians have learned to live with such
secularization and even to contribute to such a society without
losing their identity. The Russians have never had such an experience and will have to learn from the start with the establishment
of an authentic political democracy in their land.

Now, the crucial question is what means does the Russian
Church possess in order to respond to these new challenges? On
the material level, one of the consequences of such a liberalization
is that the Church has been impoverished. The return of houses
of worship and monasteries in great numbers demands very expensive restoration, not to speak of the construction of new
churches. Yet there is an advantage in all of this. In such a
disastrous economic situation as prevails in the former USSR, the
Church can no longer appear as an "opulent" institution in peoples' eyes. On the contrary, she finally has recovered the freedom
to organize charitable work of all sorts.

But it is especially on the intellectual plane that the greatest
difficulties are to be found. There are some educated pastors and
theologians, certain of them very well-trained and gifted, but these
are not united as they must be in order to respond to the demands
placed upon them. Not only are there but few such intellectual
leaders, there is also lacking a locale, a context, an intellectual
terrain for the exchange of ideas. Common reflection would allow a
quality theological and religious education to be offered at all levels.
After more than seventy years of enforced silence, which has de-
stroyed this educational and intellectual milieu, and the necessity of
clandestine work, Christian intellectuals in Russia have developed
an individualism which often engenders mutual suspicion rather

than cooperation. Consequently, the Russian Orthodox Church is bereft of its intellectual leadership, its vitality having been drained during the long Soviet period.

And from this flows another difficulty for the Russian Church. Certain "missionaries" have begun to arrive from abroad with considerable means at their disposal, attempting to attract Orthodox Russians deprived of material or spiritual resources. Among them are certain Catholics nostalgic for "union," whose activities, it should be noted, have no approval from the Catholic Church at all, as well as representatives of American "evangelicals," also denounced by the mainline American Protestant churches. To all of this must be added the activity of the American hierarchy of the Russian Orthodox Church Abroad, the "Synodal Church," which has taken over a number of parishes of the Church in Russia under the pretext of being the "proper hands" into which these parishes should be placed by the government authorities. It should be noted that the lay membership of the Russian Orthodox Church Abroad, especially throughout Europe, emphatically disapprove of this action by their hierarchy and desire that peace be reestablished among all the "factions" of the Russian Orthodox Church.

After the death of Patriarch Pimen on May 3, 1990, a local council of the Russian Church gathered on June 7-8, 1990 at the Holy Trinity Monastery in Sergeiv Posad (formerly Zagorsk). This council elected as patriarch Alexis (Ridiger), former Metropolitan of Leningrad and of Tallinn. The new patriarch, Alexis II, is 65 years old and came from a family of Baltic nobility. [2] During the Soviet period, he had to "pay" for his origins, being required, for example, to deliver particularly hateful political speeches. He is a

2 Born on March 23, 1929 in Tallinn, Alexis Ridiger studied at Leningrad until February, 1949. He was ordained priest in 1950 and spent 12 years in Estonia. In 1961 he became the bishop of Tallinn and in 1964 was named an official in the chancellery of the Patriarchate of Moscow. He became Metropolitan of Leningrad in 1986.

man of great gifts who well understands the extraordinary difficulty of the situation of the Russian Church. He immediately
became friends with Fr. John Meyendorff who very much appreciated him and wished to devote his own work to assisting Russia,
something he sadly did not have the time to accomplish.

Even though there are several bishops of equally high quality,
these are few in number, and they must deal with all sorts of
negative currents in the Russian Church—ultra-nationalists, inte-
grists, antisemites, anti-ecumenists . . . (until his election, Patriarch
Alexis had been president of the European Council of Churches.
While on a visit to America, he publicly declared that Orthodoxy
and anti-Semitism were incompatible, for which he earned severe
criticism from certain groups upon his return to Russia.)

Anti-ecumenism can be explained by a conjunction of at least
three factors. First, "missionary activity," not to say proselytism is
most abhorred. Then, there is the "good word" dispensed by
certain representatives of the Russian Orthodox Church Abroad
for whom ecumenism is neither more nor less than "the heresy of
the 20th century." Finally, and perhaps most especially, the fact is
that in the time of the USSR, the Soviet period, ecumenism was
practically a state affair. One could not have relations with official
institutions such as the World Council of Churches unless one
had the "blessing" of the government, most often even instructions from the state. "Ecumenists," then, were tightly controlled
(though this did not prevent them from escaping this control and
establishing genuine contact with their fellow Christians) and
moreover belonged to that category of the privileged able to travel
abroad (those called "outgoers"—*vyezzhaiushchii*). Thus, even
good people say: "Today, the Church isn't controlled by the state
any longer, so why continue to dialogue with all those 'heretics'?"

The breakup of the USSR and its transformation into the
Confederation of Independent States has likewise affected the
Church. Even though the Synod of bishops remains united, the

territory now is divided into numerous independent republics. Three great regions, in particular, were constituted: Russia, which remains with Moscow the center of the Russian Orthodox Church, Belorussia or Belarus with its capital Minsk and Ukraine, with Kiev, the most ancient seat of Russian Orthodoxy. The two latter republics are at present "exarchates" of the Russian Church, along with a large measure of internal autonomy. The old external exarchates of Western Europe and the East have been suppressed.

Metropolitans Philaret (Vokhromeev) of Minsk and Vladimir (Sabodan) of Kiev have had to face very difficult situations. On the one hand, there are strong nationalistic currents which tend to express themselves in "anti-Moscoism." Thus, for example, there are Ukrainian groups demanding autocephalous status (one of these is led by the former Metropolitan of Kiev, Philaret Denisenko, laicized by the Synod of Bishops of the Russian Church, a measure he continues to refuse to accept). The Patriarch and the Synod have refused to grant this autocephalous status, since the basis of the Orthodox ecclesiological principle is that of territory, not nationalism, and secondly, because such a decision requires the conciliar agreement of all Orthodoxy.

On the other hand, a source of difficulties for Metropolitans Philaret of Minsk and Vladimir of Kiev is linked with Eastern Rite Catholics (those called "Uniates," from the "Union" of Brest-Litovsk signed in 1596). In 1946, these Catholics were forced to enter Orthodoxy by Stalin with the "help" of the Orthodox Church. Naturally, with liberalization, the Eastern Rite Catholics have recovered their right to exist in full daylight, in the name of freedom of conscience and human rights. Their reappearance has led to conflicts, sometimes violent ones, with the Orthodox over the restitution of church buildings. Accords have been concluded between Rome and Moscow on this matter. Sadly, those involved do not always respect these agreements, and this conflict has damaged the international Catholic-Orthodox dialogue.

It is important to underscore finally that Patriarch Alexis II, on several occasions already, has expressed repentance, in the name of the whole of the hierarchy of the Russian Church, for the "weaknesses" displayed during the period of persecution.[3] One can only regret that the New York-based Russian Orthodox Church Abroad has never responded to this public act of repentance with a corresponding act of reconciliation, and that certain "ex-dissidents" such as Fr. Gleb Yakunin (recently laicized for his refusal to submit to the decision of the Patriarch and Synod that henceforth clerics must not stand for parliamentary election or otherwise participate in purely political activity on a full-time basis) continue to retain their criticism as in the past. (On this matter, see Fr. John Meyendorff's text above.)

In closing, we cannot but join with Fr. John Meyendorff in his hope of seeing Russian Orthodoxy saved from the great confusion into which it is presently plunged by the profound, solid faith which has sustained and still sustains the Christian people of Russia, to which are constantly added masses of the newly baptized. Here, a real collaboration with that dynamic Orthodoxy of the immigration will be most useful.

Romania: The anti-religious and, more particularly, anti-monastic drive which occurred in 1958-62 and coincided with the Khrushchev persecution in Russia has subsided and some of the Church leaders arrested during that period, including Fr. D. Staniloae, the leading Romanian Orthodox theologian, are again playing an influential role in the life of the Church. However, the Church remains under very tight state control, and witnessed by the case of Fr. Calciu, a member of the staff of the Orthodox Theological Institute of Bucharest, who was tried and condemned to prison in the spring of 1979 for active preaching and youth work.

The election of the new patriarch, Justin Moisescu, on June 12, 1977, to replace the deceased patriarch Justinian, is another expres-

---

3 See in particular the remarkable text in this regard of a pastoral letter addressed to all the pastors and faithful of the Russian Orthodox Church throughout the world at the beginning of Great Lent, 1993.

sion of the close ties between the patriarchate and the government. As metropolitan of Moldavia, Justin was known to have cooperated with government officials in the reduction of monastic life in 1958-62.

After the fall of the Berlin Wall and the execution of the Ceaucescus, the Romanian Orthodox Church has come to face, with liberalization, difficulties comparable to those in Russia. Thus, problems stem from battles over returned church buildings between the Eastern Rite Catholics and the Orthodox, as well as tensions from the work of foreign "missionaries" of the same type as in Russia.

Even at the heart of the Church, those tolerated or appointed to official posts under the Ceaucescu regime have been attacked for their past actions. Thus, Patriarch Theoktist, elected November 9, 1986 to succeed Patriarch Justin, who died July 31, 1986, himself had to resign temporarily though he has been recalled to his office by the Synod.

A projected law insuring religious freedom is in preparation, but in a tense climate, in which the Orthodox Church, seeking to regain her historic rights as the majority faith of the nation, finds herself in conflict with other Christian confessions, most notably the Eastern Rite Catholics.

The Romanian Orthodox Church is experiencing a powerful renewal of monastic life and theological work despite the difficulties described here. In particular, the Romanian Church is graced with many young bishops of high quality, many of whom were educated and have taught abroad, at the Ecumenical Institute in Bossey and at the St. Sergius Institute in Paris.

Bulgaria: The present patriarch, elected on July 4, 1971, after the death of Patriarch Cyril, is Maxim, formerly metropolitan of Lovech and earlier the prelate-in-charge of the Bulgarian Orthodox representation in Moscow.

The liberalization here has led to the appearance of groups hostile to the Patriarch, who have attacked him for his links to the former communist regime. After the unsuccessful attempt at the election of Metropolitan Pimen of Nevrokop on May 22, 1991, Patriarch Maxim once again took office, where he remains still. There also exists an anti-Moscow movement due to the domination of "big brother" Russia during the era of the USSR, a hostility as much about political matters as about the relationship between the two Orthodox Churches of Bulgaria and Russia. Patriarch Alexis II has most articulately expressed the apologies of the Russian Church for the past to Bulgaria and has called for the re-establishment of conciliar relations of equality between the two sister-churches, but this has yet to be accepted by all.[4]

Greece: The life and status of the Orthodox Church h in Greece was seriously affected in the period of the military dictatorship. The religious "movements," and particularly the powerful Zoe Brotherhood, were closely connected with the ideological position of Colonel Papadopoulos ("Greece of Greek Christians"). The latter imposed upon the Church the election of Jerome Kotsonis, one of the spiritual leaders of Zoe, as Archbishop of Athens.

Archbishop Jerome, an articulate and well-educated church leader, attempted to introduce administrative, canonical and ethical reforms which were generally needed and constructive. But his connection with the unpopular junta compromised his activity and made his resignation inevitable. As a result, the Zoe Brotherhood lost most of its prestige and influence.

At the restoration of democracy, the Church appeared to many as morally compromised. The new Constitution, adopted in 1975, significantly modified its legal status. While still considered the "dominant" religion, Orthodoxy now enjoyed less preferential treatment, but also greater administrative freedom from the government. Some observers believe that further separation between Church and state is forthcoming, and that such separation may be desirable if the Church is to regain its prestige and moral authority.

The present primate, Archbishop Seraphim of Athens, was elected on January 12, 1974, during the second phase of the dictatorship.

4 See *Service Orthodoxe de Presse*, no. 190, July-August 1994, pp. 11-13.

The situation of the Church of Greece is little changed from that described by Fr. John Meyendorff in 1981. The most difficult problem of the separation of Church and state remains the order of the day, but has yet to be thoroughly and effectively resolved.

The entry of Greece into the European Community has resulted in the presence of Orthodoxy among those forming this new Europe. An important witness of this was the official visit of Ecumenical Patriarch Bartholomew I to the European Parliament in April, 1994. His speech there was well received as an Orthodox statement. In Greece, many voices, including that of a metropolitan, have been heard, underlining the significance that an Orthodox presence at the very heart of Europe demands of Greece the deepening of a more "open" and not narrowly nationalistic Orthodoxy.[5]

Georgia: A few years ago, information about the Orthodox Church of Georgia was scarce, but there were many signs of governmental repression and internal decadence. The situation seems to have changed spectacularly with the election of a new catholicos-patriarch, Elias II, on December 23, 1977. A man of 45, well-educated and with obvious leadership qualities, the new patriarch presides over a real revival of the Church of Georgia. One may assume that Georgian public opinion was the decisive factor which made his election possible. Careful, as all churchmen in the Soviet Union, not to antagonize the authorities, Elias II during the first months of his tenure was able to consecrate several young bishops to vacant sees, reorganize the seminary and undertake a program of renewed preaching. He was recently elected as one of the presidents of the World Council of Churches, replacing the deceased Metropolitan Nikodim.

At present, the independent republic of Georgia is experiencing an extremely unstable period, due to the civil war between the Georgians and the Ossetians. Georgia's president, Eduard Chevarnadze, has declared himself a Christian and has established excellent relations with the Patriarch-Catholicos Elias II. The autocephalous status of the Church of Georgia is recognized by all today, and this was reaffirmed by Ecumenical Patriarch Bartholomew I during a

5 See *Service Orthodoxe de Presse*, no. 190, July-August, 1994, pp. 8-9.

recent visit to Patriarch-Catholicos Elias II in May, 1994. A theological academy has been added to the seminary in Tbilissi in 1988.[6]

Cyprus: To replace Archbishop Makarios, the Holy Synod elected Chrisostomos, formerly metropolitan of Paphos, as the new archbishop of Cyprus (November 13, 1977). The new head of the Church will not combine his ecclesiastical functions with the presidency of the republic, as did Makarios, since a civilian president now occupies that position.

The Church of Cyprus plays an active role in the ecumenical movement, particularly in the Council of Churches of the Middle East. Archbishop Chrysostomos remains in office.

Sinai: The archbishopric of Sinai is presently held by Damianos Samartsis, elected on December 23, 1973.

Albania: All religious life was made illegal in Albania as a result of the "cultural revolution" of 1966. According to press accounts, the last primate of the autocephalous Church of Albania, Archbishop Damian, died in retirement (or in prison?) in 1967. There are no churches officially open anywhere in the country

Such was the situation in 1981. Since then a certain liberalization has occurred and the Orthodox Church is reemerging from beneath the rubble. A most energetic Greek bishop, well educated and gifted with pastoral abilities, Bishop Anastasios Yannoulatos, was named in 1991 to lead and preside over the rebirth of this martyred Church.

Poland: The present head of the Orthodox Church in Poland is Metropolitan Basil, elected on January 24, 1970.

The Orthodox Church of Poland seems to least resent the imposing proximity of her sister Church of Russia, enfeebled as we have seen she is. She is undergoing problems again comparable to those of the other Churches of the former Eastern bloc, in particular that of "missionaries" and the reality of being considered "non-Polish," because of her Russo-Ukrainian origins.

Czechoslovakia: During Dubcek's liberal regime, which again legalized the "Greek-Catholic" Church in Czechoslovakia, a sub-

6 See *Service Orthodoxe de Presse*, no. 190, July-August, 1994, pp. 1-2.

stantial number of former Greek-Catholics ("Uniats") who had joined the Orthodox Church in 1950 returned to Roman obedience. Many conflicts over property resulted in clashes between the communities. At present, the situation seems to be stabilized, but exact numbers of faithful belonging to the Orthodox Church are difficult to assess.

An Orthodox theological faculty exists in Presov, with seven professors and 25 students. The seminary in Karlovy Vary no longer exists.

America: On April 12, 1970, the late Patriarch Alexis of Moscow signed an official act ("Tomos") granting "autocephaly" to the metropolitanate of America, which had grown up out of the original diocese created by the Russian Church first in Alaska, then after 1867, in the continental United States, for Orthodox immigrants of all nationalities. The metropolitanate had been *de facto* independent from Moscow since 1924, but this independence was now officially sanctioned by the Mother Church.

The establishment of an autocephalous American Church was always seen as a desirable and canonically inevitable goal by the leadership of the Russian Church. As early as 1905, Tikhon, then archbishop of America (and later Patriarch of Moscow), wrote a report recommending this action. His goal even then was to secure the unity of the various ethnic groups and lay the foundation of expansion and growth of Orthodoxy on the American continent. As we have noted earlier (p. 168), the crisis of the Russian Revolution and the administrative chaos in the affairs of the Russian Church (including the unilateral splitting away of the American metropolitanate from Moscow in 1924) had lead to the breaking up of the original one American Church into many ethnic units, which were now administratively dependent upon their own Mother Churches: the Greek Archdiocese under Athens (later under Constantinople), the Syrian Archdiocese under Antioch, the Serbian, Romanian and Bulgarian dioceses under their respective national patriarchates, etc. Thus, in 1970, the Russian Church could grant autocephaly to only a segment of American Orthodoxy. The explicit goal of the action, however, was to lay the foundation for canonical unity, which would result from an agreement by the various national Orthodox churches having established branches in America after 1922.

The establishment of the autocephaly provoked a fierce canonical debate especially between the patriarchates of Constantinople and Moscow, which touched upon the very nature of Orthodox canonical principles, the significance of the Orthodox presence in the New World, and the authority of Constantinople as "first among equal" patriarchs. Behind this debate on principles, there was also a much more practical unwillingness on the part of the Greeks and of the other churches to lose administrative control over their respective "dispersions" (or "diasporas") in America. Fortunately the debate did not lead to schism, and full communion and cooperation continued without interruption between the different Orthodox jurisdictions in America. The autocephalous Orthodox Church was officially and permanently recognized by the patriarchates of Russia, Georgia and Bulgaria, and by the churches of Poland, Czechoslovakia and Finland, whereas the Greek-speaking churches of Constantinople, Alexandria, Jerusalem and Greece publicly opposed the very idea of American autocephaly. The debate, meanwhile, allowed for a consensus on one point: the existence of parallel jurisdictions in one country is canonically abnormal and should be corrected.

During the ten years of its existence, the autocephalous Church has expanded and taken root. It uses English as the predominant language in the liturgy, and has welcomed into its fold large groups of Romanian, Albanian and Bulgarian parishes. It continues missionary work among the indigenous populations of Alaska and Mexico. The majority of its bishops, including its head, Metropolitan Theodosius (elected in October 1977), are America-born.

At present the three largest Orthodox jurisdictions in America are the Greek Archdiocese (535 communities), the Autocephalous Orthodox Church in America (528 communities), and the Antiochian Archdiocese (107 communities).

The elder Herman—one of the original group of monks from Valamo, who came to Alaska in 1794—and John-Innocent Veniaminov, the first bishop in America, were canonized as saints in 1970 and 1978 respectively.

The situation of Orthodoxy in America is so well described by Fr. John Meyendorff that there is but little to add.

To the number of the saints, the apostles of America, Herman and Innocent, it is necessary to add Patriarch Tikhon, canonized

October 9, 1989 by the Church of Russia. He had already been canonized on November 1, 1981 by the Russian Orthodox Church Abroad. In 1994, two additional saints were added: Fr. Alexis Toth, a Ruthenian immigrant priest of the Catholic Eastern Rite who converted to Orthodoxy and brought many faithful with him; and Fr. Jacob Netsvetov, the first native-born Orthodox priest in America and a tireless missionary.

While full administrative unity among all the Orthodox in America has not yet been achieved, there are at present some hopeful signs. On November 30-December 1, 1994, twenty-nine Orthodox bishops from all the canonical jurisdictions met at Antiochian Village, in Ligonier, Pennsylvania. In their "Statement on the Church in North America," the bishops affirmed that American Orthodoxy is one Church, and that the present division into "jurisdictions" is unacceptable. They rejected in no uncertain terms the use of the term "diaspora" to describe the North American Church. They concluded that they were already in fact an "Episcopal Assembly, a precursor to a General Synod of Bishops," and they agreed to meet annually "to enhance the movement toward administrative ecclesial unity in North America."

The initial reaction from Constantinople, based largely on inflammatory reports in the secular Greek press, was totally negative. Nevertheless, the Conference served and continues to serve as a clarion call to all the "Old World" Orthodox Churches, as well as to all the Orthodox in America, that the search for unity remains high on everyone's agenda.

It seems most important to underscore here the role of two men in particular who have contributed more than any to the edification and development of the Orthodox Church in America. (OCA) These are Fr. Alexander Schmemann and Fr. John Meyendorff himself. Both were alumni of St. Sergius Institute in Paris and were successively deans of St. Vladimir's Orthodox Theological Seminary, from which both illumined the world in a manner unparalleled in recent Orthodox history. Both were inheritors of the profound and creative religious renaissance among Russian Orthodox from the beginning of this century (Pavel Florensky, Nicolas Berdiaev, Sergius Bulgakov, Simeon Frank, Vladimir Lossky, Georges Florovsky, Nicolas Afanassieff, Kyprian Kern, to name a few). Coming from the seedbed of this renewal at St. Sergius Institute in Paris, they made it bear fruit a hundredfold both in America and throughout the world.

Fr. Alexander Schmemann, without doubt the greatest Orthodox liturgical theologian of this century, has bequeathed to both the Orthodox Church and the world the gift of what would be called after him "liturgical theology." The heart of this theological perspective is the understanding of the indissoluble unity between the rule of prayer (*lex orandi*) and the rule of faith (*lex credendi*). This unity should be understood in a double sense: *lex orandi, lex credendi* and *lex credendi, lex orandi*. In either case there is not the least contradiction between the purity of the faith of Orthodoxy and the content of the liturgy (here meaning the whole of worship) and the manner of its celebration. The content and structure of the Church's worship is theology, the "primary theology," as it has been called. If there is any divergence, it must be corrected. The entire Orthodox world, Russia especially, needs to be inspired by the teaching of Fr. Alexander Schmemann.

As for Fr. John Meyendorff, he is well known throughout the world as a gifted Byzantinist, a Church historian and a theologian.[7] Let us be content with emphasizing that even to the end he did not cease to work for the unity of Orthodoxy in America. All progress in this path is due to his incessant effort. Even if the situation in America cannot fully be said to have arrived at a thorough ecclesial solution, the considerable breakthroughs recently among the autocephalous Churches concerning the prob-

7 See in particular Dimitri Obolensky, "John Meyendorff (1926-92)" in *Sobornost*, vol. 15: 2, 1993, pp. 44-51.

lems of the Orthodox "Diaspora" or "dispersion" are in large measure the result of what Fr. John Meyendorff had said for many years about Orthodox unity in one place, about the conciliarity, the catholicity, and most generally about the very nature of the Church of Christ. All of this is particularly helpful to the Christian world at the moment when the ecumenical movement is taking up the most crucial problem of ecclesiology. Fr. John Meyendorff was always profoundly concerned with the restoration of unity among Christians. For many years, from 1967-76, he was president of the Faith and Order Commission of the World Council of Churches and also a member of the central committee of that body.

Japan: The Orthodox Church of Japan, founded by the Russian missionary, St. Nicholas Kasatkin, in the late nineteenth century, was under the canonical jurisdiction of the American metropolitanate from 1945 to 1970. At that date, simultaneous with the establishment of the American autocephaly, the Church in Japan was made "autonomous" with the right of electing its bishops and full administrative independence. The election of the archbishop of Tokyo, however, is confirmed canonically by the patriarchate of Moscow. The present archbishop is Metropolitan Theodosius Nagashima, elected on March 28, 1972.

Serbia: In the postscript to the American edition of his book from 1981, Fr. John Meyendorff did not mention the Church of Serbia. Today, one cannot pass her by in silence. The whole world knows the tragic situation of the former Yugoslavia. That will not be described at length here, but a word about the Church there is necessary. In Orthodoxy it is traditional to say that the Church is identified with the destinies of her people. Sometimes, sadly, this principle is poorly understood and the identification is transformed into an alliance of the Church with power or the strongest in that land. Thanks be to God, in the person of Patriarch Pavle (Paul), elected December 1, 1990, and his Synod, one finds an identification with the people in a manner truly faithful to Orthodoxy, that is to say, as the moral conscience, a critic when this is necessary. Patriarch Paul and his Synod have forcefully declared that one may not kill or otherwise employ violence in the name of Jesus Christ, and this is true of any war in the name of religion—such is a betrayal of the faith. But unfortunately Western media have not always cited these statements, doubtlessly to not "complicate" the simplistic vision of a war where the Orthodox oppose both the Catholic Croatians and the Muslims. Such a simplification, perhaps better a falsification, is encouraged by the traditional and privileged relationship between the Serbs and the Russians. In fact, the hierarchy of the Serbian Orthodox Church has opened up ecumenical relations with the Roman Catholic Croatian hierarchy. The civil war in the former Yugoslavia is no more a simple religious war than that fought in Northern Ireland.

Relations with Roman Catholicism

The new ecumenical openness of the Church of Rome, which resulted from Vatican II, expressed itself in a series of spectacular encounters with Orthodoxy. Pope Paul VI met with Ecumenical Patriarch Athenagoras in Jerusalem and then visited Istanbul personally. Patriarch Athenagoras paid a return visit to Rome. No such encounters had ever taken place since the schism. Furthermore, the protocol of the visits emphasized the equality of the two leaders. In another gesture made in 1964, the churches of Rome and Constantinople officially lifted the "anathemas of 1054." Although this gesture did not imply the end of the schism (the mutual excommunications of 1054 were canonically doubtful in the first place, and were followed by many other excommunications which were never "lifted"), it presented a symbolic significance of some importance, and was accompanied by many meetings between the representative of Rome and other Orthodox leaders, including those of the patriarchate of Moscow.

In fact, whereas both sides recognize that Orthodoxy and Rome are the two major branches of historical Christianity and, in that sense, can be seen as "sister churches," the theological differences which still separate them (particularly the issues of papal infallibility and universal jurisdiction) cannot be solved by symbols only. One must hope, therefore, that a serious dialogue, in an atmosphere of mutual respect and concern for Christianity as a whole, will begin soon.

One knows that the last wish, as expressed by Fr. John Meyendorff in 1981, was realized not long after. An official dialogue, at the international level, has been established. Meetings were held at Patmos and Rhodes in 1980, at Munich in 1982, in Crete in 1986, at Bari in 1987. The Catholic-Orthodox dialogue has resulted in extremely serious theological work, even though this has not happened without difficulties. The dialogue has itself undergone the consequences of the conflict situations produced by liberalization in the East. The problem of Eastern Rite Catholics has been raised in an especially urgent and direct manner. The meeting at Balamand in 1993 has produced an important text regarding Eastern Rite Catholics.[8] The commission issued a common statement, ("The Balamand Declaration") in which it is affirmed that while the Eastern Rite Catholics deserve their existence respected on the basis of human rights and freedom of conscience, the "Union" path cannot be the way to the restoration of unity within the Church. It is not surprising that those who are called "Uniates" feel themselves to have been sacrificed by the Balamand Declaration. Since then, it has been decided that representatives of the Eastern Rite Catholics should be invited to participate in the dialogue.

Beside the dialogue on the international level, there also exist commissions for Catholic-Orthodox dialogue on the national level in many countries, in France and in America as well. Contrary to the cautious approach of the international dialogue, the French commission has decided to attack the most burning issues directly. It has already begun work on a study of Roman primacy and has produced a book on this subject, which clarifies the question from an historical point of view.[9] At present, the com-

8 One can find this text in *Irenikon* 1993: 3, pp. 347-356.

9 *La primauté romaine dans la communion des Eglises,* Commission mixte Catholique-

mission is pursuing a study of the "Uniate" question with the participation of Eastern Rite Catholic representatives. The atmosphere of this commission is most warm and fraternal.

One can add that at the core of the Faith and Order commission of the World Council of Churches, in which the Catholic Church is a full participant, collaboration between the Catholics and the Orthodox is most significant. This is a sign of unity which not only includes the others, but which is leading an impressive number of Protestant representatives to deepen their rediscovery of a common sense of the Church.

Here we are led to say that what Fr. John Meyendorff expressed as a hope in 1981 with respect to the Orthodox participation in the World Council of Churches (see chapter 10) has been realized quite marvelously. Orthodox participation is being taken more seriously and two examples can serve as evidence of this. One is the last General Assembly in Canberra in February 1991, where a large Orthodox delegation under the presidency of then Bishop Bartholomew, since then elected Ecumenical Patriarch, made known its unease with the drift of the WCC from its vocation (and its Constitution) of working to reestablish the unity of Christians in the one Eucharist. This "call to order" was taken very seriously. The other example which deserves mention comes from the sixth world conference of Faith and Order, held at San Diego de Compostella in August, 1993 (30 years after Montreal), where the Orthodox participation reached a new height of impact. In particular, we have in mind the plenary address of Metropolitan John Zizioulas of Pergamum on a communal and trinitarian ecclesiology and the enormous impact of this speech on the entire conference.

Orthodoxe en France, presentation par le Métropolitan Jérémie et Mgr André Quelen, Paris, Le Cerf, 1991.

Towards an Orthodox "Great Council"?

During the past two decades, a number of conferences and consultations between the representatives of all—or most—Orthodox churches were initiated by the Ecumenical Patriarchate of Constantinople. The ultimate goal of the conferences was to pave the way towards a "Great Council," which the Orthodox are reluctant to call "ecumenical" before it actually meets and proves to be indeed the voice of the whole Church. The council will be called to solve some of the problems faced by the Orthodox Church today.

Among these problems, the relationship of Orthodoxy with the rest of Christendom, including, in particularly, the Church of Rome, is certainly and crucially important. However, the last conference held in Chambésy, Switzerland, in 1977, rightly judged that problems internal to Orthodoxy itself deserve the highest priority, including such issues as the overlapping jurisdictions in Western countries (including America), the procedures to be followed in establishing new autocephalous churches, the role of the ecumenical patriarch in the concert of the other autocephalous churches, etc. Indeed, as long as these questions remained unresolved, the witness and credibility of the Orthodox Church is seriously handicapped.

Understandably, great obstacles stand in the way to the council. Many observers question the possibility of securing an adequate and free representation of the Orthodox churches located in Communist countries, where 90 percent of all the Orthodox Christians live today. On the other hand, the connection which exists between the policies of all the patriarchates—including Constantinople—and the interests of the various nationalities is so obvious, that a dispassionate and objective approach to canonical problems is not always easy to achieve. The present consultations and conferences could nevertheless lead to a consensus on concrete issues, which could then be resolved even without the official gathering of a council. Observers from outside are often puzzled by the weakness of formal, administrative procedures in Orthodoxy and wonder how a sense of unity and common commitment can be preserved under such conditions. They generally underestimate the power—keenly felt by the Orthodox themselves—of a common perception of basic Christian truths, expressed particularly in the liturgy but also in frequent, unofficial and brotherly contacts, which hold the Church together. This inner, spiritual unity in faith and sacraments is sometimes more fruitful and even more efficient than the official diplomacy of patriarchates and synod, tied up in political entanglements and, for the most part, lacking essential freedom of action.

With regard to certain points, the situation which Fr. John Meyendorff described then (1981) has evolved radically. Fears about freedom of witness in a "Pan-Orthodox Great and Holy Council" by the churches of the Eastern European countries no longer exist since the fall of the Berlin Wall. Yet the dangers linked to nationalist tendencies have not only remained possibilities but have grown with the liberalization and breakup of entities such as the USSR or Yugoslavia, not to mention the "Eastern bloc."

At the same time, the process of preparing for the Council continues, and, as Fr. John said, some concrete problems seem to be approaching solutions without having to wait for the Council to resolve them. Thus, it seems as though a consensus among the autocephalous churches is emerging with regard to one of the most pressing problems, that of jurisdictions superimposed upon countries of the Orthodox "dispersion." In almost every case, contacts among the Churches have multiplied and deepened. Even past suspicions have tended to disappear. The 1994 assembly of bishops in Ligonier, Pennsylvania, shows clearly the strong desire, particularly in America, to resolve these issues. One can be particularly grateful for the most effective action by the new Ecumenical Patriarch Bartholomew, who, as we earlier stated, has taken quite seriously his role as the "first among equals," and who above all sees this role as one in the service of unity, in the spirit of canon 34 of those called the Apostolic Canons:

> That each bishop in each region (*etnous*), seek the first and consider him as his chief (*kephalen*) and do nothing without his accord in the administration of the business of the diocese and the area which pertains to it. He (the first) should do nothing without the consultation of all, and thus concord (*homonia*, unanimity) will prevail, to the glory of the Father and the Son and the Holy Spirit.

We would simply add that Patriarch Bartholomew's activity has been aided by the exceptional insight and sensitivity of several Orthodox patriarchs.

With respect to the actual convocation of the Council, Metropolitan Damaskinos (Papandreou), in charge of its preparation, said, in September, 1993, that the Council would convene before the year 2000.

❖ ❖ ❖ ❖

Fr. John Meyendorff fell asleep in the Lord on July 22, 1992, the feast of St. Mary Magdalen, "equal of the Apostles." A great Anglican theologian of the 17th century, Lancelot Andrewes, preaching on Mary Magdalen at Easter, said that when she anointed the feet of the Savior at Bethany with the expensive perfume, she represented in advance the entire contribution of the Fathers of the Church and of the great theologians of the Church's Tradition, whose work was an anointing of the Body of Christ, the Church. One of those, who, in the 20th century, has best interiorized and "passed on" the Tradition is without doubt Fr. John Meyendorff. He then participated in this anointing. So it was not just by chance that it was on the day of St. Mary Magdalen that the Lord called Fr. John to Himself.

SELECT BIBLIOGRAPHY

1. The Orthodox Faith

Bulgakov, S., *The Orthodox Church*, rev. trans., Crestwood N.Y., SVS Press, 1988.

Florovsky, G., *Bible, Church, Tradition, An Eastern Orthodox View*, Belmont, Mass., Nordland, 1972.

Lossky, V., *Orthodox Theology, An Introduction*, Crestwood, N.Y., SVS Press, 1978.

_____, *The Mystical Theology of the Eastern Church*, London, 1957; 2nd ed. Crestwood, N.Y., SVS Press, 1976.

Meyendorff, J., *Byzantine Theology: Historical Trends and Doctrinal Themes*, 2nd ed. New York, Fordham University Press, 1979.

_____, *Christ in Eastern Christian Thought*, Washington nd Cleveland, 1969; 2nd ed. Crestwood, N.Y., SVS Press, 1975.

Ouspensky, L., *Theology of the Icon*, 2 vols.,Crestwood N.Y., SVS Press, 1992.

Pelikan, J., *The Christian Tradition 2: The Spirit of Eastern Christendom (600–1700)*, Chicago, The University of Chicago Press, 1974.

Pelikan, J., *Christian Doctrine and Modern Culture (since 1700)*, vol. 5, University of Chicago Press, 1989.

Ware, T., *The Orthodox Church*, rev. ed., Penguin, 1993.

The Living God: A Catechism of the Christian Faith, 2 vols., Crestwood N.Y., SVS Press, 1989.

The Incarnate God: The Feasts of Jesus Christ and the Virgin Mary, C. Aslanoff, ed. Crestwood N.Y., SVS Press, 1995.

Lossky, V., *In the Image and Likeness of God*, Crestwood N.Y., SVS Press, 1974.

Icons: Windows on Eternity, Gennadios Limouris, ed., Geneva: WCC, 1990.

Go Forth in Peace: Orthodox Perspectives on Mission, Ion Bria, ed., Geneva: WCC, 1986.

Archbishop Paul, *The Faith We Hold, The Feast of Faith,* Crestwood N.Y., SVS Press, 1980, 1988.

2. Orthodox Ecclesiology

Borelli, J. and Erickson, J. H., *The Quest for Unity: Orthodox and Catholics in Dialogue. Documents of the Joint International Commission and Official Dialogues in the United States, 1965-1995.* Crestwood, N.Y. and Washington D.C., SVS Press and USCC, 1996.

Florovsky, G., *Collected Works,* vols. I-III, Belmont, Mass., Nordland, 1972-1976.

Meyendorff, J., *Orthodoxy and Catholicity,* New York, Sheed and Ward, 1966.

Primacy and Primacies in the Orthodox Church (articles by V. Kesich, J. Meyendorff, A. Schmemann and S. Verhovskoy), special issue of *St. Vladimir's Seminary Quarterly,* vol. IV, 1960.

The Primacy of Peter: Essays in Ecclesiology and the Early Church, New York, SVS Press, 1992. A symposium os articles by J. Meyendorff, N. Afanassieff, A. Schmemann, N. Koulomzine and V. Kesich.

Zizioulis, J. *Being as Communion,* Crestwood NY:SVS Press, 1985.

_____, "The Eucharistic Community and the Catholicity of the Church," in *The New Man: An Orthodox and Reformed Dialogue,* ed. by J. Meyendorff and J. McLelland, New Brunswick, N.J., 1973, pp. 107-131.

3. Orthodox Liturgy and Spirituality

Bp. Alexander, *The Life of Father John of Kronstadt,* Crestwood, N.Y., SVS Press, 1979.

Behr-Sigel, E. *The Ministry of Women in the Church, The Place of the Heart: An Introduction to Orthodox Spirituality,* Torrance CA: Oakwood, 1991, 1992.

Bloom, Metropolitan Anthony, *Living Prayer,* Springfield IL: Templegate, 1966, *Beginning to Pray,* Mahwah NJ: Paulist Press, 1970.

Breck, J. *The Power of the Word,* Crestwood N.Y., SVS Press, 1986.

Cabasilas, Nicholas, *The Life in Christ,* Translated from the Greek by C. J. Catanzaro, with an introduction by Boris Bobrinskoy, Crestwood, N.Y., SVS Press, 1974.

_____, *A Commentary on the Divine Liturgy,* trans. by J. M. Hussey and P. A. McNulty, with an introduction by J. M. French, London, 1960; reprinted, Crestwood, N.Y., SVS Press, 1977.

Clément, O. *The Roots of Christian Mysticism,* London: New City, 1994.

Evdokimov, P. *The Sacrament of Love, Woman and the Salvation of the World,* Crestwood NY, SVS Press, 1985 1994, *The Art of the Icon: A Theology of Beauty,* Torrance CA: Oakwood, 1989.

Fedotov, G. P., *The Russian Religious Mind,* I-II, Cambridge, Mass., Harvard University Press, 1966.

The Festal Menaion, trans. from the original Greek by Mother Mary and Kallistos Ware, London, Faber, 1973.

George, K.M., *The Silent Roots: Orthodox Perspectives on Christian Spirituality,* Geneva: WCC, 1994.

The Lenten Triodion, trans. from the original Greek by Mother Mary and Kallistos Ware, London, Faber, 1979.

Meyendorff, J., *St. Gregory Palamas and Orthodox Spirituality,* Crestwood, N.Y., SVS Press, 1974.

A Monk of the Eastern Church (Lev Gillet), *The Jesus Prayer, The Year of Grace of the Lord, Serve the Lord with Gladness,* Crestwood N.Y., SVS Press, 1987, 1992, 1990.

Ouspensky, L. and Lossky, V. *The Meaning of Icons,* Crestwood N.Y., SVS Press, 1983.

The Philokalia / The Complete Text compiled by St. Nikodimos of the Holy Mountain and St. Makarios of Corinth, trans. from the Greek and edited by G. E. H. Palmer, Philip Sherrard, Kallistos Ware, vol. I, London, Faber, 1973.

Quenot, M., *The Icon: Window on the Kingdom,* Crestwood N.Y., SVS Press, 1991.

Schmemann, A. *The Eucharist: Sacrament of the Kingdom, Liturgy and Tradition, Celebration of Faith,* 3 vols., Crestwood N.Y., SVS Press, 1988, 1990, 1992, 1994, 1995.

_____, *For the Life of the World: Sacraments and Orthodoxy,* rev. ed. Crestwood, N.Y., SVS Press, 1974.

_____, *Introduction to Liturgical Theology,* Crestwood N.Y., SVS Press, 1966.

_____, *Of Water and the Spirit: A Liturgical Study of Baptism,* Crestwood, N.Y., SVS Press, 1974.

Tregubov, A., *The Light of Christ: Iconography of Gregory Krug,* Crestwood N.Y., SVS Press, 1990.

Yannaras, C., *The Freedom of Morality,* Crestwood N.Y., SVS Press, 1984.

Ware, T. *The Orthodox Way,* rev. ed., Crestwood N.Y., SVS Press, 1995.

Wybrew, H., *The Orthodox Liturgy,* Crestwood N.Y., SVS Press, 1990.

4. History and Contemporary Issues

Curtiss, J. S., *The Russian Church and the Soviet State, 1917-1950,* Boston, Little, Brown, 1953.

Dvornik, F., *The Photian Schism: History and Legend,* Cambridge University Press, 1948.

Erickson, J. H., *The Challenge of Our Past,* Crestwood N.Y., SVS Press, 1991.

Every, G., *The Byzantine Patriarchate,* London, SPCK, 1947.

Frazee, C. A., *The Orthodox Church and Independant Greece, 1821-1852,* Cambridge University Press, 1969.

Hopko, T., *All the Fullness of God,* Crestwood N.Y., SVS Press, 1983.

House, F., *Millenium of Faith,* Crestwood N.Y., SVS Press, 1988.

Leong, A., ed. *The Millenium: Christianity and Russia 988-1988,* Crestwood N.Y., SVS Press, 1989.

Meyendorff, J., *Living Tradition,* Crestwood N.Y., SVS Press, 1978.

_____, *Vision of Unity, Witness to the World,* Crestwood N.Y., SVS Press, 1987.

Meyendorff, J., Breck, J., Silk, E., eds., *The Legacy of St. Vladimir: Byzantium, Russia, America,* Crestwood N.Y., SVS Press, 1990.

Nicol, D. M., *Church and Society in the Last Centuries of Byzantium* (The Birkbeck Lectures, 1977), Cambridge University Press, 1979.

Nichols, R. L. and Stavrou, Th. G., eds. *Russian Orthodoxy under the Old Regime,* Minneapolis, University of Minnesota Press, 1978.

Orthodox Visions of Ecumenism, Gennadios Limouris, ed., Geneva: WCC, 1994

Pospielovsky, D. *The Russian Church Under the Soviet Regime 1917-82,* 2 vols., Crestwood N.Y., SVS Press, 1993.

Runciman, S., *The Great Church in Captivity: A Study of the Patriarchate of Constantinople from the Eve of the Turkish Conquest to the Greek War of Independence,* Cambridge University Press, 1968.

Schmemann, A., Church, World, Mission, Crestwood, N.Y., SVS Press, 1979.

The Sense of Ecumenical Tradition: Ecumenical Vision and the Witness of the Orthodox, Ion Bria, ed., Geneva: WCC, 1991.

Struve, N., *Christians in Contemporary Russia,* New York, Scribner's, 1967.

Zernov, N., *The Russians and Their Church,* rev. ed. Crestwood, N.Y., SVS Press, 1978.

_____, "The Eastern Churches and the Ecumenical Movement in the Twentieth Century," in Rouse and Neill, *A History of the Ecumenical Movement, 1517-1948,* Philadelphia, The Westminster Press, 1954.

Index